Venturing Beyond the Campus

VENTURING BEYOND THE CAMPUS

Students Who Leave College

BY C. HESS HAAGEN

Office of Institutional Research and Career Services
WESLEYAN UNIVERSITY

378.169
H111v

Copyright © 1977 by Wesleyan University

Distributed by Wesleyan University Press, Middletown, Connecticut 06457

Library of Congress Cataloging in Publication Data

    Haagen, C   Hess, 1917-
      Venturing beyond the campus.

      Bibliography: p.
      Includes index.
      1. Personnel service in higher education.
    I. Title.
    LB2343.H22   378.1'94   77-2541

Manufactured in the United States of America
First Edition

Contents

Acknowledgements		vii
Chapter 1.	Purpose, Design and Methodology of the Study	3
Chapter 2.	Why Do They Leave?	17
Chapter 3.	Who Takes a Leave?	47
Chapter 4.	What Do They Do?	61
Chapter 5.	Was It Worthwhile?	75
Chapter 6.	Any Problems?	93
Chapter 7.	Do They Return?	105
Chapter 8.	Can Colleges Help Persons Who Leave?	129
Chapter 9.	Will Colleges Give Leadership and Direction?	151
Notes		160
Bibliography		162
Appendix I	Survey Instruments	165
Appendix II	Student Protocols	197

Acknowledgements

This book is a report of the findings of a Cooperative Research Project on "leave-taking." The degree to which it in fact has been a cooperative undertaking is illustrated by the acknowledgements that are required to identify those who have made the study and the report possible.

I am grateful to the Trustees of the Braitmayer Foundation for their initiative in identifying "leave-taking" as a phenomenon of contemporary higher education that deserves careful and comprehensive investigation and for their leadership in obtaining the participation of the institutions that cooperated in the present study. Their financial support throughout three years of data gathering and a fourth year devoted to the analysis and reporting of the results of the investigation was crucial to the development and completion of the project. Particular mention must be made of Mr. James Fraser who has been unflagging in his efforts to facilitate a better integration of campus-based educational programs with the resources for learning that exist in the larger community. Professor Robert Rosenbaum invited my early involvements in helping to define the investigation that eventually was undertaken. Throughout the course of the project he has been a resourceful advisor and an unfailing source of assistance.

Dean Lee Verstandig of Brown University, Daniel Kegan of Hampshire College, Ralph Maddry of Trinity College, Dean Nancy Milburn of Tufts University and Dean Sharon Jackiw of Wheaton College served as the representative of this project on their respective campuses. They and their staffs attended faithfully to the variety of tasks that the investigation required from its inception to its conclusion.

It is impossible to identify all those who contributed to a project of this magnitude and duration. However it would be unseemly to leave unacknowledged the work of students Annie Ewing, Lucy Flint, Christopher Thorne, Gail Boxer and Edmund Hawley who typed and coded responses, programmed analyses of data, interviewed non-respondents, and in many other ways assisted in the processing of the survey results. Mrs. Geraldine Cote has been my mainstay in the day-to-day operations of the study. Her systematic work habits, her many-faceted competencies, her patience, good humor and dedication to the project have made an impossible task workable. My wife, Marian, has given support and assistance throughout the project. Her skilled proofreader's eye helped free the text of errors and her fine sense of language spared the reader some of the infelicities of my writing style.

My greatest debt of gratitude is to the 3,100 students of the six cooperating colleges and universities who furnished the basic information from which this report has developed. The most satisfactory acknowledgement of their contribution that I can make is the accurate, forceful and compassionate reporting of the experiences, insights and concerns which they shared in their replies. For many, their leave was a time of personal testing, of openness to new experiences, ideas and relationships; a period of unprecedented emotional and intellectual growth. It is my intention to communicate to the reader, not only a summary of principal findings as they have been abstracted from the thousands of protocols, but also a strong sense of the individuality, the personal significance, and the critical importance of the leave experience to the personal and educational development of many of the leave-takers. To the extent that I have been successful in this, I will have kept faith with the students who completed our surveys and shared, in full candor and in some instances at length, their ideas, feelings and aspirations. In the writing of this report I have tried to be their faithful and sensitive spokesman.

C. Hess Haagen

Venturing Beyond the Campus

CHAPTER 1

Purpose, Design and Methodology of the Study

Historical Backgrounds: In many quarters, dropping out of college is still commonly regarded as a social loss, an economic waste and a personal failure. This negative attitude derives in part from the assumption that the purpose of a college education is the earning of a degree and that the approved time for doing this is in the four years immediately following high school graduation. In his 1962 review of the literature on Dropping Out of College, John Summerskill reported: "The dropout problem has been of continuing concern to educators and has been subject to perennial rediscovery in the research literature. Research on college student dropouts, college student attrition, has a history of at least 40 years. . . . The college's interest in attrition has at least three origins. First, there is a persistent underlying concept that the American college is organized as a training center rather than as an intellectual center. . . . This concept is given strong support in our culture by students and parents, by corporations and professional schools, by state and federal governments. When students fail to make the grade, disappointment and hostility are frequently directed at the college. . . . Secondly, with the marked increase in the size and complexity of colleges, administrators have been necessarily concerned with efficiency. The nature and extent of student losses constitute one measure of the efficiency of any educational institution. For both students and colleges, withdrawal means a waste of time, of energy and money. . . . A third reason for the study of attrition is both less subtle and less talked about: dollars leave the income side of the budget when students leave college."[1]

In the book, The College Dropout and the Utilization of Talent, published in 1966, the editors comment on the prevailing attitude toward those who withdraw from college without taking a degree. "With typical commitment, the American people are convinced both of the desirability of education and of its perfectibility. This commitment leads to general impatience with whatever stands in the way of progress and perfection. If a college education is desirable, society asks, why should any young person not seek to attain it in the appointed time? Society's immediate reactions are that the dropout has sacrificed his own future, squandered his institution's resources, and indeed detracted from the national interest itself."[2] The editors go on to urge a dispassionate point of view that would entertain the possibility that dropping out of college is not necessarily undesirable or wasteful.

By the mid-sixties, students and educators alike had begun to explore the potential values of interrupting the four-year progression of studies at a single campus in order to pursue formal studies in a different environment, or to seek experience through employment, volunteer service or self-directed activities. R. Sargent Shriver, then Director of the Peace Corps, gave expression to this changing attitude in his address to the 1964 graduating class at Wesleyan University. "If the college sophomore wants to drop out of school, let him! Let the bored or the confused or the burned-out undergraduate have a short, meaningful interlude -- a sojourn into reality -- for a year or two years, so that he can come back revitalized, committed, concerned enough to finish both college and graduate work."[3]

This exploration of the creative outcomes that might be realized from modifying the established four-year progression, some called it "lockstep," of collegiate studies had barely received popular recognition when it was attenuated and given new directions by rapidly changing social forces. The war in Vietnam reduced very severely the available options for leave-taking and created a motivation, especially for male students, to retain their student status by remaining enrolled in undergraduate and graduate programs as long as possible.

With the end of the Vietnam war and the military draft, those conditions, social and personal, that created motivations for following different and more individualized timetables could operate once again, uninhibited by the counter-pressures of the threat of conscription into the service of an unpopular war. Educators investigated with renewed commitment the educational value of various programs designed to enrich campus-based learning with opportunities for education-in-the-field. In response to the needs of an increasingly heterogeneous student body, they modified regulations and procedures to permit, and in some cases to encourage, students to follow patterns of college attendance that departed from the norm of four consecutive years of undergraduate enrollment. A special report of the Carnegie Commission on Higher Education, published January 1971 under the title, <u>Less Time, More Options: Education Beyond the High School</u>, included these major themes:

1. The length of time spent in undergraduate college education can be reduced roughly by one-fourth without sacrificing educational quality.

2. Young people should also be given more options (a) in lieu of formal college, (b) to defer college attendance, (c) to stop out from college in order to get service and work experience, and (d) to change directions while in college.

3. Opportunities for higher education and the degrees it affords should be available to persons throughout their lifetimes and not just immediately after high school.

9. Society would gain if work and study were mixed throughout a lifetime, thus reducing the sense of sharply compartmentalized roles of isolated students v. workers and of youth v. isolated age. The sense of isolation would be reduced if more were also workers and if more workers could also be students; if the ages mixed on the job and in the classroom in a more normally structured type of community; if all members of the community valued both study and work and had a better chance to understand the flow of life from youth to age. Society would be more integrated across the lines that now separate students and workers, youth and age.[4]

One of the Commission's recommendations was:"That service and other opportunities be created for students between high school and college and at stop-out points in college through national, state, and municipal youth programs, through short-term jobs with private and public employers, and through apprenticeship programs in the student's field of interest; and that students be actively encouraged to participate."[5]

The Second Newman Report recognized the importance of introducing greater diversity and individual freedom into the procedures and programs of higher education. In a preview to this report published in <u>Change</u>, Newman stated: "In terms of our institutions, one would hope that there will be a greater diversity among them, that there will be less of a sense of ivory-tower self-centeredness. . . . For our students, one would hope that there would be less of a sense of college as ritual to be gone through, to be gotten over with; for others, that college will be less of a shelter to avoid life, and for all students that they will attend college when they are ready, and go on to something else when they can no longer profit from being at college."[6]

The Cooperative Research Project on Leave-taking: In the spring of 1973, the presidents of Brown University, Hampshire College, Trinity College and Wesleyan University with the assistance and encouragement of the Braitmayer Foundation agreed to undertake a study of leave-taking by their students. In the following year Tufts University and Wheaton College joined the research effort. The first paragraph of the covering letter that was mailed to students who were requested to participate in the study states the purpose of the investigation:

> We have a request to make of you. This letter explains why it is being made. Increasing numbers of students are interrupting their college studies or are pursuing their academic programs for a time at institutions other than the one in which they first matriculated. Others seek some type of non-academic experience before beginning college. In a great variety of ways, contemporary students are departing from the tradition of four consecutive years at the same college. Some educators believe that this trend should be encouraged. However, little is known about the values and the potential hazards. In recognition of this need for more precise information, Brown University, Hampshire College, Trinity College, Tufts University, Wesleyan University and Wheaton College have undertaken a three-year project of cooperative research with the support of the Braitmayer Foundation. Its purpose is to identify the characteristics of students who are most likely to profit from such activities or programs and to specify the conditions that contribute most to personal growth and educational enrichment.

Critical to the understanding of this report is the definition of "leave" that was used throughout the investigation.

> Although individual institutions use different terminology, for the purposes of this survey we will use the term "leave" to refer to that period of time in which a person is involved in activities other than those of a full-time student enrolled in a program of academic studies at the main campus of the institution from which the person expects to receive a degree.

This very broad definition was adopted so that the investigation would include persons who left the campus to pursue formal studies at another institution, to be gainfully employed or involved in volunteer service, or to engage in self-directed activities. The intent was to define the research population by the student's behavior rather than by administrative classifications or categories.

The Research Design: In each semester from September 1973 to February 1976, representatives of the six participating colleges prepared rosters of persons who were on leave and of those who had returned from leave. An appropriate questionnaire was mailed to the address furnished by the college for each leave-taker and returnee. (Exception: students of Hampshire College received their survey materials directly from their college.) A follow-up request was mailed to all non-respondents.

For those who wish to examine the survey instruments that were used in this investigation, the items of the several surveys are reproduced in Appendix I. A summary outline of their contents follows:

Survey 1 was designed to measure the attitudes of students toward their college experiences, their reasons for taking a leave and their proposed activities while on leave.

Survey 1A, an abbreviated form of Survey 1, was mailed to persons who went on leave in the first semester of 1975-76. Since there would be no opportunity for follow-up of these persons at the conclusion of their leave, only those items dealing directly with plans and motivations for leaving were included. Survey 1 or 1A was mailed to students at the beginning of their leave.

Survey 2, which was mailed when the leave-taker returned to his or her college, included questions concerning the student's leave-time activities, judgments concerning the value of the leave and attitudes toward resuming formal studies at their college.

Survey 3 was mailed after the leave-taker had been re-enrolled for one semester. It repeated many of the questions of Survey 1, so that changes in attitudes and perceptions could be identified and assessed by comparing responses given before and after the leave.

Survey 4 was mailed to students who had been continuously enrolled at their college for five or six semesters. Questions concerning their attitudes toward their college experience were identical to those of Survey 1. Other questions explored their reasons for choosing to remain enrolled at their college.

Background Information Form accompanied the first survey that was addressed to a particular individual. It consisted of questions related to family background and personal history. Its principal use was to provide categories for the analysis of subgroups of persons who took leaves and of those who remained at their colleges.

<u>Survey 5</u> was sent to persons who had not returned to their college within one year of the beginning of their leave. Its items dealt with activities during the leave, reasons for extending the leave and intentions in regard to further formal education.

The data-gathering phase of the study began in the summer of 1973 and continued through June 1976. In 1973-74, Survey 1 was mailed to students of Brown, Hampshire, Trinity and Wesleyan who were reported by their colleges as starting a leave of absence. In the second semester, Survey 2 was mailed to persons returning from leave, both to those who began their leaves in September and to those whose leaves had been initiated some time prior to the inception of the research project. Also in the second semester, Survey 4 was mailed to all students at Wesleyan University who had been continuously enrolled for six semesters.

Tufts University and Wheaton College joined the project in 1974-75. Again, during this year, Survey 1 was sent to all persons who began a leave of absence. Survey 2 was mailed to persons returning from leave and Survey 3 was sent to persons who had completed a semester of academic work following their return from leave. In either the first or the second semester, Survey 4 was mailed to students who had been enrolled continuously for either five or six semesters. At Hampshire, Trinity, Wesleyan and Wheaton, all students meeting this criterion were included in the mailing. A random sample of students at Brown and Tufts Universities who had not taken a leave during their first six semesters was mailed Survey 4.

In 1975-76, Survey 1A was used with persons beginning a leave since there would be no opportunity for follow-up with Surveys 2 and 3. Throughout the year, Surveys 2 and 3 were mailed to returning students. Survey 5 was sent to persons who had completed Survey 1 at least one year earlier but who had not returned to their college by September 1975. The final statistical analyses have been performed on data obtained from completed surveys that were received up to June 30, 1976. The information that has been obtained through these several survey instruments has been supplemented by data obtained from the official records of Brown University, Trinity College and Wesleyan University. Analyses based on grade point average and current enrollment status include students from these institutions only.

The comprehensive character of this investigation is indicated by the following features: 1) it reflects the experiences of a large number of individuals; 2) it includes students from six private New England colleges and universities that differ substantially in size of student body, urban-rural location, curricular resources, and in policies related to leave-taking; 3) its design permits the longitudinal study of individuals and the identification of time trends; 4) it provides for the comparison of persons who take leaves with those who do not; and 5) it includes information concerning persons who do not return to their college within the originally scheduled time of the leave.

Elaborating on these points, the findings of this study are based upon the reports of 1367 persons who took a leave of absence from one of the six participating institutions in 1973-74 or in 1974-75, and of 1140 persons who returned after an absence of one semester or longer. Two hundred and fifty persons who began their leave in 1975-76 completed Survey 1A, providing a basis of comparison with leave-takers of the two previous years. Six hundred and seventy-four individuals who participated in the study completed both Survey 1 at the beginning and Survey 2 at the end of their leaves. Four hundred and sixty-five persons who had completed Survey 1 also completed Survey 3 after they had been enrolled for an academic term following their return to college.

The conclusions of this study therefore are based upon the experiences and expressed attitudes of a large number of students who had taken leave from one of the six colleges. The statements of a sizeable number of persons, obtained at different times in their college careers, make it possible to observe changes and constancies in attitudes and performance over a time period of six months to three years. Seven hundred and sixty-four students who had been enrolled at their college for five or six consecutive semesters completed Survey 4. Their responses to questions similar or identical to those included in Survey 1 make it possible to compare the characteristics of students who take leaves with those who do not.

Ninety-six persons who had not re-enrolled at their college after an absence of one year or more completed Survey 5. They included persons who had extended the period of their leave with the intention of eventually returning to their college, some who had transferred to another institution, and some who do not plan to become involved in any program of higher education in the foreseeable future.

Response Rates and the Representativeness of the Respondents: A research program that obtains a large proportion of its information by mail survey must confront the issue of the representativeness of the persons who return completed questionnaires. Are the leave-takers who did not return completed questionnaires different from those who did in ways that might limit the conclusions that may be drawn from the information supplied by the respondents?

Several lines of evidence will be considered in an attempt to respond to this question. From the records of those colleges that enroll both men and women, we know that forty-three percent of all persons who began a leave in the period 1973-1975 were women. Forty-eight percent of the persons who returned a completed Survey 1 were women. In comparison with the population of leave-takers, women are over-represented in our sample of respondents to a degree that cannot be attributed to chance.[7] For whatever reasons, being female increased the likelihood that a person would respond to a request to participate in this study. It is possible that this over-representation of women does not distort seriously much of the information received since it will be demonstrated in chapter 3 that the responses of men and women to a majority of the items of Survey 1 do not differ by amounts that exceed chance probabilities. Men and women did differ in the amount of time that they devoted to various types of activities during their leave. Since a greater percentage of the women respondents took academic leaves and a greater percentage of men were employed, the sample of respondents probably overstates the proportion of leave-takers who study at other institutions during their leave and understates the number who are employed or involved in volunteer service.

A larger percentage of persons who were on leave for a year returned completed questionnaires than did persons who were on leave for one semester.

TABLE 1

Length of Leave

	Respondents	Non-Respondents
One Semester Leave	50.6%	58.6%
Two Semesters Leave	43.2%	31.1%
More than Two Semesters Leave	6.2%	10.3%

This outcome may be related in part to the greater probability that persons who were away for a year received their mail and had sufficient time to respond before their return to the campus was imminent.

Only small differences were observed in the percentage of respondents and non-respondents when classified by the number of semesters completed before taking a leave.

TABLE 2
Semesters Completed Before Leave

Semesters Completed	Respondents	Non-Respondents
1	3.6%	4.4%
2 or 3	28.5%	30.3%
4 or 5	59.9%	56.0%
6 or 7	8.0%	10.3%

Leave-takers who did not return to their college are under-represented in our sample. In the total population of leave-takers, thirty percent either extended their leaves or withdrew from college (most to transfer to another college). Among the respondents to Survey 1 only nineteen percent were persons who had not returned to their college by the second semester of 1975-76. Several factors almost certainly contributed to this difference. For one, persons who intended to or were in the process of dissociating themselves from their college were less likely to maintain a current mailing address with their college. More importantly, many were less motivated to participate in a project that was sponsored by an institution with which they no longer felt closely identified. In the data of Survey 1, there is an under-representation of the experiences and opinions of persons who did not return to their college. Direct study of this group was undertaken, using Survey 5. A more detailed discussion of those who did not return to their college after a leave of absence is presented in chapter 7.

TABLE 3
Response Rates for Surveys 1, 2, 3 & 4
By Institutions

	Survey			
	1	2	3	4
Brown	53%	61%	59%	69%
Trinity	45%	43%	42%	49%
Tufts	51%	46%	32%	46%
Wesleyan	43%	72%	72%	66%
Wheaton	53%	48%	48%	55%
Total	49%	54%	49%	58%

Table 3 displays the response rates for the several surveys. The response rates for Survey 5 are presented in chapter 7 in the context of the discussion of persons who did not return from their leave. The percentage of Hampshire students who returned completed surveys is not included in this table because the manner of distributing the surveys differed from that of the other colleges. The Hampshire rate of return ranged from a low of thirty-five percent for Survey 1 to a high of forty-seven percent for Survey 2.

The rates of response were relatively high for a mail survey and were strikingly good for a group of instruments that were as demanding of time and thought as these surveys were. The variations in rate of response from institution to institution result from the interaction of many factors whose significance in effecting outcomes can only be surmised. One uncontrolled variable in this regard was the timing of the mailings as they related to campus activities and calendars of particular schools. Articles about leave taking and/or this particular study that were printed in the newspapers of several of the colleges may have stimulated a greater response to mailings that occurred at the time of their publication. The general accuracy of mailing addresses varied from institution to institution. Campus addresses produced a higher rate of response than did off-campus addresses. This applied whether the off-campus addresses were for the immediate vicinity of the college town or for some distant location.

To investigate more directly students' reasons for not responding to the survey, a limited number of telephone and face-to-face interviews were conducted with students who had not responded to the original mailing or to the follow-up request for Survey 2. These interviews were conducted at Brown and Wesleyan Universities by students who had been given instructions for conducting structured interviews. Some of those interviewed could not be certain whether they had ever received a request to participate in the study. Most remembered having received it. They reported that their non-reply resulted from lack of time, mislaying the survey materials, forgetting about it and other similar circumstances. No one who was contacted indicated that their non-response represented an objection to the study or a refusal to participate. As a result of this personal contact, almost all agreed to complete the survey. Characteristics of the non-respondents as revealed by the Background Information Form did not differ in any significant way from those of the respondents. Neither did this small sample of "non-respondents" differ from persons who returned a completed Survey 2 in respect to their stated reasons for taking a leave, in the nature of their leave activities or in their expressed satisfaction with their leave experiences. Personal contacts with these non-respondents produced no evidence to suggest that the absence of the protocols of non-respondents changed substantially the findings of this investigation.

Most of those who did respond to the surveys did so thoughtfully and in a manner that suggested that they took the investigation seriously. Of the 3,335 surveys, 1,2, and 3, that were returned, 2,922 or eighty-eight percent contained statements written in response to the open-ended questions that concluded each survey. Some added notes to explain their answers to specific questions. Some offered criticisms of particular items, others of broader aspects of the study. Many asked for more information about the study or requested a copy of a report of the findings. There were those who expressed gratitude that a serious attempt was being made to learn more about leave-taking. Others expressed doubts that anything constructive would be done with any findings that might be developed. Several typographical errors appeared in the surveys. Numerous respondents corrected the misspellings, a few with caustic or gleeful comments. Some persons included with their completed survey copies of reports that they had written about their leave for other purposes, brochures describing the programs with which they were associated or reprints of articles about leave-taking. There was a high degree of internal consistency in responses to interrelated items of the survey. All of these observations indicate that the study elicited a high level of interest and cooperation

<u>General Comments about the Preparation of the Report and the Organization of the Book</u>: To give organization to the mass of information that has been generated by these surveys and to assist in the interpretation of the findings of the investigation, the responses to each of the structured items of each survey were tabulated for all persons who responded to the survey and for a number of identifiable sub-groups. For purposes of analysis, respondents were classified according to: type of leave activity, length of leave, field of concentration, level of expressed satisfaction with college experience, ratings before and after leave, year in which leave was begun, institution, sex, and other variables. Statistical indicators of central tendency, variability and degree of relationship were computed. Tests were made of the significance of observed differences. The thematic content of the comments that were written in response to the open-ended questions that concluded each survey were coded and tabulated. This provided a frequency count for the topics that respondents included in their essarys. It also permitted

identification of and access to protocols that discussed a particular issue.

To make the communication of the results of this investigation as clear and interesting as possible, infrequent and limited reference will be made to statistical indicators and tests. Much of the quantitative material will be presented in tabular displays or as simple percentages. In the chapters that follow, each topic is developed by summarizing the most relevant information from the structured questions of the surveys and by quoting from the statements of respondents who addressed that particular issue in their remarks. These statements were selected to represent the range of ideas, opinions and feelings that were expressed by the whole group of respondents. The samples of statements never exhaust the response pool for a given topic and do not reflect the frequency with which a particular point of view was expressed. The text is a blend of statistical summaries and first-hand observations that hopefully presents the results of this investigation fully and accurately without losing the human dimensions of leave-taking in a series of abstractions. The generalizations that are formulated should never obscure the fundamental fact that each person's leave is a very personal experience. It has aspects that can be quantified, and elements that are common to the experience of many others. The very undertaking of this study is testimony to the belief of those who undertook it that something of value could be learned from an analysis of the responses of students to directed questions about their college and about their leave. Some respondents expressed the opinion that a structured questionnaire could not reflect elements of their situation and experience that they considered to be critical to an understanding of their leave. A few returned the survey unanswered because they felt that no survey could capture the uniqueness of their leave and its relationship to their own educational history and personal aspirations. Granted, each person's leave is an expression of an individuality that is not fully captured in numbers or adequately described by averages and coefficients of correlation. However, it is not necessary to restrict attempts at understanding to one line of evidence or to any one form of data gathering. Educators, in the formulation and administration of policy, must attempt to identify and differentiate the variety of needs within the student body and not over-respond to the claims of groups that have influential spokesmen, to the neglect of other less visible or articulate groups. Knowledge of averages, of distributions, and of trends can help to maintain perspective and balance when various facets of a complex situation are unequally represented. Students can benefit from having access to information that will extend their awareness of alternatives beyond those represented in their own particular circle of acquaintances. Parents may be influenced by their familiarity with specific instances of leave-taking that may not be wholly relevant to the proposal that their son or daughter has presented to them. Information that provides a broader perspective to the issues involved in leave-taking may relieve their anxieties and permit them to participate more constructively in the decision that finally will be made.

Throughout the book, the reader's attention is directed to three types of evidence: 1) summaries of information derived from the items of the surveys and from college records; 2) brief quotations from the free comments of respondents that were selected to illustrate particular themes; and 3) the full text of statements written in response to the open-ended questions of the surveys. Each is intended to compliment and enrich the insights provided by the others. The full statements provide a more direct, personal account of the unique experiences of a particular individual. In them, remarks about a specific issue may be examined in the context of the other comments that the person chose to make about his/her experiences in college and while on leave. These statements appear in Appendix II, grouped according to the principal leave activity of the author. Footnotes in the text identify protocols that contain comments that are particularly germane to the topic under consideration.

The book is addressed primarily to students who may wish to evaluate the possibility that time away from their formal studies at the school in which they are presently registered might be appropriate to their situation and needs. Many of the students who participated in this study stated that having access to the experience of other students who had taken a leave would have been helpful to them in their own planning and decision making.

Hopefully this study also will be of interest and value to educators who must formulate policies governing the timing of students' educational programs and their utilization of off-campus resources for learning and for personal development. It is intended to be a resource to all those who counsel and advise students: members of the faculty and staff, and most especially, parents.

CHAPTER 2

Why Do They Leave?

In September 1970, over one and three quarter million persons enrolled for the first time in an American college or university. For many, their matriculation was the culmination of years of anticipation and preparation by them and by their parents. High school courses had been selected with preparation for college in mind. Guidance conferences, admissions tests, campus visits, and the selection of schools to which application would be made became a two-year preoccupation. For much longer, their parents may have been setting aside money in anticipation of their son's or daughter's entering college. One of the "rites of passage" for 272,268 freshmen at 425 colleges and universities that year was the administration of the Student Information Blank. This is a survey instrument that has now been in use for more than a decade in a longitudinal research program sponsored by the American Council on Education.[8] An item in that survey is germane to our investigation of leave-taking for it posed the question: "What is your best guess as to the chances that you will drop out of this college temporarily (exclude transferring)?" Given the eagerness with which most sought admission to college, it is hardly surprising that only two and four-tenths percent of the freshmen enrolled at private, nonsectarian colleges answered, "Very Good Chance." At those colleges that are classified as exercising "very high selectivity" in admission, the percentage of freshmen who estimated a "Very Good Chance" was somewhat greater. At one such college, Wesleyan University, four and four-tenths percent of the first-year students of the class of 1974 forecast that there was a very good chance that they would leave the college temporarily sometime before their graduation. In fact, forty percent of the members of this class took a leave for a semester or more. This particular class was not atypical. Forty-two percent of the Wesleyan class of 1975 took a leave as did forty-one percent of the class of 1976. Other colleges and universities also have issued reports indicating that a substantial minority of their students leave for a time to engage in some off-campus activity.[9]

Why do so many young men and women, for whom getting admitted to the college of their choice had been one of their most pressing concerns just a few years before, find it desirable or necessary to leave their college for a time? This chapter will explore some of the findings of this investigation that bear on that question.

The following is the text of Item B in Surveys 1 and 1A:

> B. <u>Reasons for taking a leave of absence</u>: Each student has his or her own very personal reasons for attending college and in some instances for choosing to interrupt or terminate college work. The following are some broad categories of reasons that students give for taking a leave. Please indicate the importance to you of <u>each</u> reason by writing the code number of the most descriptive statement. Add any reasons that are important in your case but which are not included in the list which follows:
>
> Code for Degree of Importance
>
> 1. A precipitating factor, one of the most important or crucial reasons for my taking a leave at this time.
>
> 2. A contributing factor. Although not decisive, was an important consideration in decision to take a leave.
>
> 3. A minor factor, may have influenced my decision to take a leave but only in limited or peripheral ways.
>
> 4. Not a factor in my decision to take a leave, although it may be present in my personal history.
>
> 5. Does not apply in my case.

The thirteen "reasons" included in Survey 1 are listed below in three empirically derived groupings. Under each "reason" is printed the percentage of the 1367 respondents who assigned one of the codes, 1 through 4, to the item. The fifth entry is the percentage of all respondents who selected code 5, <u>does not apply in my case</u>.

> b. To obtain course work or experiences not available to me at this campus
> 1. 54%   2. 29%   3. 10%   4. 4.7%   (5. 11%)

e. My need for a change; desire for different kinds of experience and/or associations
1. 53%   2. 31%   3. 11%   4. 5%   (5. 4%)

h. Personal need for experiences that might give a perspective on myself, to college, my relations to society, etc.
1. 49%   2. 30%   3. 14%   4. 7%   (5. 7%)

Virtually all of the respondents rated these "reasons" as applying to their situation to some degree. Approximately one half of the respondents rated each of these three reasons as <u>one of the most important or crucial reasons for my taking a leave at this time</u>.

A second group of "reasons" relates to the student's attitudes toward his or her college program and experiences. For the items in this group, the percentage of respondents who state that an item <u>does not apply in my case</u> varies from a low of thirty-four to a high of sixty-seven. Except for Item c, fifteen percent or fewer of the respondents judged these items to be <u>precipitating factors</u> in their taking a leave.

c. Lack of sufficiently well-defined purposes for being in college to justify the time, effort and/or expense involved.
1. 35%   2. 27%   3. 19%   4. 19%   (5. 34%)

f. Lack of interest in my course of studies
1. 15%   2. 29%   3. 26%   4. 30%   (5. 47%)

i. Failure to find satisfying personal and/or social relationships at this college
1. 15%   2. 25%   3. 30%   4. 30%   (5. 47%)

a. A recommended or required part of my college program.
1. 15%   2. 29%   3. 27%   4. 29%   (5. 62%)

d. The seeming irrelevancy of college to issues that are important to me.
1. 12%   2. 24%   3. 31%   4. 33%   (5. 46%)

g. Lack of success in my course of studies
1. 9%   2. 20%   3. 25%   4. 46%   (5. 67%)

The items in the third group are "situation" reasons that usually are not related directly to the student's academic program or campus life. A majority of the respondents coded them as <u>does not apply in my case</u>. Forty to fifty-six percent of those who thought that one or more of these reasons pertained to their situation, rated it (them) as crucial or contributing to their decision to take a leave.

    j. Personal health, medical reasons
        1. 34%   2. 13%   3. 16%   4. 37%   (5. 90%)
    l. Personal circumstances not related to college
        1. 26%   2. 30%   3. 23%   4. 21%   (5. 56%)
    k. Financial considerations
        1. 20%   2. 30%   3. 31%   4. 19%   (5. 60%)
    m. Family circumstances
        1. 17%   2. 22%   3. 22%   4. 39%   (5. 77%)

    Sixty-two persons listed under <u>other</u>, a reason for their leave. In the main, their statements were particularizations of one or more of the thirteen alternatives. For example, some reported the specific names of courses or programs not offered at their college or described the specific circumstances that prompted their decision to leave.

    There were relatively small differences in the importance assigned to thirteen "reasons" by persons who began their leave in 1973, when compared with those who went on leave in 1974 or in 1975. Variations from year to year did not exceed the magnitude of difference that would be expected in chance occurrences. There are several non-chance differences in the responses of students who return to their college following their leave (referred to below as "persisters"), and of those who either do not return or who drop-out after their return ("non-persisters"). Thirty-one percent of the "non-persisters" cite <u>lack of interest in my courses of studies</u> as one of the <u>most important</u> reasons, in comparison to fifteen percent of the "persisters." A statistical test of the significance of the differences in the weights assigned to this reason by "non-persisters" and "persisters" yielded a probability value of 0.04. The letter "p" will be used throughout this report to signify probability. Here the notation, $p=0.04$, indicates that the observed differences in the numbers of "non-persisters" and of "persisters" who assigned each code to the alternative <u>lack of interest in my course of studies</u>, will occur by chance only four times in one hundred random samplings of this size. This observation would support the conclusion that some variable or variables operate(s) systematically to produce differentiations in the coding of this alternative by "non-persisters" and "persisters." Comparable percentages for the item, <u>the seeming irrelevancy of college</u> were: "non-persisters" 33%, "persisters" 13%, ($p=.001$).

    Throughout Survey 1, a greater frequency of statements indicating a lack of satisfying personal relationships or of social supports differentiates the responses of leave-takers who continue their studies to

TABLE 4

Index of Importance of Reasons for Taking a Leave by Type of Leave-time Activity

Reason for Leave	Leave Activity		
	Academic	Employment	Self-Directed
	Index of Importance		
b. To obtain course-work or experiences	1.56	1.97	1.84
e. My need for change	1.65	1.70	1.69
h. Personal need for experiences	1.62	1.64	1.90
c. Lack of sufficiently well-defined purposes	1.80	1.97	2.57
f. Lack of interest	2.38	2.62	2.98
i. Failure to find satisfying personal/social relationships	2.64	2.90	3.68
q. A recommended part of college program	3.23	2.87	2.58
d. Seeming irrelevancy of college	2.66	2.81	3.03
g. Lack of success in courses	2.90	3.14	3.23
j. Health	2.33	2.85	3.24
l. Personal circumstances	2.36	2.46	2.40
k. Financial	2.21	2.53	2.52
m. Family circumstances	2.60	3.21	2.81

graduation and those who transfer to other institutions or otherwise do not finish at the college at which they first enrolled. Only five percent of the "non-persisters" reported that <u>people in my living unit are congenial and sharing</u>, as compared to twenty-one percent of the "persisters" (p=.02). A larger proportion of the "non-persisters" reported that they had experienced difficulties in social relationships during the academic term before their leave. By contrast, the "persisters" stated that they have more close friends among the students of their college. The differences between the groups in the reported degree of importance that parents attach to <u>graduating from this particular college</u> could not occur by chance one time in one thousand. A significantly large proportion of "persisters" are encouraged by their parents to remain at and to graduate from the school from which they took leave.

Chi square analyses of the relationship between students' principal leave activity and the importance which they attach to the several categories of reasons indicate that the differences observed would not occur by chance more frequently than five times in one hundred except for the items, "lack of success" and "personal circumstances not related to college."

Data presented in Table 4 permits the examination of similarities and differences in the importance attributed to the thirteen "reasons" by persons who: 1) took a leave to pursue formal academic studies at another institution, 2) were employed or involved in volunteer service and 3) were engaged in self-directed activities. To facilitate comparisons, an index of importance was computed by multiplying the number of persons assigning a given code by the weight assigned to that code (i.e. most important = 1; not a factor = 4) and dividing the sum of these products by the total number of persons. The reasons are listed in the same order as above.

The foregoing analysis, which was undertaken to identify categories of reasons for taking a leave and to provide an estimate of their relative importance to identifiable groups of leave-takers, does not provide an adequate representation of the motivational forces that operate in the decision of an individual student to take a leave. The motivations for taking a leave of absence are personal and, in most instances, complex. Occasionally a leave is ascribed to one overwhelming cause such as the sickness or death of a parent, or to personal ill health. More commonly, it is the expression of a variety of interests and needs. Restating the question that this chapter addresses, we may ask: What happens during the college years to make "stopping out" desirable or necessary?

The results of this investigation indicate that only about eighteen percent of those who interrupt their studies do so for reasons that are to a large degree beyond their control: financial need, family circumstances, ill health, etc. While attending to the situation that required their leave, these students typically seek as well for ways to promote their personal development and their readiness to re-engage their studies, when circumstances permit.

The great majority of those who take a leave cite their desire for new experiences as the most potent motivator. They feel a need for fresh challenges and opportunities for growth that are not readily available within their college program and environment. For them the academic program and the total college experience does not represent with sufficient inclusiveness, directness and intensity, the world in which they expect to live, or the range of human experience to which they wish to relate. Schooling in its duration and intensity has become limiting, controlling and diverting from other important interests and concerns. Some express the belief that by being so demanding and engrossing their education does not support adequately, and may actually interfere with, their perception and understanding of themselves and their relations to society.

Emphasizing their need to disengage from a situation that seems unresponsive to their felt needs and desires, many students use words like "controlling," "repetitious," "disorienting," "suffocating" to describe their accumulating college experience. For any number of reasons, they feel the need to put some distance between themselves and the press of their college experience. They need new perspectives in order to understand and appreciate what has been happening to them in college. They need a change of pace so that they may be free to pursue interests that are not well-served by the college curriculum. Some need the experience of taking a greater measure of control of their lives. College is seen as womb-like and sheltering from the common demands of everyday living. Students react against the temptation to accept a dependent role and to allow external forces to define their interests and activities. Many complain that their life in college isolates them from the "real world" and from significant interaction with "real people."

Students are concerned about the increasing costs of a college education. They fear that they will confront diminishing employment prospects for college graduates, and greater competition for admission to programs of advanced study. In the face of wide-spread questioning of the value of higher education, particularly in the liberal arts, some discover that their own motivational supports for meeting the various demands of college are inadequate. They search for ways to rekindle their interests or to discover more personally relevant reasons for pursuing their collegiate studies.

For many, concern about the choice and/or development of a career is an element contributing to their dis-ease in college. From statements that students make about their hopes and objectives in taking a leave of absence, three broad areas of concern about careers are clearly evident. 1. Some students express the need for very basic career information and orientation. They feel the need for a greater exposure to and an understanding of the world of work. They seem to be looking for an experiential base from which they can make some very basic decisions about their own interests, abilities, preferences and needs and how they relate to the work-a-day world. Expressed in many different ways, their concern seems to be: "What is it like out there?" "Can I survive without the supports of college and family?" "How does what I am doing in college relate, if at all, to how other people live their lives and earn their living?" Twenty-three percent of the 1367 persons who completed Survey 1 chose the alternative "I have been unable to decide" in response to the question "In thinking about your occupational future, do you feel that in the long run you would have a preference for: (followed by alternatives that list seven broad career fields). 2. Others have formulated career objectives, however tentative, which they wish to test through active involvement. In effect, they state: "Before I go further with my education, I need some assurance that I have what it takes to succeed in this field." "The concepts employed command my interest and engage my abilities, but will I find the operational level of this career equally appealing?" "I think that this is something that I would like to do, but I have no way to determine this with conviction by simply reading a book or talking to people." 3. Still other students have made fairly substantial commitments to a particular career and seek ways to facilitate their progress in it. They look for situations through which they can develop or perfect job-related skills, establish contacts or relationships with persons who may aid their career development and in other ways improve and enlarge their qualifications and credentials for eventual employment or professional recognition.

These themes can be identified in the responses of students to questions 1 and 2 of Survey 1: 1. What are your objectives in taking this leave of absence? What do you hope to accomplish during the time that you are away from college? 2. What will you be doing during your leave? How do you propose to pursue the objectives that you outlined above? The responses to these questions that are quoted here have been selected to represent the range of ideas and feelings that students on leave express. The protocols of other respondents appear in Appendix 2 in the context of their responses to the other questions included in the surveys.[10]

Financial:

> I am extremely in debt and need to work and pay back some debts. Obtain a good paying job in some construction company.

> There are many objectives I wish to pursue, such as, work to earn the money that I must raise myself to return to school, --to grow stronger both physically and emotionally--to try to find a career so I can set my goals and try to gain that career when I return to school. I'm asking for a lot. Right now I hold one job at low pay--I hope to find another soon. I am also using this leave to try to straighten things out in many of my relationships, both family and otherwise.

> My main objectives are financial. However, once these considerations are out of the way, I would hope to leave the area for a while, as I have lived here most of my life (New England). Also, I would like to lend support during my parents' divorce proceedings. I would really like to do some unstructured reading and studying, for which I gave myself no time in college, but doubt I'll get around to it. I will be working full time for at least four months. I will be near my family until things get better. Only then will I decide whether to return to school or ask for an extension, or a transfer to a West Coast school.

> I am extremely in debt and need to work and pay back some debts.

Personal Medical, Health:

> Unfortunately my objectives are not educational per se. During my leave I will be giving birth to my first child and breast feeding that child. Since I live forty miles from college my leave is of indefinite duration.

> To regain my health. A greater understanding for my purposes for being in college. Resting, contemplation, reading, and involvement with people.

> Leave forced on by illness. I hope to accomplish more individual reading of interest while away.

I have taken this leave to care for my father who is seriously ill. I am taking my final semester of courses at another school, but will still be graduating from my college.

While my main objective is to develop strength lost while I was in the hospital, I also hope to use the time to do things I found it hard to make time for at school, such as reading, creative writing, etc.

Family Circumstances:

Reason for leave was parents health. My objective is to see them both back to good health but the odds are high against it. It came on all of a sudden such that it caught me off guard and kept me off my balance. I finally decided it best for me to return home. I'm working full time in a sawmill as a pony-bolter operator. I can only wait for time to decide for or against my parents health.

I will complete my degree away from the pressures I was under from family and personal problems; and a change from an all-school-oriented outlook on life. Achieve responsibility and independence. I moved away from my parents and am employed full time. I take two courses per semester this year in my major and I will receive my degree on schedule in May. I am financially and situationally and more emotionally independent of my family.

I am taking this leave to care for my father, who is seriously ill.

I hope to learn more about myself, to grow and develop in many personal ways, to redefine certain family relationships, to evaluate my academic and other interests, to gain work experience, to earn some money, to come to peace with myself and get to know myself better. My reasons for taking this leave are really quite complex and personal. They have very little to do with the university itself or the people I knew there. There are certain circumstances in my family that just recently came out into the open and forced me to come to grips with formerly dormant feelings and anxieties. My family and I are working on our problems, and I am optimistic that things will work out for us. I look forward to resuming my studies at a state university in the fall.

Academic: For some students, the primary considerations that motivate their leaves are academic and curricular. The development of their intellectual interests and the optimal progress of their academic programs may require courses of instruction or resources that are not available at their college. They seek a learning environment that will provide greater stimulation and enrichment, or they desire to experience teaching methods and conditions of learning different from those of their college. In addition to achieving these academic goals, students commonly express the hope that they will realize a number of supplementary benefits from studying at a different institution. For other students, these priorities are reversed. Their principal objectives are to have a change of pace and scene, to meet new people, to travel, to realize economies in tuition and living costs and to accomplish this without breaking the continuity of their education or at least without delaying the time of their graduation. Although the students may be conscientious in selecting an academic program that will make important contributions to their education, the choice is essentially a means to these other ends. These themes appear in the statements of students who took a leave to study at another institution and may be identified in the examples that are reproduced here and in the appendix.[11]

> My objective was to study in a Mexican University as part of the Latin American Studies major. My college offers little in this area, so courses taken here are invaluable. Too, I expect to attain greater facility with the Spanish language, which will help me in what work I plan to do after graduation.

> A necessary part of majoring in classical studies is experience in Italy or Greece, in my opinion. I hope to acquire a lot of knowledge and see a lot of things I've always read about.

> Exposure to new surroundings, teaching methods, people. The courses in international politics and economics which I am taking at the London School of Economics are far superior to those offered by my college. Also the opportunities for cultural enrichment in London far exceed those available in (college town). I hope to expand my knowledge of another culture, to enhance my intellectual and academic growth and to travel.

> I was not satisfied in the curriculum offered at the school I was attending. I found the very scholarly and competitive atmosphere and mode of teaching was really making me lose the love of learning I have possessed all my life. I will be studying and taking a variety of courses which either my school does not offer or which I did not take because of the way I found it was being taught.

> The main reason is to fulfill a strong desire to be able to really speak Chinese. To devote myself fully to it is the only way. Secondly, having lived in Taiwan before, I felt there was a lot to the country that I had missed by not knowing the language. Also going to school in the East while living in California has separated me from my family. My sister will be in Taiwan this year and I will live with her so we can try to reknow each other.

To attend a school of music that offers more than my college does.

I'm looking for an intense dance program with very stiff requirements to give me a clearer view of the professional world and my relationship to it.

I left because I wanted to pursue an interest in photography at a school of fine arts. I had been unable to successfully combine this interest with my academic work. I found my academic work interfering with my photographic work.

I am trying to find out once and for all whether and where my musical talents/interests lie by creating an intense atmosphere of pursuit without interference of other academics. I will spend a year at a conservatory of music.

To mature as a result of being "forced" to make decisions that are truly mine--to either establish or dismiss a growing interest in European History in the place where I can best get a feel for it. I will be studying at the University of Tubingen.

Change of social atmosphere and physical environment. Felt stifled, bored, needed to explore, to broaden my intellectual and social horizons or perspectives. Studying in London, England. By living in a city and being associated with people who have diversified socio-economic backgrounds.

I wanted to study at another school to get a perspective on education in a different environment (larger school, new region, etc.), to take some courses not offered at my college and to see my reaction to being in an unfamiliar environment (and what that tells me about myself). My objectives were to meet some new people, familiarize myself with an area of the country I'd never been to, take some courses unavailable at my college, form opinions about studying at a large university. While I have no regrets about coming here (the University of Colorado), I'm quite definitely looking forward to returning to my college, which I feel is more suited to my personality and academic needs.

This leave was specifically planned as an extended field work project for anthropology. This independent work is a necessary part of the thesis project, though I must say that taking a full year leave is not the regular procedure. I decided to take a full year however, because considering all, less than a year would not do justice to the unique opportunities for research I have. At this point, I am halfway through my year on leave. Up till now I have completed two months of intensive language work here in Israel, and four months of anthropology field work on location at a Yemenite Moshav here. These next five months will be spent developing my research issues by using other related sources available here in Israel. Before I return for my senior year, I plan to return to my field work location for another three month period. I am in contact with a couple of my professors - I send them field notes and they send back criticism and advice on my work as they see it through these notes and short essays I have written in letters.

I am a political science major but my interests in this area are not satisfied by this University's course curriculum. I not only want to pursue these unavailable courses but wish to gain a non-American perspective of areas in which I am already familiar. Also, future career will in some way entail an international perspective. Plus, language study and a long standing interest in Europe, etc. I will spend a semester in London and a semester in Vienna with the Institute of European Studies.

I took this LOA because I wanted a dramatic change in my life. I was also interested in course not offered at my school. I was mainly concerned with new experiences. I will be at Dartmouth on the Twelve College Exchange.

Freedom to explore myself in a new and foreign environment far from the security and advice of parents and friends. To experience this freedom and the possibilities freedom affords. I am living in a room of my own in a ten room flat. I am enrolled at Schiller College and have travelled to Ireland, France and England. I am taking courses related to my major.

The idea of going abroad was a spur of the moment one. I was having a personal identity crisis and I was contemplating many alternatives to returning to my college. I was frustrated with having to work so hard for what I considered low grades. I know I need to get far away from my parents because of their great amount of influence over me. I hope that I learn to live and be my own person while on leave. I plan to be studying at various institutions - art, psychology, and possibly French or economics. I intend to explore the many cultural opportunities available only in Europe. I hope to find some helpful expression in writing - that is I wish to devote less of my time to academics and more to personal thought and improvement.

I desired a broader program in my major - math and secondary education. I wanted to take a rest from the pressure and competition amongst students here. I also wanted to be away from home, as I was a commuter. Above all, I wanted a change of atmosphere and scenery. I will be attending the State University of New York at Stony Brook. My courses have been approved by individual professors, as well as by the University. I will be a resident student, hopefully having the opportunity to grow intellectually, socially, etc.

Personal Development: Some students come to feel the need for personal growth. They recognize the desirability of developing discipline and self-control. They see in their reactions signs of immaturity. They feel themselves to be lacking in interpersonal skills. They are frustrated by a lack of self-confidence and have a gnawing feeling that for all their learning, there is much to life that they have not experienced and which they do not know or understand. They seek to formulate a system of values and a life style that is truly their own. For them, the college campus has not proved to be a congenial environment for pursuing these objectives. They want time and space and other associations through which they may attend to these items of their personal agenda.[12]

> I left college because I needed to get away from some of the people there who were causing me to lose concentration on my work. Mainly for personal reasons of relationship dissatisfaction. I hope to be able to think things out as well as decide what I want to do with my schooling and friends. I will be studying in Italy next year.

> A basic gain in maturity. I felt settled in at my school in a specific clique atmosphere which I was comfortable in but yet I felt that I was not really being challenged. Part of my reason for taking a leave was to expand, to get out of that settled feeling. I do not know many people at my new school, and I am looking forward to making progress on my own without my own comfortable social contacts to fall back on. Location, immediate cultural advantages, and co-educational living will all be new college experiences for me.

> My one objective is to develop a sense of responsibility - to myself and therefore, for myself. By putting myself in a situation where there will be no choice but to fend for myself, I will have to develop the habit of doing what must be done, i.e. a sense of responsibility.

> My objectives as of right now, are to experience the responsibility of being completely on my own and from that, to discover more about my own ideas, desires, etc., and to act on those discoveries. Also, just to do new things, go different places, meet new people and ideas - learning what I can from whatever comes along. Sort of getting the adventure out of my system until I'm ready to accept school for what it is and get what I should out of it. There's a slight possibility that I won't get it "out of my system" but may latch onto something else in which case I would not return. I have no idea what the next year will be like. The only thing I'm sure of is that I'll have to work at various points to support myself. I have a great deal of ideas in mind, but they are all tentative. Some of these are: travelling by bicycle, getting an apartment and job in some city, possibly thereby pursuing some interest by attending classes - either sculpture or

film-making - reading philosophy novels (I'm looking forward right now to being able to pick up any book that interests me and read it without feeling guilty about neglecting something else) anything else (but avoiding classes in academic subject), maybe going to Europe, going out West for a while (living in the Midwest probably). Also, getting straight various ideas of my own.

One of my main objectives which I hope to accomplish during my leave of absence is to mature more socially and emotionally, particularly the latter. I also hope to become somewhat better than I am at forming interpersonal relationships. Another is getting employed. I've never done it before, and in some strange way, I'm hoping it will give me some sort of sense of responsibility. I suppose this is very immature of me, but I've never felt a real sense of responsibility to myself, or to anybody here at college. One of my chief objectives is to form a better sense of responsibility to myself and to other people by taking a job. I'm not sure what kind of job. Another is to try and form some closer interpersonal relationships without academics as an interference (or is it a shield I use to hide behind?). I hope to have more time to join various social or activist-type groups. A more minor goal is to straighten a few minor academic problems, such as paper writing. Looking back, I was not prepared for the pressures of a college education. I honestly feel I was, (and to some extent still am) too immature to take full advantage of the splendid opportunities available here. I was scared stiff by my instructors, I did not take my work seriously enough, and had no idea of either how to relate to other people or what the hell I was here for. I intend to change that.

I hope to succeed in giving myself a strong moral foundation through religion; learn discipline through regular jobs, paying bills, all the lessons on independence; and dabbling in special interests to see what I want to specialize in. My job at a Christian Science nursing home has given me many opportunities for religious practice plus disciplining me in the hardships of an eight-hour job. My free time is spent studying the Bible and other religious material. Not a monk's life! I have taken an acting class and dance class. I am now studying voice and guitar. I enjoy the city and feel it is a vital part of my education.

To face my total self, i.e. my angers, fears, hopes, defense mechanisms; and to experience the unreality of all that is commonly held to be real. To practice Taoism without having to learn a single chapter. To find out what I really like to do so that I can see if I should return to school.

To take time to think and do things slowly. Get to know myself better. Learn what it is I want to do in the future, and if there is any value in going to college. I hope to be living and learning in a true community--people sharing their love, life, and knowledge with one another. Also making a necessary break with my parental dependencies. I'll be living and working on a commune in California - helping build a new community - with progressive, (educated!) people. Also being in the country - doing art work, and some writing (keeping a journal, with fantasies of making it into a book someday) getting things together.

I hoped to re-enter and examine a life style that I lost when I went to college. Also, trying to do some of two years deferred reading. Performing in a band, self-regulated reading plan and writing.

I felt that I was wasting my time and my parent's money by staying in college. I also wanted to experience ways of life different than the sheltered academic community. Also, I felt the need to simply exist. I have been working, so that when I have enough money I can travel.

I wanted to have a break in the middle of my college years; to look at what I'd been doing and to think about what I wanted to be doing. I wanted to do something on my own. I felt college had been too programmed, and I was caught up in the schedules and busy work. I wanted to free myself from these binds. I travelled to Europe for two months, meeting people and experiencing new lifestyles. I got a better perspective on myself when I got to new countries where I was the foreigner. It was interesting to see how well I could get along on my previous experiences and my own sensitivity to new people.

I want things to open my eyes. I have been in school for fourteen or more years. School and TV put on the blinders more than anything else. By doing as nearly as possible what I want to do.

Better Perspective on College Education: In the course of their college years, some students are overwhelmed by a feeling of staleness. They have been going to school too long. They find it repetitive in its methods of instruction and specialized, perhaps constricted, in its outlook. It is hard for them to reconcile the high value placed upon a college education by society and their own evaluation of their day-to-day experiences in the classroom and laboratory and library. They have a sense that away from the campus, life is lived by different standards and to different ends. Yet, they have been led to believe that their access to a meaningful and fulfilling role in society is dependent upon their acquiring the credential of a college degree. They have difficulty in appraising their college experience while it is in process. They take leave of their college to gain a more basic understanding of why they are attending college and how they might relate to it with greater benefit and enjoyment. Some wish to explore the possibility that other alternatives might serve them just as well. After a time they discover that the forces that led them to seek admission to college -- societal pressures, expectations of their parents, the example of their friends, and their own unexamined assumptions about the functions and values of going to college -- are insufficient to sustain their involvements in the collegiate enterprise.[13]

> To revive the joy and pleasure I once took in learning, to renew the desire that has been taken away from me in previous educational experiences. To do this, I think that the perspective I will get away from school will be enough. Working for six months, then travel in Europe.
>
> I don't want to go to college because other people want me to go. I want to know why I'm going and what I'm going for. When I find that out, I'm bound to benefit more from the experience than otherwise. I have been and will be travelling and working. During the past year I have lived in an unheated farm house in Maine, an apartment in Philadelphia, a grass hut in Mexico. I have been a waitress, a counselor, a secretary. Through these varied experiences, I learn more about myself and other people.
>
> I hope to have time to consider which major to pursue and, whether or not to come back to this college at all, to make some money and spend time in a school volunteer project which I have been involved since I was in high school. I will be working two days a week as a secretary and three days as a teacher's aide in a school in Roxbury.
>
> I want to find out whether I really need a college education in order to be productive in a challenging full-time job. I hope to find out what, if anything, I am missing in the way of social, intellectual, or academic background. Also, how will other people evaluate my experiences if they're not documented by a diploma? I have been working as a Policy Aide in the Governor's Office in Rhode Island. It is full-time, challenging, yet frustrating position. Basically, I'm finding out what my limits are in terms of my capabilities and ability to deal with political and social situations.
>
> To better define what I wish to get out of my college experience. To expose myself to the hardships and rewards of an intellectual, adult life, and to grow as a person. Writing and playing pop music in a band. The success or failure of the band, and my relative happiness during the leave will help determine if music will be my career. This directly effects what my undergraduate expectations will be. As to personal growth, for the first time in my

life, I am not confined to a passive preparatory learning role. I am learning quite a lot but not at the expense of doing.

For fifteen years now I've gone to school. I felt, with a little financial pressure behind me, that allowing myself an alternative life-style and different opportunities might be a wise idea. I've never had the chance to plot a course other than through schooling and I want to see what may present itself. Basically I feel my leave will be just a varied style of classroom setting. I will be working in the Bavarian Alps in Germany from October through April. From April through June I will be travelling around Africa. I wish to visit certain countries, not as a tourist just passing through, but as one who, taking into consideration the time element, can get a feel for the style of life there as close as possible to the native inhabitants.

My objectives were to get away from the routine of going to school year after year and to see where I am headed. I am now working as a computer programmer trainee in the data department of the largest manufacturer in Sweden.

I want to change the pattern of my life. I went to school for thirteen consecutive years. Thus I felt for one year I'd change my pattern of life. I plan to work full time and perhaps do some travelling within the United States.

I was tired of school with its structured, pressured atmosphere. My objectives are to experience being independent financially and, otherwise, to become more self-aware and have somewhat of a sense of how to enjoy living. I would like to gain a better idea of what I like to do and would therefore like to study (i.e. Biology, Anthropology). I am now working at a lucrative job as a waitress. I have much free time and read novels continuously (my favorite pastime). Also live with two art students and am learning about sculpture. I spend time making clay pots, also. I plan to get some sort of work involved with study of wolves in the wild -- one of my main interests. Also would like maybe to do bookkeeping.

To get away from school, not because I dislike it, or find it irrelevant, but just because I am temporarily bored with it, with the sameness of the past three years. I will be pursuing basically the same course of studies, for credit, in Rome, Italy rather than at my college.

To escape from the intense academic life here, read books that I want to read and be able to learn from them without doing it for a professor, give much thought to the validity of my college experience and what I intend to do after college, be able to socialize without feeling married to my work. I'll be reading (mostly non-fiction), traveling, socializing, relaxing, generally trying to live for myself rather than others (i.e. the university) and still attain some level of productivity (intellectual and physical activity).

An interruption of academic monotony (the vicious cycle of books about books) and involvement in a real world. A chance to re-orient myself towards academic study and through my own readings to redirect the thrust of my studies. Improvement of my financial standing. I am working as a staff member of a program center for retired people, intimately involved with people, not books about books. I have time for self-directed reading and leisurely reflection upon my studies. My paycheck goes in the bank.

I left to join the Fred Harris campaign in the New Hampshire primary. This has fizzled out unfortunately. I left my university not just to join the campaign for Harris (which I knew was pretty shakey anyway), that was more a catylyst in my decision to leave. Through the first semester of my sophomore year, things were not working as satisfactorily as they might. I found myself approaching potentially fascinating courses in an overly mechanical manner, without inspiration or any feeling of inner direction. That's a waste of money and opportunities. When I got involved in New Hampshire, I saw there was a chance for a completely different life, and took it. Working now in Washington, D.C. I remain a resounding "non-student" for the first time in seventeen years.

Reactions to Pressure and Feeling of Not Being in Control: A variation on the foregoing theme emphasizes the need for relief from the pressures and controls that permeate college life. The college year is sprinkled with time deadlines. What the student does and when he or she does it is set, to a considerable degree, by instruction assignments and course schedules. An institutionally determined course load specifies how broadly one's attention and efforts will be divided. Commonly, one's living space is shared with others and one's psychological space is invaded and probed in the close and exposed relationships that characterize dormitory living. The need to withdraw is not necessarily an expression of dissatisfaction but rather of a need for recovery and revitalization. Frequently it is because students value their educations that they take actions designed to help them re-engage their college work with a greater sense of purpose and control.[14]

I took the leave with the intention of expanding my experiences on a human, non-textbook level. I also took it to temporarily separate myself from the pressures of college existence. I spent six weeks touring England, Wales, Ireland and France on bicycle. The whole idea while overseas was one of living day by day and getting totally caught up in the environment.

School had begun to seem like an endless parade of papers and exams. It seemed that I would finish school by sticking to it till it ended, and I wanted to be excited about my work, and to have more direction. I needed time to think over and make decisions concerning my academic priorities and my lifestyle. I needed to regain a feeling of mastery over my own life, as school, in its paternalism, tends to reduce one to a child with few responsibilities other than selfish ones, and I found this irresponsibility permeating relationships with college students. I wanted to try to be a "real person" (knowing that I could always run back to school and that charade of life). I have been working at the Sandy Hook Marine Lab in New Jersey. I will be leaving there, either to travel or to study, I'm not sure just yet. I find now that my plans are no longer defined as they might be were I still at school or highly achievement oriented. I feel more confident that what I do will be worthwhile to me, no matter how it looks or sounds to my college. It is true that one learns a lot outside of school, but if one's head is still too intensely academic, much of what there is to learn will pass by. It is important to change your attitude once you leave school, to try to discover your own values and needs outside of the definition laid down by the College experience.

I want to get away from the pressures of college and have time to justify to myself my undertaking of the social, academic and financial burdens there. I will work at my summer job -- family business -- substitute teach at the local high school, read and exercise and just try to get back to the mental state I was in at the end of high school (not so disillusioned).

I hope to collect my thoughts and orient myself without the pressures of the college environment, these pressures being misdirected and confusing to me. Presently, I am working in an office and in a few weeks I plan on travelling to Europe. I hope to pursue the above objectives by divorcing myself as much as possible from my achievement oriented college.

I have found that being in college leaves me no time to be anything other than a student. I took a leave in the hope that I would have time to think and just generally get my head together and figure out the reasons and direction of my future as well as past activities. School left me no time for that.

Time to be away, gain perspective and come into contact with my needs and desires as opposed to those that I feel in college. Continue informal study of nutrition and plant ecology and work towards putting together a self-sufficient experimental garden. Knowing these subjects a little better will indicate if this is where I want to make the committment and investment. Basically, I was just getting too "off center" to feel good about my direction. As a result of this, the fever and creativity with which I could approach my studies and living situation was on a decline. Stop the bus at this point and check a map.

I'm not sure yet what I hope to accomplish. I took a leave because I was wasting my time (academically): getting good grades but putting little effort into work and getting little out of it. Also, I'm in a state of indecision about what I want to do with my life. I want to be working full time, but as yet I have not found a job. By living in a different environment, some different (and fewer) friends, I hope to be able to come to some conclusions about what I want to do, etc.

I left because I was dissatisfied with the curriculum. I lost my love for learning. The atmosphere was highly competitive and stagnant. I will enroll at another university. I will be studying and taking a variety of courses which my school does not offer.

My primary objective is to achieve some sort of perspective; because college is a sort of "ivory tower" (although I'm very happy in it), I felt it necessary to take a break and experience a more realistic world with more decisions and less protection. Initially, I'll be working on a farm. For the following three months I plan to do a major research paper in my concentration field (art history) and work with a professor on a film. This is all to take place in France. Living in France will also be beneficial for my other major, comparative literature, for which mastery of three languages is necessary. This semester will fulfill my objective in that I'll be pursuing study and work that are related to my academic field at school.

All my life I have been a student and summer vacations have (with only one exception) been spent in my immediate home community working or doing volunteer work. During my leave of absence I would like to become acquainted with different people, values, lifestyles; gain perspective on myself and the world. Summer '74 travelled throughout Europe. Fall '74 working in a law office in downtown D.C., working in political campaign.

Wider experience, especially in areas more relevant to living in present day society. Growth. Gain more definite knowledge of direction career-wise. Clearer idea of what I want educationally. Working as a community organizer, gaining experience in dealing with people from different backgrounds. Constructive approach to socio-economic problems in inner city. Experience in working world. Wider, different experience -- knowledge of choices.

To return to college with an improved attitude, better prepared to do extensive study and research. To get a better idea of my future plans. To ease the financial burden on my parents.

Career Concerns: Career aspirations are the pole star by which many students and their parents hope to chart their college program. Beneath whatever rhetoric they may employ concerning the value of forming lifelong friendships or establishing a love of learning that will enrich their lives, the bedrock of their expectations is the belief that college will be the avenue through which they will have access to some self-fulfilling occupation in the world of work. Some look to the college experience to provide a clarification of their career goals. In an economic society, feelings of self-worth are closely related to how one earns a living. The search for self pivots about the question of one's vocation. Issues such as "what am I good at?" "where do my interests lie?" "do I have what it takes to succeed in a particular calling?" become critical to self-discovery and to self-acceptance.

Others have selected a career to which they aspire: tentatively, or with deep commitment. Their expectation is that college will contribute to their career preparation, directly in the acquisition of knowledge and skills, or more subtly in the formation of attitudes and elements of character. For those with professional ambitions, securing favorable recommendations from professors and compiling a transcript that is "competitive" can easily become goals that overshadow other considerations of what the college experience might be.

Students who attend colleges of the liberal arts frequently are distressed to discover that there is a great institutional ambivalence about their vocational concerns. The relationship of their course work to their career objective is not readily apparent and, with few exceptions, their instructors are unable to or uninterested in explicating the connections. Whatever measure of academic success students enjoy, their classroom achievements provide few useful cues in evaluating their vocational fitness. The college community provides limited role models for the aspiring lawyer, accountant, investment counselor, physician, artist, community organizer or any other of the hundreds of vocations in which college students will be employed.

In times of relative affluence, students feel less pressured to make career decisions and are less concerned with optimizing their credentials. But in times when admission to graduate and professional study is highly competitive and graduation from college gives no assurance of an attractive entry position in the labor market, the relationship of college to career becomes a focal point of anxiety that directs and sometimes distorts the college experience of many students. Recognizing deficiencies in their earlier developmental experiences, and finding the college environment poorly suited to providing experiences that give instruction and testing in relation to career suitability or vocational readiness, some students find it helpful to leave the college, for a time, in order to address more directly their concerns about a career.[15]

> Full-time employment, with the bulk of my earnings going towards next year's tuition. Time devoted to laying out plans for next year and the years after graduation from college.
>
> To decide upon a career. Regular business employment, possibly entering a non-collegiate training program or deciding at which school and in which program I would resume my studies.
>
> I hope to make my final decision about my future career; to gain more independence by doing something totally on my own without the support of my parents or best friends; to have time alone to think about my life, and to do things I haven't had time for in college (music and dance lessons, art, bicycling, reading). I will be living in an apartment in Connecticut with three other girls and working as assistant to field botanist at the University of Connecticut. Biology is a possible future profession for me. I will be able to take lessons (music, etc.) at the University of Connecticut unofficially.
>
> I am trying to make the decision of going into a career of scientific research or film making. Right now I am working in a lab. After the summer I hope to be working in a T.V. studio.
>
> I hope to use this time to think more seriously about my future plans. I have been looking into career opportunities for college graduates in my field, and other colleges which might be better able to meet my needs. I would like to get the restlessness out of my system through travel and by pursuing things which I like to do. Above all, I hope to miss college very much and to return with an improved attitude. I don't want to waste my college years.
>
> To decide whether or not to apply to medical school. To get away from school for a while so I can take a more objective look at the direction that my life is taking. To earn money. Working in a candy factory. Volunteering in a hospital.

I hope to decide what to do with my life. I want to improve my ability as a guitar player. I wanted to live with my girlfriend, as we were deeply in love and I missed her at school (we lived together the previous summer). Unfortunately, the romance died. Working, thinking, travelling and practicing.

I wanted to explore the architectural field while still an undergraduate and see if that was what really interested me. I wanted to leave my college for a while in order to get some sort of perspective on it and determine what I wanted to get out of my last terms there. I wanted a year of something very different from my previous two years at my college -- to learn and think in a different way in a different environment. I went to the Architectural Association in London, England and took a year's study in their intermediate school.

I hope to put to practical use in the area of mental health some of my academic preparation. Another important objective is to see if I am capable in this work and to see if my interest will increase or decrease when actually confronted with the situation. Aside from my career development I feel strongly that a break is needed from the usual four year college environment. I am living and working in a therapeutic community for emotionally disturbed individuals. Twenty-four hour a day exposure to the workings of a mental institution in addition to the stresses and/or pleasures of the patients themselves will surely be evident after six months.

I took my "leave of absence" to gain some practical experience in the field of Environmental Engineering before I had completed my course of study. This way, I could be sure that I wanted to pursue this field of study. I have been working in my field of interest to make sure that this is the field of engineering that I am interested in. The practical on the job experience that I have received in recent months has proven to be invaluable.

I hope to have enough experience in a teaching situation this term to enable me to decide whether or not to continue pursuing my goal -- teaching and academics. I hope to regain a degree of strength through meaningful relationships with committed people -- a rare commodity on a 20th century college campus. Relieving my parents of the financial burden of college for at least a year in hopes that there will be work next year from various sources -- summer work and financial aid. I want to gain a better awareness of all my options not only in careers but in lifestyles. The first term of my leave will be spent as a teaching intern in a secondary private school. My specific duties are as of yet unclear, but they will include teaching, reading and writing, lectures and counseling. I will be working with many committed individuals. The second term will be spent in low cost travelling in Great Britain.

> I hope to gain experience in the areas of law and politics
> particularly in relation to using these processes to effect
> change in society. I want to understand what people in-
> volved in these areas actually do, how they go about
> doing it, and what type of goals they have. College
> fails to give students any kind of healthy dimensional
> view of a working life, especially one tied to specific
> social goals. I decided I needed this type of experience
> to make my own career decisions. I am a staff member
> for the Governor's Commission on the Status of Women in
> Massachusetts. My work centers on legislation, research-
> ing, monitoring, and lobbying for bills affecting women.

As these statements illustrate, the decision to take a leave is prompted by many individual interests and needs. The particular activities in which students engage are a resultant of many circumstances: some related to the college's willingness and ability to give guidance or substance to the leave, some reflecting the student's own initiative, resourcefulness, and desires, some that are beyond the direct influence of either college or student. One group of leavetakers pursues enrichment of their academic programs by participating in educational opportunities not available to them at their college. Others seek some form of personal growth or healing that they feel requires a different schedule, or environment, or commitment. These are students whose leave is primarily a retreat from a situation that they found unsatisfactory in some regard. There are those who use their leave to search for another college or situation that may better serve their interests. Still others seek for personal growth that will permit them to participate in college life with a greater sense of accomplishment and enjoyment. Almost all identify positive goals which they expect to be able to pursue more effectively during a temporary absence from the college campus than they could through consecutive enrollments, term after term, until their graduation.

A further perspective on the complex of factors that motivate leavetaking is provided by the responses of students who do not consider or who choose not to act upon this option. Circumstances that motivate some students to take a leave of absence cause other students to remain in college. Students who had been enrolled in college for five or six consecutive semesters reported reactions to their academic program and to their broader college experience that were in many respects similar to those of leave-takers. However they made the judgment that their interests were better served by maintaining the continuity of their academic program and in some cases by completing requirements for their degree in the shortest time possible. Approximately one-half expressed satisfaction with their decision to remain at their college.

In response to the question, With the wisdom of hindsight and the opportunity to choose again whether to continue your program of studies at this college without taking a leave, would you . . . ?, thirty-two percent indicated that they definitely or probably would take a leave. Nineteen percent were uncertain and forty-nine percent indicated that they probably or definitely would not take a leave. Twenty-three percent of those who did not take a leave reported that they had investigated the possibility of taking a leave. An additional eleven percent actively attempted to arrange for a leave but remained because they were unable to work out a leave situation that was satisfactory to them or to the college.

The reasons most commonly cited for not taking a leave were: the desire to finish as quickly as possible, judged to be an "important" or "determining" consideration by fifty-four percent of non-leave takers; undesirable discontinuities in program of studies, cited as "important" or "determining" by forty-one percent; available leave activities not sufficiently attractive, by forty-three percent; financial considerations by thirty-eight percent, and loss of association with college friends by thirty-five percent.

Twenty-three percent said that opposition of parents was a determining or important consideration, while forty-five percent stated that this was not a consideration in their decision. For twenty-two percent inability to participate in college activities that are important to me was important or determining; forty-seven percent said that it was not a consideration for them.

The suggested reasons for not taking a leave that the smallest percentages of respondents coded "important" or "determining" were: unsatisfactory leave experience of other students, only three percent with seventy-six percent stating that it was not a consideration; friends advised against taking a leave, five percent with seventy percent coding it as not a consideration; faculty advisor(s) recommended against taking a leave, six percent and seventy-eight percent; loss of association with particular members of the faculty, nine percent and sixty percent; and college regulations made taking a leave difficult or unattractive, eleven percent with sixty-nine percent reporting it was not a consideration.

Many of these observations are repeated in more graphic and personalized form in the statements that students made about their reasons for not taking a leave. A few of their comments are quoted here to illustrate the wide range of opinions and feelings that were expressed. Students who did not take a leave experienced the same external pressures and internal emotionalized state that other students had mentioned as having contributed to their decision to take a leave. Some of those who remained did not feel that leaving college was an option for them because of financial constraints or the need to complete their work as quickly as possible. Some had enjoyed the benefits of a leave before they entered college and others considered it prudent to postpone such activities until after their graduation from college. Still others were able to alternate summer activities with those of the collegiate year in a manner that satisfied their needs for different kinds of involvements and satisfactions. There were those who remained because of parental or peer pressures or because of their own inability to exercise initiative or because their academic program required it. Finally, there were those who remained at their college because they were pleased and satisfied with their life there. College was meeting their needs to a degree that no other alternative was equally appealing.

> I am the oldest of seven children. Taking a leave would be outrageous because of the financial factors involved and the wasted time involved. Taking a leave gives no academic credit towards a degree and is totally useless academically. If colleges eased up on their pressures and requirements and gave academic credit towards a degree for things learned outside the academic world, then I would consider taking a leave.
>
> One of the major reasons I do not plan to take a year off is that the cost of attending college is rising at such a great rate, it would be ridiculous not to finish as soon as possible and pay less in the process.
>
> A leave would have put me in danger of being drafted. My selective service number was twenty-three.
>
> I was married the second semester of my sophomore year to a student in the same year of schooling as myself.
>
> I took a year off between high school and college which is one reason I haven't taken a leave yet.
>
> At present, I plan to take time off between college and graduate school. Although I have never taken a leave, it is very important to me to work in the summers doing non-academic things.
>
> My primary reason for not taking a leave was to graduate as soon as possible -- will have completed college in two and one-half years as of January.

I attended a public "free" school during my junior and senior years in high school. For eight months I worked in a law commune in New York City. It was an area of interest and also a possible career option. Also I have spent a number of summers in activities that, for me, served the purpose of a leave. All of these acquainted me with the practical side of my interests. I have chosen to stay at school to pursue the academic and theoretical aspects of these areas.

I am about to graduate after three years. I never seriously believed I could take a leave, or else I might have considered it. I was very affected by the lock-step view, and initially guided myself in large measure in that light. Now I might do things very differently, but I think what has happened has also been good.

I thought about taking a leave or transferring many times but it takes an effort and a commitment that I haven't been willing to give. I have met a number of good friends here and do not really want to leave them.

I think that leaves are extremely important and feel that for my own growth and confidence, I probably should have taken one. Had I been more willing to take risks without needing unrealistic guarantees of how well the leave would work out, been willing to trust my own judgment and not felt the need to justify my leaving by some rigid, not necessarily applicable, criterion, I would have.

I play varsity sports in both the spring and fall and this prevents me from leaving campus either semester. I feel that the college years will be my last chance for this type of athletic activity and I would not like to forfeit it.

I'm working to obtain my certification to teach secondary school in the fields of history, social studies and French. This has required that I spend my last two years on campus in order to fulfill all the requirements. I would have liked to take a semester off somewhere to do community work, but this was not feasible in terms of my priorities.

Taking time off mid-college seems to do some people a lot of good, and I've thought of doing it a lot myself, but I think that it would have been disruptive of my educational and social life. At the time I thought most of doing it, everything turned upwards and I felt no reason to. As it turns out, I have become less sure of myself as far as career and educational goals go, and if I were not as far along, I probably would take time off now. I have satisfied my "taking time off" desires to some degree by my summer activities.

I did not want to take a leave until I had more or less decided on my major field. Now that my goals have jelled, I am actively planning to take a semester leave

> in which I hope to do independent research or obtain field work experience in my major field -- psychology.
>
> I stay at college because I like it here. I am close to my best friends, cordial and friendly with most others. I feel I am learning -- sometimes <u>despite</u> the institution -- but learning, nonetheless. I have numerous positive relationships with faculty -- both personally rewarding, as well as intellectually stimulating. Sure the place gets me down sometimes, but anything would.

Contemporary American college-attending youth face a number of critical developmental tasks. They must acquire competence and establish the bases for personal achievement and social usefulness. This commonly involves the identification of a general career area or a more specific occupational objective for which the individual prepares through appropriate educational programs and work experiences. Many students do not have the level of self-understanding or the awareness of the world of work that permits them to make vocational commitments with confidence. They know that their acceptance into programs of graduate or professional training will depend, in part, upon the level of their academic performance in college and that the competition for favorable employment places an increasing importance upon the acquisition of appropriate credentials. Both the student's self-regard and the eventual career opportunities that may be available to him or her are related to the measure of academic success that is achieved in college. Indicators of academic accomplishment and of progress toward establishing qualifications for a career contribute substantially to the student's sense of identity and personal worth, for what one can do and how one makes a living determines, to a degree, one's social status and provides a foundation for functioning as a mature, economically independent adult.

A second developmental task involves the mature resolution of problems of authority. Maturity implies the flexibility and the judgment to function both independently and cooperatively: the capacity to exercise authority, to be self-motivating and self-directing, and to accept instruction, direction and control as may be appropriate in a given situation. The contemporary college campus presents a confusing array of demands for conformity and independence. Students are expected to exercise personal initiative and to assume responsibility for their education, their personal conduct and their social relationships in a context of rules, procedures and requirements that often place them in dependent and subservient roles. Students who have not already made substantial progress in achieving a mature resolution of their independence-dependency needs find themselves conflicted by the contradictory demands of the college environment and may experience a degree of stress that interferes with their growth in this aspect of their personal development.

A third task involves moving from self-centeredness to a capacity for intimacy, to an ability to give and to receive love in its many forms of expression and in ways that respect the personhood of each of the parties. The college campus provides unusual closeness to large numbers of people and affords many occasions for sharing. But some find the social environment oppressive and limited by its homogeneity and unrepresentativeness of the larger society. Fulfilling the role of student forces them to concentrate on their intellectual development to the neglect of their emotional and spiritual growth. The intrusiveness of the college's demands leaves little time or energy for the cultivation of close personal relationships.

The reasons that students give for taking a leave may be read as a statement of the many ways in which the experiences of "growing up in America" and of being educated in its institutions of elementary and secondary education bring students to college unprepared to respond fully to the rich opportunities inherent in the college experience. It is also an indication of the many ways in which colleges frustrate some of their students in their quest for wholeness and the full development of their personhood.

CHAPTER 3

Who Takes a Leave?

Who takes a leave? Freshmen, sophomores, juniors and seniors do. Men and women do. Students who are skirting academic probation and potential Phi Betes do. Students with majors from art to zoology are numbered among the leave-takers. People who were happy in their college situation take leaves and so do some whose college years have been filled with raging discontents. The number of students enrolled in colleges of the liberal arts and sciences who spend at least one semester away from the campus is so large that no sizeable sub-group of students is unrepresented among those who take a leave of absence.

Students who take a leave do not differ greatly, in respect to their personal and family characteristics, from students who remain in college without taking a leave. There are small differences that do not exceed chance probabilities in the proportions of the two groups that graduated from public high schools or from various types of private secondary schools. Minority students are less likely to take a leave than are those not identified with a minority group. There are suggestive but inconclusive indications that leave-takers, on the average, come from more affluent family backgrounds. Equally worthy of observation is the great amount of overlap in the distributions of the two groups on all of the characteristics that are inquired about on the Background Information Form. It would be tedious and unprofitable to the interests of many readers to present a detailed review of this information. For those who wish to examine some of the data obtained from this form, the responses of leave-takers and of persons who had been continuously enrolled for five or six semesters are presented in table 5.

TABLE 5
Percentage of Students Within Various Sub-groups Who Selected Given Alternatives to Items of the BACKGROUND INFORMATION FORM

Listed for the following groups:
1. Employment the principal activity during a significant portion of leave
2. Employed a substantial or moderate amount of time during leave
3. Limited or no time devoted to employment during leave
4. All leave-takers who completed Survey 2
5. All respondents to Survey 4 (Continuously enrolled for five or six semesters)

	Groups				
	1.	2.	3.	4.	5.
Item 1. From what kind of secondary school did you graduate?					
Public high school	61%	63%	60%	61%	66%
Alternative school	2	3	1	2	1
Independent private school	24	24	28	26	19
Private school, religious affiliation	11	7	9	9	13
Private school, other sponsorship	2	3	2	2	1
Number of cases	333	245	562	1140	764
Item 2. Are you:					
White/Caucasian	94	92	94	93	89
Black/Negro/Afro-American	2	4	2	3	7
Other minority groups	4	4	4	4	4
Item 3. Are you:					
An only child	5	7	3	4	7
The oldest child	37	33	31	33	35
The youngest child	23	28	31	28	31
An in-between child	35	32	35	35	27
Item 5: Your sex:					
Male	60	54	35	54	55
Female	40	46	65	46	45
Item 6. Which of the following is currently true about your parents?					
Both alive and married to each other	83	79	85	83	84
Both alive and divorced or separated	10	14	8	10	8
One or both parents deceased	7	7	7	7	8
Item 7. Which of the following categories comes closest to your Father's occupation?					
Profession requiring advanced degree	34	29	34	33	29
High level executive	24	25	25	25	20
Profession requiring bachelor's degree	10	15	12	12	16
Owner, manager, officer	15	19	20	19	17
Other	17	12	9	11	18

TABLE 5 continued

	Groups				
	1.	2.	3.	4.	5.

Item 8a. How much formal education does your Father have?

Highest graduate or professional degree	26%	25%	31%	28%	25%
Master's degree	15	13	13	14	15
Advanced study without degree	7	8	8	8	7
Bachelor's degree	25	28	27	26	21
Attended college	9	15	9	10	10
Other	18	11	12	14	22

Item 8b. How much formal education does your Mother have?

Highest graduate or professional degree	5	2	4	4	3
Master's degree	16	14	16	15	16
Advanced study without degree	4	4	7	5	4
Bachelor's degree	29	31	36	33	25
Attended college	22	24	18	20	18
Other	24	25	19	23	34

Item 9. What is your best estimate of the total income last year of your parental family? Consider annual income from all sources before taxes.

Over $50,000	24	20	28	25	22
$30,000-$50,000	27	26	32	29	25
$20,000-$29,999	23	24	24	24	25
$10,000-$19,999	18	23	13	16	21
Below $10,000	8	7	3	6	7

Item 10. What is your best estimate of when you will return to this college from your leave?

One term	43	48	50	47	Does not apply
Two terms	41	34	41	40	
Three or more terms	3	9	2	4	
Duration cannot be decided	9	6	5	6	
My present expectation is that I will not return to this college	4	3	2	3	

Item 12. Have you ever lived or traveled outside the limits of the continental United States?

Yes	77	78	87	82	72
No	23	22	13	18	28
Lived or Traveled in:					
Western Hemisphere	43	33	37	38	45
Europe	51	52	69	60	42
Middle East	8	8	15	11	8
Far East	5	4	6	6	4
Africa	3	4	5	4	2

Because there are some interesting differences between leave-takers whose principal activity was employment and those who were not employed, the record of these sub-groups is presented in this table also. Note particularly that a greater proportion of men than of women had employment as their principal leave activity. There was little relationship between family income and amount of time on leave that was spent in gainful employment. Although some students' employment was motivated primarily by financial need, for many it represented a learning experience undertaken to foster personal development (greater independence, self-reliance, competence in managing personal affairs) and to facilitate career exploration. Fewer persons who were employed had, previous to their leave, traveled outside the continental United States. Of those who did, the largest percentage had traveled in the western hemisphere whereas the largest percentage of those who were not employed had traveled or lived in Europe.

As can be observed in appendix I, most of the questions of Surveys 1 and 4 are very similar or identical in wording. The responses to many of these common items by leave-takers (Survey 1) and by persons in continuous enrollment (Survey 4) did not differ by amounts that exceeded chance probabilities. The high degree of similarity in their responses can be observed in tables 6, 7 and 8. In these tables and throughout the chapter, students who were in continuous enrollment for five or six semesters will be referred to as "controls." The responses of the two groups were significantly different on several items related to the importance attached to formal education and to opportunities for personal attention and the pursuit of individual interests. Leave-takers did not place as great a personal importance upon the earning of a college degree and were less confident of their plans for formal education beyond college.

How important is it to you that you obtain a college degree?

	Leave Takers	Controls
1. It is essential to my development and to my future	28%	39%
2. It is extremely important to me.	24%	31%
3. It is fairly important to me.	30%	22%
4. It is not very important to me.	11%	4%
5. I would not attend college if a college degree were not a social and vocational necessity.	7%	4%

After obtaining your bachelor's degree, do you expect to continue your education in a graduate or a professional school?

	Leave Takers	Controls
1. Definitely yes	21%	39%
2. Probably yes	53%	45%
3. Probably not	21%	12%
4. Definitely not	4%	2%
5. Do not intend to complete bachelor's degree	1%	0%

The amount of time that leave-takers and those who did not leave devoted to activities directly related to their program of studies was essentially the same, as was the time devoted to non-curricular activities and to employment.

During the present term or the last in which you were enrolled, how much time per week, on the average, have you devoted to activities directly related to your program of studies (include class and laboratory time, reading, papers, problem sets, field or studio work, etc.)?

	Leave Takers	Controls
1. Less than 20 hours per week	10%	9%
2. 20 to 29 hours per week	17%	16%
3. 30 to 39 hours per week	28%	30%
4. 40 to 49 hours per week	29%	29%
5. 50 or more hours per week	16%	16%
Average number of hours per week	37.2	37.5
Percent of respondents answering "so variable" that an average is meaningless or "don't really know."	16%	13%

During the present term or the last in which you were enrolled, how much time per week, on an average, have you devoted to activities that you pursued with some degree of regularity and commitment (e.g., organized extra-curricular or community activities, personal projects such as writing, music, personal exercise, etc.)?

	Leave Takers	Controls
1. Practically none	9%	9%
2. Less than 5 hours per week	16%	17%
3. 5 to 9 hours per week	31%	30%
4. 10 to 19 hours per week	29%	28%
5. 20 or more hours per week	15%	16%
Average number of hours per week	10.7	10.8
Percent responding too variable or don't know	14%	10%

During the present term, or the last in which you were enrolled, how much time, on the average, have you spent in gainful employment or in a work-study (bursary) program?

	Leave Takers	Controls
1. None	48%	50%
2. Less than 5 hours per week	10%	10%
3. 5 to 9 hours per week	19%	22%
4. 10 to 14 hours per week	15%	11%
5. 15 or more hours per week	8%	7%
Average number of hours per week	8.9	9.1
Percent responding too variable or don't know	6%	3%

As can be observed in table 6, leave-takers placed somewhat less importance upon their coursework than did those who remained at college. In turn, they place greater importance upon self-directed activities as is indicated by their average rankings of alternatives 6, 7, 3, 5 and 8. The two groups did not differ significantly in their average ratings of difficulties except for the alternative, handling the content of my courses, a difference that probably relates to the importance attached to doing well, as indicated by the grades received (see table 8). Fifty-five percent of the leave-takers stated that they attached quite a bit or a great deal of importance to getting good grades in contrast to sixty-four percent of those who did not leave.

Of the twenty-two aspects of college life that students were asked to rate in terms of their degree of satisfaction, only five elicited significantly different expressions of satisfaction-dissatisfaction from the two groups (see table 7). Leave-takers were less satisfied with the availability of faculty and with the availability of courses, etc., in field of their principal interest. The average number of faculty members that respond to you as a person and show a personal interest in you was reported to be the same by members of the two groups, but leave-takers were less satisfied with their colleges' ability or willingness to respond to their individual needs and requirements. They also experienced the social environment of their college as less fulfilling to their interests. It was noted earlier that leave-takers assigned a higher priority of importance to social life and social relationships but a greater proportion found themselves frustrated and dissatisfied in this regard. Their greater frequency of dissatisfaction with their college living arrangements was reflected in the larger percentage who describe the social relationships of their living arrangements as superficial or mixed: forty-seven percent

TABLE 6

Mean Index of Importance of College Activities
Based upon Survey 1, Item Y and Survey 4, Item U

Judging by the amount of time, effort and attention that you have given to each during the present term (or the last in which enrolled), what relative degree of importance do (did) you attach to the activities listed below? (Activities in which persons did not have some degree of involvement were not ranked.)

1 = ranked as most important

9 = ranked as least important

Listed in order of importance to leave-takers

		Leave Takers	Controls
1.	Course work in my major field	2.7	2.5
2.	Coursework in general	3.2	2.9
6.	Social life and social relationships	3.1	3.5
7.	Self-discovery, self-insight, discovery of new interests, talents, life-style, etc.	3.5	3.9
3.	Individual study, research, writing, artwork, etc.	4.0	4.7
4.	Organized extracurricular activities	5.2	4.9
5.	Concerts, exhibits, seminars, lectures	5.3	5.8
9.	Gainful employment	6.1	6.1
8.	Active involvement in community and/or political affairs	6.2	6.7

TABLE 7

Satisfaction-Dissatisfaction Index
Based upon Survey 1, Item AA and Survey 4, Item W

Please rate your degree of satisfaction with each of the following aspects of college life as you have experienced them during the past academic term.

1 = Highly satisfied

5 = Highly dissatisfied

Listed in order of mean satisfaction rating of leave takers

	Aspect of College Life	Leave Takers	Controls
s.	Degree of personal freedom permitted by the college	1.4	1.5
t.	Opportunity to form friendships and to experience satisfying personal relationships	2.1	1.9
u.	The help with academic or personal problems that students give to one another	2.1	2.0
l.	Academic regulations and requirements	2.1	2.3
k.	The adequacy of health services	2.2	2.8
r.	Opportunities to participate in extracurricular activities that are of interest to you	2.3	2.1
g.	Accessibility of faculty for consultation and academic assistance	2.3	2.0
d.	Opportunities to pursue your own intellectual, cultural and/or artistic interests	2.3	2.3
v.	Your living arrangements	2.4	2.1
c.	The relevance of your coursework to your own interests and concerns	2.4	2.3
f.	The recognition that your academic efforts and abilities have received from your instructors	2.4	2.4
a.	The quality of instruction	2.4	2.2
p.	Opportunities to know students who hold ideas, values and interests different from your own	2.5	2.4
b.	The intellectual leadership and stimulation provided by members of the faculty	2.6	2.4
m.	The level of academic motivation and commitment that characterizes students at your college	2.6	2.5
j.	The adequacy of professional counseling	2.9	2.8
i.	The adequacy of academic advising	3.0	2.9
*q.	Opportunities to know students from socio-economic backgrounds different from your own	3.0	2.6
*e.	Availability of courses, seminars, laboratories, independent study, etc. in fields of your principal interests	3.0	2.3

TABLE 7 continued

	Aspect of College Life	Leave Takers	Controls
n.	The amount of academic competitiveness among students	3.0	3.2
h.	Accessibility and responsiveness of the administration to students and to issues of student well-being	3.1	3.1
o.	The level of political and social awareness of students	3.2	3.1
	Mean Satisfaction Rating	2.5	2.4

TABLE 8

Mean Rating of Difficulty
Based upon Survey 1, Item Z and Survey 4, Item V

Rate the degree of difficulty that you have experienced in each of the following problem areas during the present term (or the last in which enrolled).

$\qquad$ 1 = A serious problem

$\qquad$ 5 = Not a problem

Listed in order of seriousness of difficulty to leave-takers

		Leave Takers	Controls
c.	Trying to "find myself in the sense of personal meaning and identify	2.5	2.7
d.	Making decisions concerning my career	2.7	2.7
a.	Managing my time	2.8	2.9
g.	My relationships with particular person(s) of the opposite sex	3.2	3.2
f.	Social relationships	3.4	3.5
* b.	Handling the content of my courses	3.5	3.2
h.	Finances	3.7	3.5
e.	Some aspect of parent and/or family relations	3.9	3.9
i.	Health - medical	4.5	4.4

of the leave-takers compared to thirty-five percent of the students who remained. A larger percentage also was dissatisfied with the <u>opportunities to know students from socio-economic backgrounds different from their own</u>. Although falling short of a rigid criterion of satistical significance, the greater dissatisfaction of leave-takers with <u>opportunities to form friendships and to experience satisfying personal relationships</u> is consistent with areas of noted differences between the two groups. In their systems of values, leave-takers place relatively greater importance upon social relationships and self-directed activities, while those who do not leave tend to place a greater importance on the achievement of academic recognition and the attainment of a college degree. However, as stated before, the similarities that are found among students who leave and those who stay are more extensive than are the observed differences.

All fields of concentration were represented among persons who took leaves. In relation to the major interests or programs of undergraduates, the performing arts and especially the humanities were over-represented among the leave-takers and correspondingly, persons majoring or intending to major in the social sciences, the natural sciences and in mathematics were under-represented. The declared majors of students who took leaves from Brown, Trinity and Wesleyan were:

Fine Arts	9%
Humanities	47%
Social Sciences	18%
Behavioral Sciences	9%
Natural Sciences	13%
Inter-disciplinary Majors	5%

Sixty-eight percent of the fine arts majors who took leaves were women. Women constituted fifty-one percent of the humanities majors who took a leave, twenty-nine percent of the social science majors, fifty percent of the behavioral science majors, and fifty-three percent of those with inter-disciplinary majors. These differences in the proportions of men and women who were identified with the several areas of concentration parallel rather closely the proportions that obtain among students who remain at their colleges.

There was a significant relationship between undergraduate major and principal leave activity. As may be observed in table 9, relatively few natural science majors were enrolled in formal academic programs of any kind and a larger percentage than of any other major group were employed. The principal leave activity of forty-seven percent of the inter-disciplinary majors involved something other than formal academic programs or employment. In table 9, the category "academic" includes enrollment as a student at another college or university, including enrollment for the purpose of permanent transfer, and field study that was carried out under the supervision of an advisor recognized by and responsible to the leave-granting college.

TABLE 9

Principal Leave Activity of Students
Classified according to their field of concentration

	Principal Activity			
	Academic	Employment	Self-Directed	Other
Fine Arts	59%	12%	23%	6%
Humanities	57%	21%	11%	11%
Social Science	68%	22%	6%	4%
Behavioral Science	62%	23%	3%	12%
Natural Science	35%	35%	17%	13%
Inter-disciplinary	41%	12%	24%	23%

Students majoring in the six areas of concentration did not differ in the degree of importance that they ascribed to the thirteen reasons for taking a leave that are listed in Item B, Survey 1, except in their responses to alternative "b." A significantly larger percentage of the fine arts majors (71%) stated that <u>one of the most important or crucial reasons for taking a leave at this time</u> was <u>to obtain coursework or experiences not available to me at this campus</u>. Only forty-two percent of the natural science majors considered this to be an important reason.

Among the several major groups, the fine arts and the natural science majors included the smallest percentages of those who were undecided about their career preferences: twelve percent of the fine arts majors, nineteen percent of the natural science majors and twenty-eight percent of the others stated that they were undecided. Fifty-seven percent of the fine arts majors who had a definite career preference aspired to a career in the creative arts. Fifty-four percent of the natural science majors preferred a professional career and twenty-seven percent selected an academic career. By contrast, twenty-nine percent of social science majors were undecided. Of those expressing a preference, fifty-two percent preferred a professional career, thirteen percent a career in business and only four percent preferred an academic career. The record of career preferences expressed by students within the six major fields and by persons who did not take a leave is presented in table 10.

TABLE 10

Career Preference of Students by Major Field and by Leave-Status
Percentage who selected alternatives 3 through 9 of Item X, Survey 1 or Item 5, Survey 4

In thinking about your occupational future, do you feel that in the long run you will have a preference for:

Career Preference	Major of Leave Takers							Leave-Takers	Controls
	Arts	Human-ities	Soc. Sci.	Beh. Sci.	Nat. Sci.	Inter-Disc.			
3. An academic life (teaching, research, other scholarly work).	20	31	4	22	27	34		21	20
4. A business life	--	6	13	4	2	8		7	12
5. A professional life (physician, lawyer, engineer, etc.).	17	31	52	44	54	25		31	45
6. A life of a trained technician or craftsman	--	--	2	--	4	8		3	0
7. A life centering upon some aspect of the creative arts	57	18	15	9	6	25		23	11
8. A life centering upon a home and a family	--	4	2	4	--	--		2	2
9. Other	6	10	12	17	7	--		13	9

The frequency with which persons who have a strong personal commitment to the fine arts find it desirable to take a leave of absence and sometimes to transfer to other institutions is discussed in greater detail in subsequent chapters.[16] Also deferred to chapter 5 is a discussion of the academic performance of persons who take a leave of absence. Here it will be sufficient to note that persons who take a leave were not differentiated by their respective grade point averages from those who remained in continuous enrollment. In the semester preceding their leaves, sixty-two percent of all students at Brown, Trinity and Wesleyan earned a grade point average of 3.0 or higher which is equivalent to a letter grade of "B" or better. It should be noted that this percentage is based upon the averages of all persons who took a leave in the academic years 1973-74 and 1974-75, including non-respondents to the surveys. Students who took leaves expressed a variety of discontents and dissatisfactions with their curricular programs and/or with their own academic performance and accomplishments. No doubt for many, their academic efforts did not represent the best of which they were capable and in this they were not unique in relation to the rest of the student body. However, if grade point average is accepted as a measure of effectiveness as a student, there were not significant differences between the averages of those who took a leave and those who did not. By this criterion, there is no basis for regarding leave-takers as less satisfactory students.

To leave college before receiving its degree, whether that leaving is temporary or permanent, is an outcome that runs counter to expectations, attitudes and values that are widely held in the academic community and in the larger society. Deeply imbedded in the thought and planning of individuals and in the policies of institutions is the assumption that following high school, students who aspire to upward mobility or to maintaining the socio-economic status already achieved by their families will attend college until they graduate, usually four years later. Many parents make personal sacrifices to assure the opportunity of college to their sons and daughters. Their childrens' inability or unwillingness to continue in attendance often is perceived as weakness or willfullness that threatens the very advantages that the parents had worked so hard to provide. Society looks to the colleges to occupy the time of millions of high school graduates who cannot be absorbed into the labor market immediately. By the end of this "holding period," the colleges are expected to have developed a ready pool of certified talent for business and industry and for the graduate and professional schools. Much of

American higher education, except for the junior colleges, has build this four-year expectation into its physical facilities and into the structure and operation of its curricular programs. Any substantial changes in the time of life at which people attend college or in the duration of their attendance at a particular institution could have far-reaching effects on how colleges are financed and operated. Given the powerful incentives that exist for maintaining four consecutive years the standard for college attendance, it is understandable that persons who do not conform to this norm are thought of as exceptional or deviant.

The editors of <u>The College Dropout</u> recognized this quickness to call into question the motivations, capabilities, and personal stability of students who leave. Inadequate attention is given to the ways in which colleges fail to meet students' needs and in so doing contribute to student dissatisfaction and disaffection. There is a tendency, in accepting the established structures and procedures of the academic community, to underestimate the serious purposes and the unfulfilled needs that motivates the leave-taking of the majority of the students.

> . . . the causes of dropping out lie not only in the student but also in the institution and in the interaction between the two. This view challenges those in the colleges who have been content with the simpler assumption that the trouble is always to be sought in the dropout himself.[17]

Who takes a leave of absence? Individuals from almost every major sector of the student body do. Contrary to the belief commonly held that students who don't stick it out are somehow different, the evidence developed in this study indicates that persons who take leaves do not have an identity that distinguishes them from those who remain at college.

CHAPTER 4

What Do They Do?

Having decided not to return to their colleges for a semester, a year, or longer, they stayed at home -- they made their way around the world. Some enrolled as full-time students at other colleges and universities. Some took courses while doing other things. Some carefully and deliberately isolated themselves from anything academic. They immersed themselves in hundreds of different occupations and places of work to earn money to support themselves or to finance their return to college. Others worked to support and promote a cause in which they believed, or to serve other persons, or to gain new insights and understandings of themselves, of "the real world," or of careers that they might wish to pursue.

Most of the respondents in this study spent their leave in the United States and/or in the countries of western Europe. Some travelled or lived in Canada, in Central or South America, in countries of the Middle and Far East, in Africa, in islands of the Atlantic and the Pacific, and even in Antartica and in the northern reaches of Alaska. As cases cited in this chapter and those presented in greater detail in the appendix will illustrate, students engaged in an extraordinary variety of activities.

They attended classes at the major universities of the world and at the community college in their home town. Some worked for major corporations, some in small businesses and a few in enterprises that they had organized themselves. They worked as factory operatives, as clerks and secretaries, as administrative assistants, as research technicians, and under a host of other job titles. They worked in many branches of government, at the federal, state and local levels. They worked in extragovernmental organizations such as community action groups, environmental and consumer action organizations, and with groups promoting feminist, minority, and other public-interest concerns. They were employed by schools, museums, courts, prisons, research laboratories, hospitals and community clinics. They were engaged in agriculture, in manufacturing, in sales, in clerical and accounting operations, in public relations, consumer services and in other functions of business and industry. Some held jobs that were routine and undemanding. Others were in positions that utilized knowledge and skills that are not particularly recognized or valued in an academic community. There were still others that held positions of substantial responsibility and trust.

It would take many pages simply to enumerate all of the things that people did while on leave. To give the reader some sense of the tremendous range of activities in which students were engaged during their leaves, summaries of statistical records and lists of representative activities are presented in this chapter. In appendix II, statements that students made about their leaves have been reproduced in their entirety with the kind permission of their authors. In them, the activities often are discussed in relation to the circumstances that motivated the leave, the benefits that the persons obtained from the experience, and difficulties that may have been encountered, either during the leave or upon return to college. The statements were selected to illustrate different kinds of leave-time involvements and to suggest the variety of situations within the several categories of leave activities that are used to give a degree of organization to this report. Since many persons did a variety of things during their leave, the placement of some statements is rather arbitrary and, at best, the classification titles are imprecise. It should also be noted that the selected statements do not begin to exhaust those that hold a high level of interest and are worthy of inclusion in this report.

There were large, non-chance differences between institutions in the percentage of students who took a particular type of leave. Institutions that sponsored active study-abroad programs enrolled a greater proportion of their own students in these programs. Colleges that had formalized programs of supervised field study had relatively more students whose leave involved "education-in-the-field." There were sizeable differences from school to school in the percentage of leave-takers who were exploring the possibility of transferring to another college. The responses to this item and evidence developed in other elements of the study lead to the conclusion that colleges can influence the type of leave-time activities in which their students engage by the selective inducements and constraints that they employ.

In this sample of 1367 respondents, 188 persons or fourteen percent of the group spent their leaves in a program conducted by their colleges at locations other than the main campus, or they were engaged in education-in-the-field projects. The latter typically were supervised or monitored by a member of the faculty or by a committee of the student's college. In most cases, credit for participation in a college-sponsored program or for field study was conditional only upon the satisfactory completion of the course of study or field project.

An additional thirty-one percent of the leave-takers enrolled as full-time students at another college or university. They took a leave, usually for one or two semesters, with the expectation that they would return to their colleges to complete their undergraduate programs and to receive their baccalaureate degrees. Some registered through programs designed to facilitate study at another institution. New York University's Semester in New York, American University's Washington Seminar, the Twelve College Exchange or any of the 699 programs listed in the 1976 edition of U.S. College-Sponsored Programs Abroad,[18] are examples of this type of academic program. Others arranged for their enrollment at another American or foreign institution of higher learning through their own direct negotiations with the appropriate administrative office at that particular school. The policies concerning the award of academic credit for courses taken at another college vary greatly among the six colleges that participated in this study. Award of credit generally required preliminary approval of the student's proposed program of studies and an evaluation of the student's accomplishments in the program when completed. Students frequently complained of the grudging and inconsistent manner in which credits earned at another institution were accepted toward the satisfaction of the degree requirements of their own colleges.

An additional ten percent of the leave-takers enrolled at another college or university with the intention of transferring to that institution. Sometimes this was done in the spirit of not "burning bridges" until the new territory was explored and found satisfactory. In other cases, the student could not be accepted as a degree candidate by the new college until after a waiting or probationary period. By taking a leave, these students retained the option to return to their college in the event that the transfer was not consummated for one reason or another. The record indicates that some who took a leave with the clear intention of transferring, did in fact return to their original institution to complete their studies. Some who left with the expectation of returning after a semester or a year, found it advantageous or necessary to remain at the school that they attended during their leave.

Twenty-five percent spent the major portion of their leave in full-time employment or in volunteer service. Many more, not included in this count, worked part-time or were employed briefly in pick-up jobs that were taken to "make ends meet." Sixteen percent engaged in self-directed activities that cannot be categorized simply without doing violence to their uniqueness and variety. Examples are cited later in this chapter and others appear in the appendix. The remaining four percent of leave-takers do not fit any of these classifications. They include persons whose principal leave-time activity was convalescing or being involved in some form of extended therapy, care of a friend or relative, or other situations that so completely commanded the persons' time and energies that they were unable to engage in any other activities with more than minimal involvements.

While in many cases it is possible to identify a principal leave-time activity, the reality is that most persons pursued a number of interests during their leave, either simultaneously or in successive periods of time. Commonly for persons who were gone for a single semester, their leave activities extended over a period of seven or eight months, made up of the semester of leave and the adjoining summer. Those who were absent for a full academic year typically had a period of fifteen months through the use of the summers before and after the year in which they were not enrolled. As is illustrated by the protocols that are quoted in chapter 2, the responses to Items 1 and 2 of Survey 1 indicate that most students had in mind, before leaving school, a list of objectives that they hoped to pursue through various activities and participations.

The descriptions of leave activities, written after students had returned to college, furnish ample evidence that principal leave activities were supplemented by involvements in many subsidiary interests. Those who focused their attentions upon a single major commitment throughout their leave typically used their free time to pursue additional interests. More commonly, students were engaged in a succession of "principal activities." For example, a person might work through the summer, register as a full-time student in the fall, devote the spring

TABLE 11

Number and percentage of students
Who selected each alternative of Survey 1, Item A

Please indicate which of the following categories of "leave" most accurately describes the type of activity in which you will be engaged.

		Number	Percent
1.	Enrollment in a program of study conducted by this college at a location other than its main campus.	54	4%
2.	"Education in the Field" or "Work-Study" activity to be supervised or evaluated by the college for possible academic credit.	136	10%
3.	Enrollment in a program of study at an institution of higher learning other than the one from which you expect to receive a baccalaureate degree.	125	31%
4.	Full-time employment or volunteer service.	333	25%
5.	Self-directed reading, research, work in the creative or performing arts, travel, etc.	220	16%
6.	Other (including transferring)	199	14%

TABLE 12

Amount of time during leave spent in specified activities
Percentage of students selecting each code
In response to Item A, Survey 2

During the period that you were not in residence at this college, how much time did you spend in the following types of activities? For EACH activity record the code number of the most descriptive statement.

Code 1. Major amount of time
2. A substantial amount of time
3. A moderate amount of time
4. A limited amount of time
5. Little or no time devoted to this activity

	Activity	1	2	Code 3	4	5
a.	Formal academic study	19%	17%	17%	15%	32%
b.	Individual study	14%	25%	26%	23%	12%
c.	Volunteer service	6%	6%	6%	12%	70%
d.	Employment	29%	13%	9%	8%	41%
e.	Travel	13%	23%	22%	20%	22%
f.	Recreational activities	5%	25%	40%	24%	6%
g.	Personal matters	3%	9%	17%	27%	44%
h.	Health	2%	2%	2%	5%	89%

months to extensive travel and finally resume employment in anticipation of return to college. This variety of students' leave activities is quantified through their responses to Item A, Survey 2 (see table 12).

Excerpts from the answers that persons returning from leave wrote in response to the question, <u>What did you do during your leave?</u>, are quoted here to restate the generalities of table 12 in terms that are more specific and individual. Beyond this listing of what individual leave-takers did, more extended statements are available in the appendix. In these, many of the respondents not only describe what they did during their leaves, but also tell how and why they chose these particular activities and what benefits they gained from the experiences of their leaves.

> I was drafted and spent two years in alternative service, at the Rhode Island State Medical Center in Cranston, and at the Jewish Hospital in Crite, Ohio. I worked as an orderly in Rhode Island, and was trained as an operating room technician in Crite.

> I took a course in music therapy and did field work at Brooklyn State Mental Hospital. I also continued my training in music performance.

> Worked as a child therapist at Michael Reese Hospital in Chicago and attended Roosevelt University and University of Chicago during off hours.

> Psychiatric attendant in a hospital, working midnight to 8 a.m. from late January through May.

> I worked in the New York City Health Department studying the ecology and problems of people who live on the street. I did all the field work which consisted of observation. The project is continuing with interviews of street people and of people who run food programs, etc., for them.

> I worked in a medical clinic learning para-medical skills and counseling skills. I worked counselling people who were trying to kick heroin and also completed a research project on sex and drugs that has been submitted for publication.

> I worked full time as a research assistant at the Institute of Brain Research, Zurich, Switzerland.

> I was a "math analyst" assisting the Video Imaging Science Team for Mariner 10, at the Jet Propulsion Laboratory in Pasadena, California.

> I worked as a lab technician in the micro-paleontology lab at Woods Hole Oceanographic Institute, Woods Hole, Mass.

> My job consisted of supervising and generating computer programs used in engineering research done under government contracts by GTE Sylvania in Needham, Mass.

> I worked at a museum. My duties were multivarious but mostly I was connected to an exhibition of African Art. I did a lot of research and helped to write the catalog for the exhibit.

Worked forty hours a week at the U.S. Army N. Labs as a chemistry aide and fifteen hours a week at McDonalds. Studied transportation at Boston University night school.

During my leave I worked for five months at a girls' high school in New York City tutoring in remedial math. The level was often on the elementary school level. I also worked two months in a museum giving tours and demonstrations to elementary school age children.

Worked as an intern with an outdoors program called Project Adventure that was attached to a public school.

Student teaching at an Infants School in Bristol, England -- full time for four months.

During my leave I attended Dartmouth College for three terms. I followed a program to earn certification in elementary education. I took several education courses and was a student teacher in the third grade.

Took night courses at Johns Hopkins and substituted in public high schools during the day.

I worked in a classroom at the Walker School in Needham, Mass. as a full-time student teacher/intern. Walker School is a residential and day school for emotionally disturbed boys whose behavior has been disruptive in other settings. The class I worked in included ten boys 7-9 years of age who were, in addition to being emotionally disturbed, mildly to severely learning disabled, hyperactive and anti-social in behavior.

I spent the majority of my time working at English High School (Boston) as a transitional aide. I worked in the schools with the kids making sure they went to class, etc.

I spent seven months at the Catholic Worker in the Bowery in New York City. It was a house of hospitality in which people from the Bowery area with no other families lived. We had a family of fifty people.

I worked part time in the "Boston Court Resource Project," a counseling program for kids 18-22 who have been arrested. I was an "educational counselor." I got kids into schools or training or tutoring programs if they wanted it. It was a volunteer job. I also was a classroom aide in a bilingual third grade classroom in a Boston school.

I worked as a student intern at Western Mass. Health Planning Council. This internship was in the field of alcohol and alcoholism.

While on a three year leave I did volunteer work in Scotland (community work -- one year), Switzerland (mentally retarded children -- one year) and then taught English and studied in Taipei.

I was an intern for Senator Javits to the Senate Health Subcommittee of the Committee on Labor and Public Welfare.

I spent the fall as a paid research assistant for the U.S. Senate Subcommittee on Constitutional Rights in Washington, D.C.

I worked for the EPA Office of Toxic Substances Quantative Analysis of National Problems.

I worked at the Council on National Priorities and Resources, a liberal public interest group serving as a coordinating organization for other liberally-oriented organizations. I did research in various areas which were pertinent to activities currently going on on Capitol Hill, including writing up statements of position, and factual articles for member's use.

I worked for a public interest group, the Health Research Group, which is part of the Ralph Nader organization Public Citizen, in Washington, D.C.

Worked at Environmental Action, Inc., a public interest environmental lobby group in Washington, D.C. Worked with organizations lobbying efforts on a number of bills in Congress, helped with other research and projects. Conducted an independent project on an area of interest to me (effect of oil crisis on developing nations) which resulted in a published article.

I worked in the Press Office of the Governor of Mass. doing writing, summarizing and general clerical work. The internship was arranged by the Mass. State Internship Office which paid me $100 per week.

My leave was devoted to military service (U.S.C.G.).

For four months I interned at the Jerusalem Planning Office, assisting in various analyses on demographic trends and implications for Jerusalem.

I worked as a draftsman for an architectural firm (as an architectural draftsman) and for an engineering firm as a mechanical draftsman.

I worked for an English language newspaper in Mexico City as a translator and feature writer.

Worked for a Boston Radio Station (WBZ) as a producer.

I was general manager of the campus newspaper.

I worked in a professional theatre company.

I made films and wrote film-criticism and related articles during my semester leave.

Played in rock and roll band, studied ancient Greek.

Went to Mt. Rainier National Park to work as a ranger.

Worked as a sheep herder and did general ranch work.

During the time I was out of school I worked for the great majority of the time as a laborer in a conservation area on Cape Cod. The job consisted primarily in cutting trails for workers and access roads to a beach area.

I worked from May to September at painting houses, contracting most of the work myself and hiring kids to help. On Sept. 21st. I left New York on a chemical tanker and arrived in Belgium two weeks later.

Poured cement for three months and travelled through Europe for five months.

During the leave I spent six days a week at work in a Chemical Engineering Pilot Plant which entailed seventy hours a week.

In early summer I lived in New York; drove a delivery van by day and attended architectural school at night. In the fall I worked for a regional planner.

I spent September through April driving a truck on which I transported forklifts, and I was a forklift mechanic as well.

During my leave I lived at home and worked in a paper mill.

During my leave I spent four months studying German language at a language institute in Germany and then two months working in a factory in London.

Worked in a factory, making wax earplugs. Did some quality control and lab work.

I worked for my father in his New Jersey warehouse as a shipping clerk and packager.

I worked for the International House of Philadelphia, an independent private institution which houses 400 graduate students at local colleges, two thirds of whom come from seventy different nations. I was the Assistant Program Director, responsible for originating, publicizing, and implementing all kinds of social, cultural and educational events.

During my leave I worked as a trainee-level computer programmer.

Employed at the Prudential Insurance Company as an acceptance tester responsible for two computer subsystems -- a portion of their Expense Management Information System.

I worked full time as a claims examiner in a large insurance company as well as waitressed at night at a nightclub.

I was employed by the "Central Labor Employment Bureau" (ZAU) of the German Government in Frankfurt, Germany. I was a clerk in the division which places foreign students in jobs within Germany and my duties were clerical in nature; occasionally I was given material to translate into English for offical letters.

I worked ninety hours a week as a manager in a confectionery store.

Full-time employment in retail sales: Calculator Department at a department store.

I worked on the Navy Base at Bainbridge, Md. I was responsible for the mobile canteen. I drove it, initiated maintenance, stocked it, and sold the food. I was also responsible for the cash. After six months I returned home and worked in a factory.

I worked as a short-order cook in a second-rate restaurant on the Maine coast.

During my leave I worked first at home for a month. I then flew to Europe where I spent two months travelling on an Euro-Rail pass with friends from college and another two months working in a German bakery.

My leave of absence was spent in an Alpine ski resort in Italy, working in a restaurant and learning the language.

Waitressed, managed, cooked, worked in a small informal Mexican restaurant -- sixty hours per week.

I spent one year at a professional art school in NYC (Pratt).

I took my leave of absence at the University of Penn. to take anthropology courses which were not offered at my college.

Attended the University of Vermont for one term, studying botany and pedology, areas in which my college is surprisingly weak.

I enrolled at MIT as a special student in Urban Planning for 1st and 2nd semester. Full time first semester, half time second. Second semester I also enrolled in Harvard as a special student, studying Judaica.

I spent one semester at the National Theatre Institute in Waterford, Conn., studying acting and related fields (directing, dance, eurythmics, puppetry, kabuki, fencing, tumbling, music, etc.).

I attended Mills College on a formal exchange program. I carried a normal course load which included interning in a San Francisco Law Office twice a week. I eventually stayed there for the summer.

I took graduate courses in marine biology at Woods Hole, Mass.

I spent my time at the University of Colorado, studying group and class piano pedogogy with Dr. Guy Duckworth. Was not registered at the university which was nice as I might have been subjected to bureaucratic hassles.

During my leave I made great pictures and started to understand art. I made a thousand photographs.

I did slightly skilled archeological field work, i.e., digging, passing buckets of dirt, pick work, wheelbarrow work. I did a lot of physical work and loved it.

I studied the classical guitar, working on technique and studying the music.

I used the five months to concentrate solely on writing fiction. I took a writing workshop at Brandeis University. Also took an advanced Spanish class.

Essentially I went on leave so as to pursue my work in typography (under the guidance of a printer in Northampton, Mass.) and to take two courses through continuing education at the U. of Mass.

I spent the time working in an office and pursuing various interests mostly in the fields of music and literature, such as building a harpsichord.

Read extensively on nutrition and exercise - designed a diet, exercise program. Lost thirty pounds.

During the fall I studied weaving intensively seven days a week, eight hours a day at Penland School of Crafts in North Carolina. In the spring I studied Spanish and weaving at the Institute Allende in San Miguel de Allende, Mexico.

I learned to play Shetland fiddle, a self-appointed task for a discouraged classical musician. Because my teacher was also teaching it to school children, I helped him and between the two of us we spent four days of the week teaching ninety-six beginning students.

The leave itself was spent studying James Joyce, Irish drama and Irish culture in Dublin.

For twelve months I lived in Japan studying the language and culture. I spent most of the time in Tokyo University but also spent the summer in the mountains studying language, spent some time on a farm, spent the winter near Kyoto studying pottery and living at a Zen Temple. Also had time to travel within Japan and Korea.

Conducted independent anthropological field research in Cavca, Columbia while affiliated with the Experiment in International Living.

During the leave I was in Puerto Rico. My activities consisted mainly of auditing two classes at the University of Puerto Rico, helping in a research project at a mental health clinic outside of San Juan, taking a course in ceramics, doing some photography and travelling.

As an anthropology major I went to Barbados where I took two courses at the University of the West Indies and designed a research project.

Studied for ten weeks at a school in Antigua, Guatemala learning to speak and read Spanish.

During my year off, I lived in Southern France studying painting and drawing with a seventy year old German artist and his following of several younger American painters.

During my leave I attended Chapman College's World Campus Afloat Program and travelled around the world.

I attended a course in Switzerland and Belgium at which I was personally qualified as a teacher of Transcendental Meditation by Maharishi Mattesit Yogi.

It was an attempt to experience a Tibetan Buddhist community by inter-acting with them, and undertaking the meditational discipline.

This list of leave-time activities and the protocols of appendix II hardly require comment concerning the constructive manner in which most of the students used their time. Their activities reflected the many different needs to which they were responding and the manifold interests and objectives that led them to seek an off-campus involvement. Their accomplishments were substantial, sometimes evident in art works created, research studies reported or academic or employment records established. Achievements less demonstrable but of equal or greater importance were new perspectives, appreciations, insights and understandings. The unique demands of the leave activities induced growth in personal maturity and in psychological strength and resiliency. Chapter 5 is devoted to an appraisal of the benefits that students derived from their involvements in these leave-time activities.

Forty-seven percent of the respondents spent the greater amount of their leave time in principal cities of the world. An additional thirteen percent lived in the suburbs of a major city. Twenty-three percent lived in towns or cities with a population of less than 100,000. Six percent spent the greater part of their leave in a rural area and seven percent remained in the immediate vicinity of their college. Four percent moved about with such frequency that no single category of community described their situation. Sixteen percent of the students lived with their parents or with close relatives during the greater part of their leave. For thirty percent, living accommodations were provided or arranged for by the group or agency associated with their principal leave activity. Thirty-eight percent negotiated their own living arrangements and sixteen percent had no single type of living arrangement that lasted for an extended period of time. Those who spent the major portion of their leave in full-time employment differed greatly, in respect to living arrangements, from those who spent little or no time in employment. The majority of the employed negotiated their own living arrangements. About one-quarter lived with their parents, relatives or family friends. Seventeen percent had a succession of living arrangements. Only three percent had their living accommodations arranged by their employer. In contrast, the majority of those who spent little or no time in employment had their accommodations arranged for by some agency. About one quarter arranged these matters for themselves, seven percent lived with parents and fourteen percent had a succession of different living arrangements during their leave.

How did students learn about the activities in which they became involved? A comprehensive answer to that question would be long and involved for they used many different methods and agencies. Some persons did not seek help; others did not find it available. Many did acknowledge receiving assistance from individuals and/or organizations. However, there was a broad consensus that the decision to take a leave and the initiatives in arranging for it, properly belonged with the student. They found that making the decision to take a leave and carrying through with the arrangements for it was, in itself, a valuable learning experience that contributed to personal growth. A simple listing of some of the resources that leave-takers found helpful may suggest avenues of search that could be useful to others.

1. Catalogs and bulletins describing off-campus academic programs, opportunities for volunteer service, employment, etc.

2. Directories and sourcebooks such as those mentioned in chapter 8 and listed in the bibliography. Copies may be available in the college library or in special collections and may be purchased at a bookstore.
3. Announcements posted on the bulletin boards of departmental and administrative offices of the college.
4. Reports published in newspapers, magazines and professional and scholarly journals identified projects or undertakings of interest. Students followed up with inquiries concerning the possibility of becoming affiliated with the project.
5. Personal contacts on campus with students who had returned from leave or with faculty and administrators who have personal knowledge of opportunities or who can furnish letters of introduction.
6. Although some students reported that these offices were not helpful to them, others received useful assistance from the office of the Dean, the alumni office, the counseling or placement offices, the financial aid office, the student employment office and the campus representative of the Venture Program.
7. Read classified ads of newspapers, magazines, or journals carefully, thoroughly and regularly. Registered with the Employment Service Office of the Labor Department in the area in which they were seeking employment. Identified and utilized the services of organizations that provided placement services or that acted as a clearing house for the types of situations in which they wished to be employed.
8. Used telephone book or other directories to identify organizations that might have opportunities appropriate to students' interests. Wrote, telephoned and eventually secured an interview to state interests, qualifications and availability.
9. Discussed interests and objectives with parents, friends and acquaintances. Members of family and/or their business and professional associates furnished leads or contacts which eventuated in successful placement.

A useful starting point for students who are thinking seriously about alternatives to registering for another term at their college is the book titled <u>What Color Is Your Parachute?</u>[19] It could be an exceedingly useful aid in organizing their thoughts and in planning a strategy of search. As its sub-title indicates, it is a practical manual for job hunters and career changers. Its information and advice is equally cogent and sound for those who are looking for temporary employment or for an internship type of experience.

A very valuable reference for persons who wish to be abroad is <u>Whole World Handbook, A Student Guide to Work, Study and Travel Abroad</u>

published by the Council on International Educational Exchange. As is true of many of the directories that list work/study/travel opportunities, a new edition is published annually. Be certain to consult the most recent publication.

Stopping Out, A Guide to Leaving College and Getting Back In by Judi Kesselman contains an extensive listing of directories, guidebooks and other references in the appendix, pages 123-134. A few additional publications that have been released since the writing of Kesselman's book and which may be of value to persons interested in leave-taking are listed below. Consult the bibliography for the full citation for these references.

> Director of Internships, Work Experience Programs and On-the-Job Training Opportunities, 1st Edition, Alvin Renetzyk, Renetzyk, editor.
>
> The 1977 Student Employment Directory, The "How to Find Summer Employment" Handbook
>
> National Register of Internships and Experiential Education, Ross C. Lewchuk, editor.
>
> The New Guide to Study Abroad, John A. Garraty, Lily Von Klemperer, Cyril J.H. Taylor, editors.
>
> The New York Times Guide to Student Adventures and Studies Abroad, Howard S. Rowland, Beatrice L. Roland, editors.
>
> World Guide to Higher Education, A Comprehensive Survey of Systems, Degrees and Qualifications, UNESCO

CHAPTER 5

Was It Worthwhile?

> My leave was clearly the most stimulating and valuable experience of my college career.
>
> The experiences of my leave proved to be vital for both my personal development and my motivations for continuing my education.
>
> I think my leave from college was one of the wisest things I ever did. It took a certain amount of courage to make the decision and now that I can look back on it, I'm very glad I decided to stay out of school for a year.
>
> Although my leave of absence proved to be a very difficult time in my life, it was probably one of the best things I have ever done, and has proved very worthwhile.
>
> My leave of absence lasted two years and contributed more to my personal development than any period before or since.
>
> My leave turned out to be much more than I ever imagined it could be.
>
> My experience while on leave was a turning-point in my life.
>
> I view my leave, not as a leaving of academia, but rather as a first step into reality.
>
> Leaves of absence are a good thing but it would be still better if people stayed out of college till they really wanted to be there rather than staying in until they really want to be out.
>
> I wish it were possible to stress, not leave-taking, but going somewhere -- perhaps call it a "come." The significant part for me wasn't leaving college, to which I have no special attachment, but in coming into a new set of experiences and perspectives.

How representative are these strong statements of appreciation and approval? Do they express sentiments that are shared by large numbers of students who have been on leave?

Answers that 1130 persons gave to Item D of Survey 2 offer one perspective on the manner in which students evaluated their leaves when they first returned to their colleges. Table 13 displays the number and percentage of respondents who selected each alternative to Item 2D.

Eighty-five percent of the respondents selected one or the other of the two unequivocally positive evaluations. Only three percent selected the statements that expressed disappointment or dissatisfaction. Another indicator of the positive attitude that the great majority of students had concerning their leaves was their willingness to recommend a leave to other students (see table 14).

To the degree that willingness to recommend their leave activities to others can be construed as an expression of personal satisfaction, almost all of the 1135 respondents expressed satisfaction with the experiences and outcomes of their leaves. Eighty-eight percent indicated that their leave experiences had been sufficiently worthwhile to them that they would recommend them, either selectively or generally, to other students. To test whether the initial evaluation of the leave might be modified by the experiences of being back at their college for a semester, several follow-up questions were included in Survey 3, the responses to which are displayed in tables 15 and 16.

Six to eight months after they had returned to college, seventy-five percent of the respondents stated that they either probably or definitely would take the same leave if they could choose again. Sixteen percent would take a different kind of leave. This group was composed chiefly of those whose leaves had been precipitated by illness, family circumstances or financial difficulties, and included some who found their leave situations not well-suited to their objectives in taking a leave. Although they obviously would have preferred that the circumstances of their leaves had been different, they valued their time away from college. Only seven and one-half percent of all the respondents stated that they were uncertain as to how they would choose or that they would not take a leave if the decision could be made again.

Less than ten percent of all persons who took a leave did not find the benefits of their leave sufficiently great to justify the difficulties and inconveniences that were involved. Eight percent thought that their college experiences were more satisfactory in the period before their leave (see table 16) and nine percent stated that, in the semester following their return to their college, they enjoyed their studies less than they had anticipated that they would (see table 17).

TABLE 13

Number and Percentage of Respondents
Who Selected Each Alternative to Item D, Survey 2

Considering your objectives in taking a leave, how valuable were the experiences associated with your leave from college?

		Number	Percent
1.	They exceeded my highest hopes and expectations.	368	33%
2.	They fully justified my taking a leave.	588	52%
3.	They were satisfactory although disappointing in some respects.	140	12%
4.	They were not nearly as satisfactory as I had hoped they would be.	21	2%
5.	For most intents and purposes, my leave was time poorly spent.	13	1%
	Total answering question	1130	

TABLE 14

Number and Percentage of Respondents
Who Selected Each Alternative to Item E, Survey 2

What would be your most probable reaction to students who sought your advice concerning the desirability of their taking a leave similar to yours?

		Number	Percent
1.	Would recommend it to almost any student.	573	50%
2.	Would be selective in the students to whom I would recommend it.	432	38%
3.	Would caution student concerning conditions that might counter-indicate this type of leave.	67	6%
4.	Would actively discourage most students from considering this type of leave.	19	2%
5.	Can't say.	44	4%
	Total answering question	1135	

TABLE 15

Number and Percentage of Respondents Who Selected Each Alternative to Item A, Survey 3

With the wisdom of hindsight and the opportunity to choose again whether to continue your program of studies at this college, would you:

		Number	Percent
1.	Definitely choose the same type of "leave."	472	58%
2.	Definitely choose to take a "leave" but one involving some other activity.	99	12%
3.	Probably choose the same type of "leave."	151	18%
4.	Probably choose to take a "leave" but one involving some other activity.	37	4.5%
5.	Uncertain	23	3%
6.	Probably would continue my program of studies at this college.	23	3%
7.	Definitely would continue my program of studies at this college.	14	1.5%
	Total answering question	819	

TABLE 16

Number and Percentage of Respondents Who Selected Each Alternative to Item B, Survey 3

In comparing your college experiences since returning to the campus with those of the period immediately before your "leave," which statement describes your feelings most accurately?

		Number	Percent
1.	This past year has been much more satisfactory.	397	49%
2.	This past year has been somewhat more satisfactory.	254	31%
3.	I am aware of little difference.	97	12%
4.	The year before my leave was somewhat more satisfactory.	52	6%
5.	The year before my leave was much more satisfactory.	19	2%
	Total answering question	819	

TABLE 17

Number and Percentage of Respondents
Who Selected Each Alternative to Item C, Survey 3

In general, are you enjoying your studies this term as much as you had expected to?

		Number	Percent
1.	No, I am definitely enjoying them less than I had expected.	79	9%
2.	No, but I am only mildly disappointed.	121	15%
3.	My expectations for this term are reasonably well satisfied.	485	59%
4.	I am enjoying my studies this term much more than I had expected.	137	17%
	Total answering question	822	

TABLE 18

Percentage of Respondents
Who Selected Each Alternative to Item Q, Survey 3

How important is it to you that you obtain a college degree?

		Before Leave	After Leave
1.	It is essential to my development and to my future.	31%	29%
2.	It is extremely important to me.	27%	29%
3.	It is fairly important to me.	29%	29%
4.	It is not very important to me.	7%	5%
5.	I would not attend college if a college degree were not a social and vocational necessity.	6%	7%
T	Total answering question	465	465

Contingency Coefficient = 0.63

Analyses were made of the responses to these questions to determine whether the level of reported satisfaction with the leave experience was related to the type of leave activity. Persons who spent the largest amount of their leave-time in employment or volunteer service chose the alternative, *. . . fully justified my taking a leave*, more frequently than did those who were enrolled in a formal academic program or commitment. Persons on an "academic" leave more frequently selected the more extreme alternative, *. . . exceeded my highest hopes and expectations*. However, the observed differences in response to this item fall short of a rigorous criterion of statistical significance. Leave activity did not affect the advice that students would give to others concerning the desirability of taking a leave similar to their own. Equally high percentages of the two groups stated that they would take a leave were they facing that decision anew. However, eighty-two percent of those in the "academic" group would probably or definitely choose the same type of leave in contrast to sixty-eight percent of the "employed" group. Twenty-three percent of the "employed" group probably or definitely would choose a leave involving some other activity. Those who expanded on this evaluation in their comments indicated most often that they would hope to find employment or volunteer service that was more closely related to their academic interests and/or to their career aspirations. Many students who began their leaves in 1973-74 and in 1974-75 found the job market very tight. Some had difficulty in locating positions with job content relevant to their interests and others had their employment terminated or changed because of economic reversals experienced by their employers. The leave activity groups did not differ, either in their judgments that their post-leave semester had been more satisfactory or in the percentage that expressed enjoyment of their studies since their return.

The surveys were designed to permit pre-leave, post-leave comparisons of attitudes, perceptions and behaviors relating to their colleges and to their academic programs. There was a moderate to high degree of correlation between the pre-leave and post-leave responses that individuals gave to questions dealing with the importance that they placed upon their academic programs. Following their leaves, there was an overall tendency for students to attach less importance to getting good grades. There was a high correlation between pre-leave and post-leave ratings, indicating that individuals tended to keep their relative position in the distribution of responses. As can be observed in table 18, there were only slight differences, before and after the leave, in the importance attached to obtaining a college degree by the group as a whole. However almost half of the individuals changed their ratings, twenty-three percent giving less importance to the college degree and twenty-four percent assigning more importance to it after the leave.

The number of persons who expected to continue their education in a graduate or professional school did not change, but the level of certainty that they would pursue graduate studies increased following the leave. There was not a significant change in the rated importance of coursework in general or of coursework in the major field of study.

There were significant differences in the pre-leave and post-leave responses to items dealing with evaluation of faculty and with ratings of satisfaction with various aspects of college life. As will be documented in greater detail later, many students returned from their leave, more self-confident, and with a better understanding of the relationship of their continuing education to the life of the larger community and to their own personal goals. They had better-defined objectives and a stronger sense of independence which expressed itself in a more critical and discriminating attitude toward their college experiences.

Before taking their leaves, twenty-nine percent of the respondents thought that less than half of the faculty were genuinely interested in students and their problems. After their leaves, thirty-seven percent held that opinion. On all of the aspects of college life that pertained to faculty and academic program, there were significant differences before and after leave in the numbers of persons who expressed satisfaction or dissatisfaction. Following their leaves a significantly greater number expressed dissatisfaction with: <u>the intellectual leadership and stimulation provided by members of the faculty, availability of courses, seminars, laboratories, independent study, etc., in fields of your principal interests</u>, and <u>academic regulations and requirements</u>. After their leaves a significantly smaller number express dissatisfaction with: <u>the relevance of your coursework to your own interests and concerns, availability of faculty for consultation and academic assistance</u>, and <u>the adequacy of academic advising</u>. Having achieved greater independence and self-confidence, persons returning from leave were less timid and possibly more effective and resourceful in relating to members of the faculty. Having achieved a better understanding of their own educational objectives, they were less dependent upon faculty advice and direction or were able to profit more from consultations with members of the faculty. On the other hand, they tended to be more concerned that the faculty and the academic program respond to their educational and intellectual needs. These differences cannot be explained away as changes that would naturally occur as students advanced into the upper levels of the curriculum. The responses of persons who had been continuously enrolled for five or six semesters were similar to the pre-leave ratings of the leave-takers.

The majority of students reported that the semesters following their leave were more productive and enjoyable. They had a better idea of what they wished to accomplish, were more successful in ignoring distractions and in resisting pressures that might impede their efforts, and were more confident both of their decisions and of their ability to execute them. They felt themselves to be more in control and consequently were more involved and responsible.

However, it would be a mistake to conclude from this that students' academic performances, as represented by grade point averages, were substantially improved following a leave. There were students who achieved startling changes in their academic records. Deans and faculty and students on most campuses know of persons whose collegiate careers were transformed after a period of absence from the college. These arresting and gratifying cases lead some to prescribe leave-taking as an effective antidote for poor grades. However, dramatic cases tend to obscure what is true for most persons. In the present study, as was the case with students taking leave of Harvard University,[20] there was not a significant difference in the mean grade point average before and after leave. Relatively few increased their grade point by as much as two grading units. Almost equal numbers experienced declines in grade point that were as extreme. The greatest numbers of students earned averages that deviated only moderately from their pre-leave record. Considering the many factors that determine the assignment of grades, this outcome is not surprising.

The pre-leave grade point average determines the range of the grading scale that is available to the individual student for improvement or loss. For the majority of students, there was more grading scale on the downside of their pre-leave academic average than there was above. Another consideration that complicates the use of pre-leave, post-leave comparisons of grade point as an indicator of academic performance is the inequality in the demands of the students' programs before and after leave.

Some students carried a substantially heavier course load in an effort to remain with their class, having fallen behind in credits required for graduation. There were students who attempted to accelerate their undergraduate programs because they had identified new objectives that make it desirable to complete college as quickly as possible. As a result of altered educational and/or career objectives, some drastically reoriented their program of studies following their leave. Many students modified their attitudes about competing for grades and the importance of grades in their own system of values. A theme that appeared repeatedly in the comments of returnees was that they were better able to put their college activities and involvements into the broader perspective of their lives rather than allowing college to be their life.

More subtle measures than the grade point average will be required to reveal what actually happens in terms of the students' effective use of the resources and opportunities that colleges provide in promoting their personal and intellectual development. Although the grade point average did not change substantially, the common experience was that returnees were better able to cope with the college environment and to respond more constructively to its opportunities and challenges than they could prior to their leaves.

In reporting the benefits that students felt they had realized from their off-campus experiences, it would be artificial and distorting to treat the various outcomes as separate and distinct. While their importance varied from person to person, most leave-takers reported a number of interrelated benefits which for the purposes of exposition will be listed and then illustrated by quotations that touch on one or more of these themes.

The leave provided a fresh perspective on the educational processes and upon the student's own educational objectives, as well as a better appreciation of the relationships of formal academic study to the larger dimensions of the individual's life and place in society. These perceptions sometimes resulted in a more critical attitude toward educational methods and the college environment, but the attitudes, whether more critical or more appreciative, reflected a greater awareness and a greater sense of personal direction and control. Students often commented that as a result of having attained a better definition of their own educational objectives, they were able to approach their continuing studies with renewed enthusiasm and with stronger, better focused motivation. In other cases, they identified goals that delayed their return to college or set them on new directions which often involved their transfer to another institution that was better equipped to meet their educational needs. From the student's point of view, the leave was valued because it provided the opportunities to re-evaluate educational and personal objectives and to test out alternatives that proved to be more satisfactory to their requirements.

The leave situation often permitted students to demonstrate abilities and traits of character that were not given scope within the college environment. They received "feed-back" that helped them to clarify or revise their self-images and to affirm elements of their personalities that college associations had not reinforced. One of the most frequently mentioned outcomes of the leave experience was growth in self-confidence, self-acceptance and an improved sense of well-being and of personal worth.

A closely related aspect of personal growth was a greater sense of self-mastery and of control. Students felt more able to accept responsibility for themselves and their decisions. They developed a stronger self-discipline that was particularly evident in their management of their time and money. In their comments, many students indicate that before their leaves they had been anxious about their ability to function in a less protective and secure environment. The experiences of their leaves permitted them to demonstrate their ability to survive in a world very different from that of their home campus and the sheltered, supportive conditions that most had enjoyed in their earlier years.

The testing of already developed competencies in different, more realistic settings and the acquisition of new skills with attendant improvement in feelings of adequacy and self-sufficiency was a benefit that many persons noted and valued. Leave activities often presented opportunities/demands for persons to acquire new skills or to perform in ways that were not required in college. It was not uncommon for students to discover that they could draw upon classroom knowledge and upon skills developed in academic contexts to deal with situations that had never been perceived as related to their formal studies. The old cliche about "learning how to learn" took on a new significance when the transferability of learning became a part of the students' own immediate experience.

Some students reported that the leave helped them to clarify their career objectives. The liberal arts college campus is a very selective mirror of the larger society, giving exaggerated prominence to some features and providing a very dim and diminished reflection of others. Although it may be an important training and proving ground for later careers, the campus reflection of the world of work is obscure and even distorted. The educational mission of the liberal arts college disavows vocational goals. For the most part, the curriculum lacks clear occupational relevance and during the present period of economic recession, the almost automatic respect previously given to college attendance has been challenged by searching questions concerning its economic utility. Intelligent young people know that one of the important bases of their own social identity and status will be their occupational attainments. One of the well-springs of their own self-esteem and personal satisfaction will be the way in which they make their living. It is difficult for them to accept the counsel, "don't be in a hurry to decide what you will do," no matter how sage that advice might be. It is hard to tolerate continuing uncertainty on a matter so central to their prospects and welfare. Particularly in a time in which the future seems uncertain and insecure, many students cannot be content with building foundations without having some conception of what the structure to be erected upon those foundations will be, or whether it will be possible to secure a permit to build after the foundation is in place.

The contemporary liberal arts campus is a paradox in that it attempts to keep itself free from the control of the demands of a vocationalism that would divert attention from more fundamental learning and commitment to the development of knowledge. At the same time, the day to day life of the campus reflects the professional ambitions and orientations of its faculty and the competition among students for credentials that may have an occupational payoff. Underlying the pursuit of knowledge is an unvoiced but powerful substratum of preoccupation with academic and professional careers that does not respond to the broader requirements of the student body.

In response to these situations on their respective campuses, some leave-takers left to acquire experiences more directly related to their career concerns. They learned through first-hand exposure something of the job-content of careers that had attracted their interest. They tested their abilities, interests and temperamental suitability. In some cases they confirmed their tentative selection of a career. In others they discovered incompatabilities that sent them searching for new possibilities. In still other cases, interests and talents that had gone unrecognized or unattended were discovered or seen in a new light. In many different ways, persons who took leaves were able to carry their thinking about their occupational futures beyond where they were prior to their leaves.

Some students returned from their leaves with improved social skills and a greater capacity to form satisfying social relationships. Prior to their leaves they had felt isolated from large segments of society by the insular nature of campus life and the social segregation of their pre-college years. Many had had few personal contacts with working people, with older people, with people whose approach to living is not intellectual and analytical. They had grown up in the society of peers who came from similar socio-economic backgrounds. They were over-practiced in the relationships of teacher and learner and of student with student. They had had few opportunities to experience relationships that were based upon other interests and functions. Their leaves gave them the opportunity to perform in different roles and in new relationships with persons who were more diverse in respect to values, life styles and cultural traditions.

A closely related benefit was an increased appreciation and a better understanding of other cultures, peoples, life styles and systems of values. By living and working in close relationships with others not normally encountered in the college community, or within their "natural habitat," students developed a more vivid and vital understanding of national character and of social and cultural differences than they could obtain through reading and discussion that took place in the context of their own culture.

Many students had interests, some of them highly developed and of great personal importance, that could not be pursued in competition with all of the other demands that college attendance places upon the students' resources of time, energy and money. Some were unable or unwilling to postpone giving attention to these interests and needs. Others found that they could not dismiss these concerns. The competition of academic and non-academic commitments often resulted in neither being satisfied or fulfilled. Sometimes the leave was taken for the express purpose of giving adequate time and suitable attention to these concerns, as was the case for several students who left college to train for olympic-competition. To others, the leave simply provided conditions more congenial to the pursuit of special interests in conjunction with other commitments, as illustrated by persons who worked at crafts or did volunteer work in hours not commanded by their employment. In either one, students were able to return with the feeling that they had been able to "get something out of their systems." Something that could not be attended to satisfactorily while a student had now been resolved. They had accomplished something that was important to them and could then return to their studies with greater equinimity and engage their college work with greater singleness of purpose.

> Now that I have returned, I feel a new freshness about college. I feel generally excited and most of all, I feel very comfortable and that this is my place. I think that my leave was necessary for this new perspective.

> I had felt, somewhat subconsciously, for about the last four years of my school experience, that I was temporarily losing the real desire to learn. I think it was because I had no questions which I wanted answered. The answers were being fed to me with no apparent stimulating reasons. The year of absence gave me some of the time which I needed during which I could find some questions I wanted answered. "Time" seems to be the key word. In an academic environment, unfortunately, one rarely feels like he has "time." And yet it is the broadness of the time sense which yields to a strong education and a broad understanding of things. I took a leave of absence, mostly to acquire at least temporarily, the feeling of having time, and I think that the leave did indeed fill that need. I feel that leave taking is one of the most important parts of a college education. Important for reasons of time and perspective. The perspective that a non-academic environment offers is of vital importance to the student, both while in college and after.

> My appreciation for a life devoted to intellectual study is greatly increased since I don't see it as a permanent state of being (as do most students who have never been away from school) but rather as a temporary interlude between jobs, to be lived to the fullest while still possible. Yet at the same time, I realize the limitations of an intellectual outlook -- it's only one side of life, not the only side as many people here believe.

> I am ready to return to school with energy and enthusiasm. I now can see the weaknesses of school but can also disregard them and will concentrate on all the things college has to offer, hopefully to get all I can out of my last two years.

> My leave (study at Indiana University for one year) provided me with an opportunity to explore a particular area of interest in depth. It enabled me to step back from my college experience and view it with a bit more objectivity. My experience was both a cultural and intellectual challenge. I feel far more confindent about my capabilities as a person and as a student. I realize that my "major" will never be the field in which I do graduate work.

My leave -- my exposure to Europe -- did create a new thirst for knowledge which I'd thought had died. I was almost ready to quit school before. Now I'm almost ready to begin my education over again. Now I have something to balance and compliment my academic knowledge -- a little more knowledge of "real life" and human beings.

I am now more "motivated" in my studies. I feel more of a sense of personal responsibility toward myself, my character, my career, my studies, etc. I conceive of the university more as a tool which can help me to realize my goals. Some of the initial mystique of the university and its professors has definitely waned. I took a calculated step against the grain (against the normal pattern of four solid years, against my parents desires, society's expectations, etc.) and accepted full responsibility for what I was doing. I than chose to return to school, an option that was very much in doubt for a while, and chose to finance it the rest of the way myself.

My attitude toward college changed in the following way. I worked harder and socialized less. By the same token, I had a strong feeling of the irrelevancy of my education to later life and of the privileged position of the college student, perhaps out of the continuous exposure to working peoples and to non-academic ways of life while on leave. As an extension of this feeling, I feel dissatisfied with my academic performance and interests prior to my leave, and feel now that either I should have worked harder throughout college or not have gone. To go mostly for social reasons or class expectations, as many students appear to have done, seems to me to be very wrong.

I found what an easy life one leads when at school as compared to out working and on your own. It also is becoming obvious that a college degree is not as important as I had always been taught it was and that you can do what you want if you plan for it, whether college is part of those plans or not.

Taking time out of school broke up the inevitability and lock-step nature of education for me. It made me feel much more in control of my life and what happens to me. It gave me much needed time to think about and to decide about things before being pushed into doing them by some ephemeral pressure. When I came back to school, I felt more enthusiastic about courses and everything else that college offers and sought things out much more actively rather than allowing education to be a passive process. This year I've done great in all my courses and with a minimum of hassles and headache. In the semester before my leave I was incomplete in two courses.

I can't say that I've returned with a specific direction in terms of a major or occupation. I can say that I'm a little more content with my situation. . . I'm not quite as thrown, and emotionally effected by all the confusing, sad, lonely things going on around me. . . . I'm a lot stronger.

By living in a situation where I was on my own, I gained an insight into the average American's working life, and gained confidence in myself through the knowledge that I _can_ survive without my parents.

I learned a lot about people. I know that there's a heck of a difference between reading about someone or something, and living in that situation. When I get back I'll be able to separate the bullshit from the facts and valuable learning experience much better than before.

My leave was by far the best thing that I could have done for myself both in terms of personal and academic development. I am much more independent now than I was before I left, much more satisfied to spend time by myself instead of feeling it necessary to constantly be with people. I find that I am more committed to developing myself and less determined to fit in with the rest of the crowd. My leave also definitely motivated me towards continuing my education in graduate school.

My leave made me refreshed, gave me a sense of MYSELF as a distinct personality again, made me aware of where my real interests lay (in terms of how I chose to spend my free time) gave me perspective so that upon returning my education seemed less monumental. Thus, I feel less "swallowed" up by the university and more able to take it for what it is and enjoy my education.

Leaving school for me was the best thing I possibly could have done. In the two years I was first at school, I was the stereotype picked up, lonely, alienated, suicidal, liberal arts student that spends all his time wondering what the hell one is doing in school in the first place. I was interested in my courses but they had no real meaning for me. I found it hard to justify the money and effort I was putting into them.

Now for the first time ever, I feel as though I am working towards something in school. I have a better awareness of life around me if not a profession. I can't say that I still don't question my being in college sometimes or that I am completely together and happy all the time, but relative to two years ago, I'm doing pretty well.

I have not been handicapped in any but bureaucratic ways. Personally my leave made all the difference in the world in so far as my self-confidence, sureness as to career, and friendship with people whom I met on leave are concerned. It furthered my determination never in my education to be trapped by structure, or to think any organizational entity is absolute.

I don't believe that one can grow emotionally while in college. After achieving what I set out to do which was to grow up a little, I could return to college with the self-confidence to continue my education. Without the leave, I would have been wasting my time to continue college.

I have read much, written some, and spent ten months as a journeyman diesel mechanic in my home town. The experience has reaffirmed my ties of birth with farmers and working men.

I left school because I wasn't working as I felt I should. During my working years I felt matured. The experience of supporting myself was extremely important to me. Now I have returned to school with a strong idea of what I would like to do professionally, something I didn't have when I left and hence the degree has taken on a more personal relevence.

My leave made me more aware of my own personal commitment and needs. I more and more discount academic solutions and a purely cerebral approach to problems. I am more independent-minded, less concerned with external appraisals of my capabilities. I am less concerned with fulfilling a traditional/professional career and flexible in my attitude towards possible future activities.

I had to rely on my own resources in ways I never could have imagined while leading my life in the U.S. Generally I guess that's what, ideally, a leave is all about. Relying on old lessons learned, internalizing new ones, growing -- and returning a more whole and diversified person.

I feel that I learned more about life in that one semester than in all the previous time I spent in college. College life to me is very sterile and protective. It really doesn't prepare you for the world.

College gives me little spare time, spontaneity in my life. I had been in school for thirteen or fourteen years, since the age of four. It was nice to see that a real world, with real people who weren't students, existed. I enjoyed relating to and learning from this world and these people. I think a leave of absence is a good experience for students. I know it was good for me.

My leave was extremely constructive in developing my own career interests and in giving me a solid ground from which to pursue them. I returned to school with a comfortable notion of the academic pursuits that I wished to follow and the manner in which I would go about it. The leave on the whole, was the most important event in my academic and career development to this point in my life.

The time spent away from this college was probably more profitable than all my years here put together. I had an opportunity to get to know another culture, to learn to speak a new language, and to meet some great people. Educationally it couldn't have been better. What better place to study ancient history than in Italy? I came back to school with a renewed interest in my studies. My department here was very flexible and happy to let me pursue work that I had started overseas.

The significant aspect of the leave was that I took upon myself complete responsibility for my own welfare in a working environment. During my first two years in college, I never took my studies seriously, not seeing any relevence in a college degree for myself. I had no specific goals or directions; no real reason for attending college. My leave gave me a chance to work out a career decision and to understand the personal importance of a college education.

I worked as a research assistant in a biological laboratory. I gained invaluable experience and solidified my intentions to pursue a graduate degree in the field of physiology.

I worked in a psychiatric hospital, which helped me to decide about clinical psychology as a career (decided against it, at least tentatively).

Leaving school was a valuable experience for me in that during this I experienced and worked towards personal growth and inner peace and stability. School was no longer a distraction and my activities at work contributed much to my personal development. By feeling more secure as an individual, my attitudes towards school improved and I have done much better since returning, partially because I'm no longer worried about doing well. I'm confident that if I work enough, I will do well. I learned a lot about psychotherapy, medicine and myself. My job gave me an insight into the politics of medical care. These were things I could not have learned in college and I am grateful to have had these experiences and the perspective that they gave.

I took the leave out of financial necessity. I acquired a number of "marketable" skills. I am sure that my employment has contributed to the great increase in self-confidence that I have experienced over the past year. My leave gave me valuable work experience, increased my faith in myself, demonstrated that I do have the ability to support myself and that I can handle relationships with others of all ages and in all capacities, not just student to student ones.

I was for the first time completely independent financially. I learned a lot about money; what it can buy and what it can't. It was a good change of atmosphere to get out of the academic sphere. I think it helped to put my studies into perspective as well as give me some perspective before making career choices.

I worked at the closest thing to a "scholarly" bookstore that New England has to offer. The background of information that I had to acquire and the resources that I have learned about and use have been invaluable to me. The business experience I have gained is unique. I learned basic clerical skills and bookkeeping. In terms of its contribution to my future, I think my time has been efficiently spent.

For part of my leave I lived in central Arizona and contributed to the building of a model city, Arcosanti. Living conditions were primitive; the workcamp isolated and "he-man" oriented. I found the work refreshing and challenging after the frustration of academic work. I learned to appreciate sense of care, efficiency and accuracy. I was often forced to trust my own judgment. Living in the desert, I finally began to understand the importance of taking care of my body with enough sleep and food. Previously I ignored my body, just so long as my mind kept going so I could read/write/think. The people I lived with were older, 25 to 30 years old, yet I was not treated as being younger. I think the greatest benefit from my leave was that I began to develop a sense of perspective on academics. Additionally, I know that there is life outside of the institution.

Some persons reported the benefit of their leaves as being primarily one of physical and/or psychological restoration. They were able to regain health, psychological equilibrium, and in some cases come to grips finally with a condition that had impaired their efficiency in doing college work or that had clouded the enjoyment of the college experience. Relief from the pressures of college life was enough to permit a spontaneous recovery for some. Many found other activities and interests to be therapeutic. Some sought the professional assistance of physicians or counselors or other therapists, spending significant portions of their leave in active treatment. Some had a religious experience or enlightenment that transformed their conceptions of themselves and their relationships to others. An outcome associated with their absence from college that was of special significance for some leave-takers was the amelioration or removal of conditions that had been handicapping or limiting, the restoration of health and the release of potentials for further growth.

> Being ill perhaps made me see things in a different perspective. I returned to campus with a mature attitude and felt as if I was "different" from my colleagues. School was no longer the tantamount concern in my life. I had come to view college life as an end in itself but being hospitalized made me realize that there was a "real world" outside of college.

> I gained from the year in a very personal way. I needed the space to grow and think independently. By gaining a new perspective on myself and my education, I have been less encumbered this year by the competitiveness and social run-around that abounds here. Facing my personal problems and being on my own much of the time were invaluable aspects of my leave.

> I spent much of my time dealing with personal and family problems which seem to have become more or less resolved as a result. I was able to gain a much better perspective on the relative values of college and those values I have been brought up with. I find it easier to maintain my personal integrity without becoming totally confused, which in my opinion, is one of the most valuable things a person can learn. I can now detach myself from the social structures/strictures set up by my peers.

> During my leave I became a Christian which changed to a drastic degree my outlook on life. Since my return, I have found more satisfaction with my social life and my academic work. I now take much more pleasure in my studies and get much more out of them. In my personal life, the year away has taught me a great deal about relating to people.

A principal finding of this study is that most students who took a leave from their colleges engaged in constructive activities that proved to be beneficial to their personal welfare and to their educational development. Their experiences illustrate the potential value of breaking the educational lockstep in favor of engaging, for a time, in activities that present new challenges and that invite different modes of response than those of their well-practiced role as student.

CHAPTER 6

Any Problems?

Good as the leave experiences were for the great majority of students, they also held their measure of problems. In addition to questions about the values and benefits of their leaves, returning students were asked: <u>What difficulties or disappointments did you experience during your leave?</u> After a semester, they were asked: <u>Have there been ways in which you have been handicapped or disadvantaged for having taken a leave?</u> Difficulties associated with leaving college and re-enrolling are discussed in chapter 8. The nature of these problems is intimated in the comments of two students.

> I was handicapped financially by the loss of my scholarship. They could make the bureaucratic red-tape less forbidding, make more room for late decisions and last minute changes in plans. The regulations governing leave-taking should be more oriented to meeting students' needs and less authoritarian. I see the need for an advisor; someone who will work <u>with</u> the student.
>
> They do not clearly tell you what to do about returning to college and getting transfer credit. The whole process is very unclear, disorganized, and a pain in the . . .

This chapter will be devoted to a summary of problems that leave-takers encountered and to some of their reflections on ways in which difficulties might be mitigated or managed to reduce their negative impacts. At the outset it is important to stress that difficulties and benefits cannot be set in opposition to each other. Many students qualified their descriptions of problems that they had faced with observations to the effect that working through the difficulties had provided them with some of their most valued learning experiences and had stimulated important elements of personal growth. One student put it very forcefully:

> The only disappointments/difficulties were self-induced and anticipated. The basic idea of my leave was to escape all safety, to tear the ground from under my feet, to deal with a new existence and, oh joy, MANY NEW PROBLEMS.
>
> On my leave I was very lonely and I really missed academic/intellectual stimulation. The independence I gained from working through my loneliness has let me get along with less social life than before. I don't see this as desirable for long periods, but I need that independence now.
>
> I was somewhat disappointed in that the intellectual climate of the school that I attended during my leave was not what I hoped it would be. I had expected it to be at least comparable to that of my degree-granting college. However, this did not seriously affect my leave experience. In fact, it may have been an advantage because the lower academic demands afforded me the opportunity to do more extracurricular activities and see more of the country. I consider that my leave was a very productive one for me.
>
> I feel that any difficulties or disappointments turned out in many respects to be benefits. I was disappointed by the French people and how the Parisians in particular were very cold toward strangers of any nationality. I was forced into a very lonely existence at times, but I feel much more confident about myself and my ability to get along in any situation now.
>
> Difficulties were the difficulties of exploration: Loneliness, lack of money. I wouldn't say I was disappointed, however.

Students reported a considerable variety of problems that they had encountered on their leaves: difficulties in securing satisfactory employment; discovering that academic programs in which they had enrolled did not meet the claims of the promotional literature or the students' expectations and needs; living quarters, diet, and social relationships often were so radically different from those to which they were accustomed that major modifications in expectations and in lifestyle were necessary. Some students experienced difficulties in communication, arising in part from lack of facility in the native language but also produced by differences in customs, class attitudes, and the stereotypic modes of thinking to which persons of different national identifications and social classes are bound.

> My only difficulty during my stay was that of alienation. Despite friends, I often felt very foreign indeed and the Germans aren't the most hospitable of hosts. The experience of feeling not part of a culture or a people was novel and shaking, since you can travel 3,000 miles here and still feel when you reach Los Angeles that you belong. I see my American upbringing a bit differently now.

> I had to live with some people who didn't handle responsibility well. This was a problem, but it will help me in dealing with people in the long run.
>
> I found adjusting quite easy, generally, but I had difficulty accepting the attitude of the men toward me as an American, as well as toward women in general. Another problem that we had was in meeting the Mexicans, women in particular.
>
> I lived with a Colombian family. The experience was a miserable one, while living in the house, but one which was very informative. The problem lay in the very different customs and traditions of each culture, American and Colombian. Obviously these differences are to be expected. As much as I tried to be compatible with my family's habits and customs, they were unable to respect my need for privacy and independence.
>
> It was often difficult living in an environment so different from what I'd been used to, but it was never disappointing.

Many students reported experiencing a kind of "culture shock" in the early stages of their leave, whether they were studying/working/traveling overseas or were located in a community very different from the ones in which they had lived previously and were engaged in activities that were "foreign" to their earlier experiences. A problem that many leave-takers encountered was social isolation and loneliness. Often this was a new experience for which they were unprepared and to which they reacted initially with varying degrees of personal distress and dislocation. However, most welcomed the opportunity to relate to a radically different social environment and expressed the belief that coming to terms with social isolation and the broad demands for self-sufficiency that it required, although painful, had contributed significantly to their personal development.

> I felt lonely at times, and isolated from friends. It was very hard to make new relationships.
>
> I was often lonely, very lonely, but this helped in introspection.
>
> The social aspect of my leave was discouraging, for while I did meet interesting people, for the most part they were much older than myself. In fact, it was rarely that I encountered a contemporary.
>
> It was difficult for me to be away from most of my friends, but I tried to visit as often as possible. Another difficulty I encountered was that a couple of people with whom I worked strongly resented my background (rich college kid) and held it against me. I certainly don't blame them or hold it against them, but it created some anxieties and embarrassment on my part.

> I found it very difficult to make French friends, although I did have a few. The French are not welcoming to foreigners. Therefore, making friends required great perseverance and self-confidence.
>
> There were many frustrating times. Also there is never enough time to do everything one wants to do. And being so very far away from home and relatives and friends can make you feel very lonely at times.
>
> I think the only disappointing thing about my leave was not being able to immediately share things with people I care about, but that too was a learning and growing experience for me.

There was not only the separation and loneliness of the leave, but the disruption of valued social relationships at the college. Many students found that they could resume social relationships without difficulty on their return. The loss of contact with college friends was less of a problem for those who left college in the early semesters of their college careers and for those who returned after a semester, or even a year. Those who took a leave in the second semester of their junior year or in the first semester of their senior year and those who were gone for more than a year commonly found that the students that they had known had graduated and that their associates in classes and in living quarters were strangers. This loss of contact with people at the college also applied to relationships with faculty. The implications that this had for departmental examinations and for securing letters in support of graduate and professional school applications varied from persons to person according to length of leave, college class and the particular circumstances of their major department.

> I find a large number of close friends no longer here and am dissatisfied socially.
>
> One disadvantage of taking a leave is that there often is a feeling of having been left behind -- especially if most of your friends, the ones you've gone all through school with, are graduating and you've still got a semester or a year to go. It's not a great problem, nor one that affects everyone.
>
> The only handicap that I experienced in taking a leave was in the severing of social relationships. This was not a serious problem and strong relationships were in fact strengthened.
>
> I felt isolated from the general campus and my class. None of the professors in my major department knew me which leaves a lack of interaction and makes it difficult when I want advice, recommendations, etc.

> My major source of handicap was within my major department. Being away in my junior year resulted in my missing "seminar contacts" with professors. This makes it hard to get to know the workings of the department and to prepare for general examinations.
>
> The only handicap I perceived is the breaking of ties with certain faculty members who are no longer at the university.
>
> I have felt at a slight disadvantage this year because of my leave. A whole year away has isolated me both from department members, faculty and personal friends. I felt somewhat like a stranger or a freshman starting out all over again, because so many of the faces and even buildings on campus had changed. Moreover, I had to readjust my lifestyle from that which I had adopted during my leave. It took a while to adjust to all these feelings, but towards the end of the semester I felt I had overcome many of them. I still feel somewhat "left out" of my department.
>
> Being away in my junior year year resulted in my missing seminar contacts with my major professors. It makes it hard to get to know the workings of the department and to prepare for general examinations. Also, the pressure of American universities hits in different ways than do the British universities. I was forced to restyle my working habits.

Many respondents judged the experiences of their leaves to be among the most significant of their lives. They had developed insights and understandings that they wished to evaluate and develop through their cousework and their informal discussions with faculty and with other students. They had new feelings and appreciations which they wished to share. Many returned with changed attitudes toward college and their academic programs; with a different conception of what the life of a student might be; with an altered sense of values and a new set of priorities for their day-to-day living. The leave experience stimulated change and growth in so many aspects of the person's life that he or she felt the need to assimilate and integrate and relate the welter of ideas and emotions and values. They hoped to make their leave a part of their continuing education. However, once they were back on the campus, they found that in contrast to their experiences of newness and change, things were much the same. The academic preoccupations of the faculty and the peer culture's pressures for conformity to prevailing values and age-bound interests and involvements in campus activities shut out serious consideration of matters that had become important to them.

> The main disadvantage of taking the leave of absence was returning to a campus that seemed very small and limiting

> after exploring a breadth of experiences that were essentially non-academic. There was a feeling that I had outgrown this kind of collegiate life-style. I had just had a fantastic leave which was becoming more and more an unreality -- idyllic memories which were now confronted by hard-edged realities. I wanted to integrate my leave of absence with my other college experiences -- make it part of my education rather than a separate entity.
>
> I would have been much more appreciative of the college had they attempted to involve themselves in my experience both during my leave and upon my return. They seemed uninterested in what I had done during my leave and did nothing to help me relate those interests to my remaining college program when I returned. I question the faculty's and the administration's true concern with the educational motivation of the individual student.
>
> I have found very few opportunities to use my "new" knowledge within this academic community. Perhaps more occasions would arise if the professors were aware of the fact that I have lived and studied in Holland, Denmark and Sweden. In short, I've found little continuity between my leave and my present academic work.
>
> The college should arrange meetings in which students who are thinking about going on leave could talk with students who have been on leave. There should also be an attempt to help the student coordinate the benefits of his experience while on leave into his academic and extracurricular life, because many returnees have acquired experiences and skills which could be developed, utilized, and shared.

For some, the problems of adjustment associated with returning to college were of an intensity that in some ways resembled a kind of reverse "culture shock." They found the social environment of the campus uncongenial or unacceptable. Having experienced a greater degree of control of and responsibility for their own lives, they found the strictures of college regulations galling. Having clarified their own goals and objectives, they were impatient with or resentful of curricular arrangements and educational procedures that appeared to be wasteful or even exploitative of their time and resources.

> My preoccupations at school since my return exclude the application of those benefits which my leave afforded me. I feel very much alienated from student "culture," i.e., parties given by students alone, the smugness which at times arises here from students of "privileged" backgrounds. There seems to be no one person, group, or activity upon which I can try to duplicate or recreate the peace-of-mind that I experienced away from school. The present realness of studies and the academic environment is another world to me in which my wants and needs often seem at odds with that which is offered me. I am more aware of this now than before taking a leave, so this may

be termed a harmful effect of my leave--ignorance of the world outside of college was bliss in a sense.

Returning was not easy. It was a test of perseverance. The problem with the college is that it remains the same while you have changed, so it is hard to relate in the same way as before you left.

I was forced to face many traumatic experiences, economic, social and personal. But the "highs" were extremely high, and the "lows" very low. All in all, it is the richest experience that I have ever had. One of the largest disappointments was my return to college. I realized just how un-catholic it is, and how little it is oriented towards the students. Consequently, I have at this point been burying myself in my work. But I would definitely recommend time off to students who would use it to broaden themselves.

At first when I came back, it was hard to study, and it seemed silly to burrow in books when life was all around, so vibrant. But the boredome of the college town brought me back to routine. Studying this year hasn't been hard. I can wade through the pointlessness much more easily, knowing that outside of books and outside of college, there is so much more.

I am handicapped only insofar as I've discovered that life at an English university is far more rewarding than life here. But I am stuck here for one more year. If I hadn't gone to England, they would have locked me up long ago.

Upon my return, I was greatly disoriented in the academic community, and found myself highly resistant to its demands. I did, however, settle down to work and accomplished a satisfactory amount. Now, again, I feel that I have perhaps over-burdened myself with academic responsibilities and have negated the social and personal side of my development.

It was awfully hard to come back. This college is so impersonal, its so expensive, there's so much red-tape, it's such a factory! I can't wait to get out of here. I learned something very valuable from my leave: I'm happier when I'm not a student.

I return to academia altogether conscious of the sick, pernicious and pervasive influences which drove me away, and thus am prepared to live with these influences for as long as absolutely necessary, that is, until such time as I am in a position to combat them.

I got away from the stagnation of my home college and studied music in a concentrated and productive way. My return has been very disappointing in that the entire attitude of the instruction fosters an unimaginative, status quo intellect that is reactionary and fearful of challenge and change. The leave was a four-month fantasy for my mind.

After having taken the leave, I felt I was ready to jump right back into my studies. I anticipated returning to school and taking all sorts of courses both towards my degree and just for the pure joy of learning. Unfortunately, the competition in all classes is so great, one all too easily just slips back

> into the old routine of learning material just to do well on exams; to "get ahead" is eventually the only thing on one's mind.
>
> My year in France made it somewhat difficult to return in that I often felt apart from the college life and a stranger in a familiar place. In a sense, it gave me a strong motivation to quickly complete my undergraduate studies and move on.
>
> I must admit that my leave has decreased my desire for a college education, if that is to be regarded as a "difficulty." I can't help but feel that I've gained more from my time in the "real world" than from that spent in colleges' surreal, country-club like atmosphere.
>
> I've become totally disenchanted with college. I do not think it is structured for education. This idea has been strengthened by my leave-taking.

A significant number of students reported that initially their parents had questioned the wisdom of their leaving college or actively opposed it. Most eventually were able to win their family's acceptance and support. Some, however, encountered parental disapproval and recriminations that continued through the leave and even after their return.

> The only disadvantages have been relative to my family. I still have to demonstrate to them the beneficial aspects of my leave (which seems to have to be in pragmatic form).
>
> Difficulties were minor really. They were mostly with family and to a degree with friends. I did something they didn't expect when I took a leave. I stepped out of the rosy, predictable picture they had painted for me. In the long run, I feel that this was a healthy thing to do and a healthy time to do it.

Most of the persons who reported being disappointed at having to give up their participation in extracurricular activities regarded this as a minor sacrifice compared to the benefits that they had derived from their leave.

> The only way I have lost out because of a leave is in campus activities. Others took over leadership in activities I might have led had I stayed on campus. I would never trade my leave for these trivial things, though.
>
> There were certain disadvantages to my leave, certain events on campus last year that I would like to have been part of, or certain people I would have liked to know better through knowing them last year, but these factors are outweighed by my experiences on my leave.

The timing of the leave and the value of advanced planning were two issues on which leave-takers commented frequently and on which they arrived at quite different conclusions. Some persons felt that the benefits that they derived from their leaves were directly related to the preparation or lack of preparation that they had made for their leaves.[21] Others argued with equal cogency that for them it was important to make a dramatic break with their past, to venture into new territory without commitments or guarantees, to open themselves to new experiences without the constraints of a schedule or prearranged obligations that would set limits upon their experiences.

> I would NOT recommend leave-taking to a student unless he: 1) had strong conviction in the need or desirability of taking a leave -- a self-induced conviction; 2) utilized leave to accomplish something distinctively unconventional and rewarding. I have observed that those friends who remained in familiar territory and held conventional jobs during their leave were most often disappointed and regretted the time "wasted"; 3) had a clear, conscious idea of why he was taking leave and what he expected to gain from it; 4) had clear notion, realistic estimation of potential risks and disappointments vs. potential gains.

> I did not leave my college because I was dissatisfied with anything. I simply knew, I could both think it and feel it, that the time had come when I could do something different with my college life and gain from it. My leave was totally successful. I got everything out of it that I could have wanted. It was productive because I was in touch with myself. I knew what I wanted to do, how I wanted to do it, when the time was right, and why I would be doing it. I believe that the key to my productive time away was that, unlike many other students, I had definite ideas and plans and worked to fulfill them.

> I needed a break from school, to think about where I was going in life and to break up academics with some practical experience. My activities were largely unplanned. I could have put more effort into planning just what I wanted to get out of my leave.

> I didn't plan my leave well at all. The utter confusion that was whirling in my mind a year ago didn't allow me to define a positive plan of action. Still, I found my leave beneficial in that I was able to get some traveling in, and got some things out of my system like heavy partying with friends.

> I might have planned more specifically, but still don't feel I wasted any of that time. Part of the beauty was not having a schedule, of rolling with the opportunities that arose and being able to make impulsive decisions and following them. A certain timelessness made all the newness I was experiencing a little more real instead of part of a plan.

> My only objectives were to have fun, to travel a little, read some and open myself to new viewpoints and experiences. My purpose was to get away from formal education for a while. Sixteen straight years of it requires some sort of personal reflection from outside the system. Anything programmed would have defeated the purpose of my leave.

Clearly the degree of planning, preparation and structure that is appropriate is a highly individual matter that is related to the person's own temperament and psychological disposition and to the requirements of a particular leave situation. Some objectives cannot be realized without careful preparation; other purposes might be defeated by an attempt to pre-determine the character of the leave.

The timing and duration of a leave requires the balancing of numerous variables and again should be responsive to the needs and circumstances of a particular individual. The academic calendar and the normal progressions of the college year present special problems.

> I feel that students should go for a full year, since one term simply isn't enough time to adjust and become a part of the new university. The time spent abroad was rewarding in both a scholastic and a personal sense.

> I know now that one-half year is not enough time in an over-seas program. One year is just about enough time, though certainly not too much.

> I think my leave would have been a better experience if I had stayed for a full year instead of a single semester.

> I only wish that I had taken a leave earlier in my college career, or directly after high school. My most valuable experience was that I learned what life was like outside of college. This I consider invaluable.

> For the first time in my life I had time to learn. I adjusted to a slower pace of life, learned to sleep well, discovered what it is like to function at peak performance by being in good health. I had time for my studies, cultural events in the city, spending time with others and with myself. This was a highly positive and valuable learning experience. I wish I had taken my leave a year earlier.

> I came back in February and found it impossible to meet any people, they were not interested. Groups of friends solidify in September during the first semester and you can't break in.

> I realize that a leave during your senior year can be dangerous for seriously considering your future. One is often out of contact with the post-graduate demands.

> My leave gave me a much needed break, and much needed thinking time. I regret that it was in the spring semester as I feel this is my most productive time of year, but I couldn't wait.

> The college is very locked into semester by semester sequencing of courses. This makes returning mid-year difficult. Considerable shuffling of courses was required in order to meet the prerequisites of my physics major. It is hard enough to resume formal study after time away from college without having scheduling problems too.

> Coming back in the middle of the year was difficult for me since everyone's patterns of life were already set and didn't include me. Fortunately my old friends were very welcoming. But as they are all now three semesters ahead of me, I am a little apprehensive of the future when they are gone.
>
> If allowed to do over, I would choose to finish my undergraduate education in three years and then take a leave travelling abroad. I found the break in my junior year disruptive to my program and intellectual work. This year, it has been extremely difficult to focus attention on academic work.
>
> If I could do it over again, I would take a similar leave, only earlier. Instead of waiting until my senior year, I'd like a leave after my freshman or sophomore years. I think that colleges should consider impressing upon students the advantages of taking time off. A leave of absence could help a lot of students here.
>
> In my case, I feel that it would have been better if I had taken off earlier. I was not ready for college, and I now find my previous failures difficult to ignore.
>
> My leave has enabled me to understand how an "intellectual-activist" integrates the academic with the action-oriented part of themselves. My leave afforded me the chance to experiment with the pieces and to fashion the whole. I would not have had the internal or intellectual strength to do this, however, without spending the previous $2\frac{1}{2}$ hours in rigorous study and challenging work (mostly out of the classroom) while in college.

Students who took a leave for a single semester in order to minimize the discontinuities and loss of contacts at the college, often found that the potential advantages of their leave situation could not be fully realized in so short a time. The greater the adjustments required, as for example in study at another American or foreign university or by a job that has a lengthy training period, the longer the time needed to develop the associations and skills that are necessary to make full use of the opportunities present in that situation.

There are those who recommend that students do something non-academic before entering college, but others argue that, in their experience, they needed a semester or more of college to sensitize themselves to the issues that eventually made their leave both desirable and productive. There were many among those who had not taken a leave who postponed taking a leave until after their graduation in the interests of preserving the continuity of their undergraduate program or simply to acquire the baccalaureate degree in the shortest time possible. Others found that they simply couldn't wait. The timing and duration of a leave should, in the final analysis, be determined by the needs and circumstances of the person taking the leave.

A long list of inconveniences and hardships could be catalogued from the reports of leave-takers. Some might be alleviated by changes in college regulations and services. Some could be avoided by more careful planning. Many are unpredictable and some that can be anticipated cannot, with that foreknowledge, be avoided. In some cases, the inherent difficulties present the challenge and excitement of the leave and their mastery is the reward that makes the effort worthwhile. Among the more than 1,000 respondents, there were fewer than fifty who felt that the problems that they had encountered as a result of their having taken a leave outweighed the benefits that they had derived from the experience.

CHAPTER 7

Do They Return?

A question concerning persons who go on leave that touches the concerns of society, of educators, of parents and of the students themselves is, "Do they come back?" "Will the leave in fact be a temporary absence from the campus or is it the first step in a process that will eventuate in permanent withdrawal from college?" The editors of <u>The College Dropout</u> highlight some of the widely held attitudes toward dropping out that fuel this concern.

> When a student leaves college before graduating, he evokes a variety of responses from the social milieu, from his college, from his parents and from himself. These responses may to some degree be appropriate and reasonable, but they are often strongly colored by the kind of emotional excess that an individual's deviation from some widely accepted and institutionalized value system is apt to evoke. . . . The dropout is often referred to as a drain on national resources. He is presumed to represent wasted talent, so that a dropout rate of fifty percent is taken to mean the loss to the national economy and welfare of fifty percent of the most talented population, which then becomes a cause for national concern.
> . . . Just as the college dropout can be viewed nationally from an economic perspective, so can he be viewed by the college in terms of the economic implications for facilities, faculties and students . . . parents interpret dropping out according to their own life experiences. For many, the child's admission to college, particularly a select college, represents a fulfilled dream and the fruition of years of struggle and hope. Any interruption of the smooth course of this dream shatters the image of hope created during the worthwhile years of effort. . . Students' attitudes toward withdrawal are rarely independent of parental feelings. Not only the event of dropping out but also the expressed reasons may be influenced by factors of which the dropout is not fully aware. . . . Over the years the predominant conventional wisdom has frowned on dropping out. . . . These negative attitudes have not only had the effect of placing the dropout under increased pressure but have also often determined policies, particularly those concerning readmission and even concerning transfer students.[22]

As Alexander Astin observes, "many decision makers -- students included -- legitimately want to know more about how to increase students' chances of finishing college, whether this concern is based on the loss of talent, the waste of limited educational resources, or the vocational and personal setbacks that result from the student's impeded career development and futile expenditure of time and effort." [23]

The evidence developed in this investigation indicates that, at least for those students who attend highly selective colleges of the liberal arts, fears that "stopping out" will end as "dropping out" are for the most part unfounded and contrary to what actually happens. For the students who took a leave of absence from one of the colleges participating in this study, the answer to the question "Do they come back?" is a simple and unequivocal, "Yes, most of them do." More specifically, two hundred and ninety-one persons of the three hundred and eighty-one who had taken a leave of absence from Brown University in 1973-74 had re-enrolled at the Brown campus on or before September 1975, this representing a return of seventy-six percent of those who had gone on leave. Of the one hundred and seventy-one persons who took a leave from Trinity College in 1973-74, one hundred and twenty-nine, or seventy-five percent, had returned by September 1975. Wesleyan University's return rate was eighty-five percent. Two hundred and sixteen persons went on leave and one hundred and eighty-four returned. Of the six colleges participating in the study, the program and policies of Hampshire College are the most supportive of the concept of students becoming involved in some form of off-campus learning. Approximately eighty-one percent of the student body take a leave at some time during their undergraduate careers. Further, a larger percentage of students who take a leave from Hampshire engaged in self-directed projects which tended to have less well-defined time limits. Because a larger number of Hampshire students extended their leaves than did students of the other colleges, the return rate of fifty-nine percent that was observed within the time limits of this investigation may seriously underestimate the number who eventually receive their baccalaureate degree from Hampshire College. A follow-up study of persons who had taken a leave from one of these four colleges and who had not returned by September 1975, revealed that approximately ninety percent either had plans for returning at a later date or had chosen to continue their studies at another college or university. These findings will be presented in greater detail later in the chapter.

Because Tufts and Wheaton entered the project a year later, the number of persons who were on leave for a period longer than one year is relatively small. In 1974-75, three hundred and one students took a leave from Tufts University. By the second semester of 1975-76, one hundred and twenty-four had re-enrolled, representing a return rate of forty-one percent. In the same time period, one hundred and twenty-one Wheaton students went on leave. Eighty-one, or sixty-seven percent, returned within six to twelve months. In comparing these rates with those of Brown, Trinity and Wesleyan, it must be remembered that the time period is shorter for Tufts and Wheaton students. Accordingly, the observed return rates understates the number and percentage of leave-takers who will return during a longer time interval.

If we examine the data developed in this investigation to determine whether there are identifiable characteristics that distinguish those who did not return, we find that similarities are more extensive and profound than are differences. Persons who returned to their college after a leave, and those who did not, were not differentiated by their responses to most of the items of Survey 1, or by their answers on the Background Information Form. Some of the questions that did elicit significantly different reactions from members of the two groups were identified and discussed in chapter 2 on page 20. As noted there, a larger proportion of the students who did not return from leave, than of those who did, assigned greater importance to the seeming irrelevancy of college to issues that are important to me, and to lack of interest in my course of studies as reasons for taking a leave of absence. A larger percentage also stated that in the semester before their leave, they had enjoyed their studies less than they had expected to. A significantly larger percentage of persons who did not return reported that handling the content of my courses had been a serious problem in the semester prior to their leave. A larger percentage also indicated that making decisions concerning my career had been a serious problem for them. To the question: In thinking about your occupational future, do you feel that in the long run you will have a preference for: the percentage of persons who selected the alternatives a life of a trained technician or craftsman, or a life centering upon some aspect of the creative arts, was greater for the non-returning group. A larger percentage of those who returned to their college selected the alternatives: an academic life (teaching, research, other scholarly work), or a professional life (physician, lawyer, engineer, etc.). As noted earlier, those who returned placed a greater importance upon completing their college work and on continuing their schooling in graduate or professional schools. These educational plans are consistent with the requirements of the career areas to which the greater numbers in each group are inclined.

The rate of return was essentially the same for persons whose principal leave activity was employment or volunteer service for those who attended another college or university as a full-time student. Students whose leave activities were self-directed were more likely not to return or at least not to return on schedule. The great majority of those who stated that they took a leave with the intention of transferring did not return. Approximately twenty percent of this group did return, however, either because they decided this was preferable to transferring or because they were unable to make satisfactory arrangements for changing schools.

There was a large, non-chance difference in the ages of members of the two groups at the time that they began their leaves, the students who did not return being younger. They differed also in their response to question ten of the Background Information Form:

TABLE 19

What is your best estimate of when you will return to this college from your leave?

Answer Given Before Leave	Current Enrollment Status	
	Returned	Did not Return
One Semester	42%	14%
Two Semesters	37%	22%
More than two semesters	4%	4%
The duration of my leave cannot be decided at this time	8%	23%
My present expectation is that I will not return to this college	9%	37%

Later in the chapter the differences in age and in students' estimates of the duration of their leaves will be discussed in relation to the number of semesters that had been completed before the leave was begun. Here we may note that nine percent of those who returned had not expected to. An additional eight percent had been unsure of the length of their leave. Seventy-nine percent expected to return to college within the year. This is very close to the proportion of all leave-takers who actually did return to their college following a leave. Among those leave-takers who had completed a Background Information Form at the time that they began their leave but had not returned to college by September 1975, thirty-seven percent took their leave with the expectation that they would not return and an additional twenty-three percent were unsure of the duration of their leave. Thirty-six percent were unable or did not choose to carry through with their original plan to return to their college within one year.

TABLE 20
Response Rate to Survey 5

	Sent	Returned Undelivered	Returned Completed	Response Rate
Brown	89	12	21	27%
Hampshire	113	1	40	36
Trinity	42	4	11	29
Wesleyan	32	5	20	74
Total	276	22	92	33%

In an effort to learn more about the leave-time activities of those who had not returned, to explore their reasons for extending their leave and to learn of their intentions in regard to further college attendance, Survey 5 was mailed to all students who had begun a leave in 1973-74 and had not returned to their college by September 1975.[24] As with all other surveys in this study, a follow-up mailing was sent to those who did not respond to the first request. As can be observed in table 20, the response rates varied widely from college to college for reasons that we have not been able to clarify to our own satisfaction. The failure of mail to reach the person to whom it was addressed almost certainly was one important factor contributing to the relatively low response rate and to the variability from school to school. In those instances in which an accurate current address was not available, we used the last known address, often the address of the parents, with the notation, "Please Forward." The number of letters that were returned as undeliverable probably is not an accurate reflection of the numbers actually received by the persons to whom they were addressed. A second factor that no doubt contributed to a response rate lower than those of the other surveys was the negative attitudes that some students almost certainly had for the college from which they had taken leave. Whatever the reasons, the analyses that follow are based upon the report of only one-third of the persons who did not return during the time period specified. In that group, students who attended Wesleyan University are over-represented in relation to those who attended the other three schools. Persons who took a leave from Tufts and Wheaton were not polled because not enough time had elapsed since the beginning of their leaves.

Of the ninety-two persons who returned a completed Survey 5, thirty, or thirty-three percent, indicated an intention to return to their college at a date later than originally planned. Fifty-two persons, making up fifty-six percent of the respondents, had transferred to another institution or were in the process of attempting to arrange a transfer. Ten, or eleven percent, reported that they did not plan to take a baccalaureate degree at any college or university in the foreseeable future. There were substantial differences among the colleges in the percentage of students who had transferred to another college and in those who planned to return. Hampshire College had the highest percentage of students who planned to return and the smallest percentage who had transferred. In contrast, Wesleyan University, which had the largest percentage of students who returned on schedule, also had the largest percentage of leave-takers who transferred to another college or university.

TABLE 21 Item B
Present Plans for Undergraduate Education

	Brown	Hampshire	Trinity	Wesleyan	Total
Return	24%	53%	27%	5%	33%
Transfer	67	37	64	80	56
No B.A. Degree	9	10	9	15	11
Number of Students	21	40	11	20	92

If the observations based on this sample can be generalized to all those who did not return, more than ninety percent of the students who take a leave will either return to graduate or will receive a baccalaureate degree from another college or university

Among those students who reported that it was their intention to return to their college to complete their undergraduate program of studies, only thirteen percent did not set a definite time for their return when they began their leave. Of those who transferred, twenty-six percent were unsure about their return. An additional twenty-one percent took the leave with the intention of arranging a transfer, if this could be accomplished to their satisfaction. In the small group of students who have no present plans for taking a Bachelor of Arts degree, six had intended to return to college, two were undecided, and two had expected, at the time that they began their leaves, to transfer to another college. These percentages are based upon the responses to Item A of Survey 5 and are summarized in table 22. This item is a paraphrase of Item 10 of the Background Information Form which has been referred to earlier.

TABLE 22 Item A

Originally, how long did you expect to be away from the institution from which you took leave?

	Intend to Return	Transferred	No Degree
One Semester	37%	11%	20%
Two Semesters	43%	38%	10%
More than two Semesters	7%	4%	30%
Uncertain	10%	26%	20%
Did not intend to return	3%	21%	20%
Number of Students	30	52	10

It is worth noting that developments during the period of the leave altered the plans of persons in each of the groups. Some who took their leave with the intention of returning, encountered circumstances that prevented their return. Others in this group discovered interests and opportunities that caused them to reorient their plans. Among those who took a leave for the express purpose of arranging an alternative educational program there were some who found it desirable or necessary to return to the school from which they had intended to withdraw. Some who left to explore the possibility of achieving their objectives without finishing their college work, re-enrolled after a time.

We already have noted a significant age difference in the three groups under consideration. These differences relate directly to the fact that persons in these groups tend to begin their leaves at different times in their undergraduate careers. Students who eventually transferred began their leaves, on the average, after a shorter period of enrollment. Thirty-two percent took a leave after they had completed two semesters. Only ten percent continued at their colleges beyond the fourth semester. Relatively early in their college careers, many of the persons who transferred found their college environment uncongenial or unsuited to their personal and/or educational requirements and were motivated to search for alternatives.

Those who intended to return began their leaves somewhat later. They were motivated by a need for perspective, or enrichment, or respite. These motivations developed in response to the experiences and stresses of college attendance. Twenty-nine percent began their leave in the second half of their sophomore year and thirty-five percent in the first half of their junior year. Those intending no degree had the longest period of enrollment. Their decision to leave was associated with the emergence of new interests and/or with a reassessment of the college experience as it related to their personal situations and interests. Table 23 presents the percentage of students in each group who began their leave after the completion of a specific number of semesters. The column listing the cumulative percentage can be read to find the total percentage of students who had completed a given number of semesters before going on leave.

TABLE 23 Item H

Semesters Completed Before Leave
Percentage and Cumulative Percentage Completing

Completed Semesters	Intend to Return %	Cum	Transferred %	Cum	No Degree %	Cum
7	9%	9%	--	--	--	--
6	9%	18%	8%	8%	25%	25%
5	6%	24%	2%	10%	25%	50%
4	35%	59%	44%	54%	37%	87%
3	29%	88%	14%	68%	13%	100%
2	12%	100%	28%	96%	--	100%
1	--	100%	4%	100%	--	100%
Average Number Completed Semesters	4.0 sem		3.4 sem.		4.6 sem	

There are rather striking differences in the frequency with which these groups of leave-takers indicated each of the eight categories of reasons as <u>one of the most important or compelling reasons for extending my leave</u>. For each reason table 24 records the percentage of students who rated it as being <u>most important or compelling</u>. Since a person may state that more than one reason was important, the total of the percentages for all reasons exceeds one hundred percent.

Only a small percentage of the respondents who intended to return to their colleges, and also of those who did not intend to return to any college, cited dissatisfactions with their college as a <u>most important</u> reason for extending their leave. In contrast, thirty-seven percent of those who transferred to another college rated it <u>most important</u>. Sixty-two percent of the transferred and fifty-five percent of the no degree respondents rated as <u>most important</u> the alternative: <u>College does not meet my educational-academic needs</u>. Only fourteen percent of those who intended to return cited this as a compelling reason. Fifty-five percent of the no degree respondents and thirty-eight percent of those who intended to return indicated that <u>the need for more time for current interests and activities</u> was for them a <u>most important</u> reason. The intend to return group considered completion of their college program to be necessary to their long-range goals but twenty-four percent felt that various psychological constraints impeded their immediate return to campus. Psychological readiness was a less important reason for other respondents. More than one-half of respondents in each of the categories rated as <u>most important</u>, <u>Have discovered alternatives to returning that are more attractive or better suited to my requirements</u>. Many of the <u>other</u> reasons listed were in fact individual, specific statements that related closely to alternatives b, f, g, or h, singly or in combination. The following are illustrative:

> I wanted to live in another part of the country and wanted to be closer to my boyfriend.
>
> I took a leave because my college was too expensive and I was not studying. I did not return because it offers no cinema arts which I got into during my leave.
>
> Was in Europe on my leave and had a chance to sail across the Atlantic in the fall. I'm in no hurry to finish studies.
>
> Need for exposure to professional world of music.
>
> Wanted to go into nutrition and dietetics. My college does not have such a program.
>
> I want to be a clock-maker -- that's not academic but still educational. Someday maybe a B.A., not now.
>
> During my leave I found I did not want to continue with my major and had no alternative major in mind. Did not want to continue school not knowing my future career.

There were few differences between the students of the four schools in the frequency with which they cited particular reasons for extending their leave. A greater percentage of Hampshire students stated that they <u>need more time for current interests and activities</u>, consistent with the fact that more Hampshire students did actually extend their leaves. Half or more of the students from each of the four colleges rated as <u>important or compelling</u>, Item h: "<u>Have discovered alternatives to returning that are more attractive or better suited to my requirements.</u>"

Many of the respondents gave additional information about their leave activities and elaborated on their reasons for extending their leaves or for not returning. A few of these statements will be quoted to illustrate some of the circumstances that were described and the attitudes that were expressed.

There were students who extended their leaves because of illness, because of financial difficulties, or because of family requirements. For the same reasons others transferred to another college or university. For them, the geographical location of another college was more convenient, the costs lower, or the person was able to meet family responsibilities or to maintain desirable employment while attending the new school. More commonly than with those who plan to return, persons who transferred also expressed dissatisfactions with the institutions from which they took leave and/or indicated that their college had not met their educational-academic needs.

> My main reasons for leaving college are given in question C. I do want to say that my two years there were years that I would never have traded. Not only was my academic knowledge increased but I also learned about myself and about a culture quite different from my own. I feel that I am a more mature understanding person because of my experience. I will always consider Wesleyan my alma-mater. (Transferred to UCLA because of financial and family considerations.)

> During my leave I became seriously ill. I am convalescing now and am looking forward to returning to my college when I am fully recovered.

> Basic dissatisfaction with college. It was not meeting the expectations I had been led to believe existed there. I left after my sophomore year because of dissatisfaction with the school but had intended to return for the second semester of my Junior year. Because of budget problems, they would not let me live off campus on my return. Disenchantment with campus housing having been part of my "misery" at college, forced me to look at other alternatives. I decided to attend the University of Kansas for the semester and then return. I found the social life a considerable improvement and the academics as strong (in fact, the quality of teaching was better). So I am graduating this semester with a BA in classics from K.U.

> The major reason for my leave was marriage -- my husband graduated in June of 1973, and when we were married early in the fall I did not return to college. Since then, marriage and geographic location have been the reasons I did not return. At first we lived in, and were both employed in Philadelphia. Later, my husband got a

job in the Los Angeles area, which is where we are now. (Plans to take degree at another institution.)

> I was on leave as defined by your definition above, for only one semester. I transferred to another institution and completed my undergraduate work in the semester following my leave. I left feeling inferior to most of the student body and uninterested in academics in general. I am not by nature a devoted scholastic achiever. But I worked one semester at odd jobs and found that despite the reading I was doing I was feeling unfulfilled. When I decided to return to college my finances would not allow me to return to my college. I was able to get tuition remission at American University because a member of my family was a professor there. I have finished my B.S. in biology and will complete my M.S. in physiology next year.

Some persons found it desirable to extend their leave because activities in which they were engaged required more time than had been anticipated in their earlier plans. Some, who for a period of time had entertained the idea of not returning to college, discovered needs and interests that motivated their return. Some returned to college eagerly while others accepted their return as necessary, but anticipated it without enthusiasm.

> I spent my junior year abroad at Tufts University in London. After I finished my year in London, I had absolutely no interest in returning to the United States, much less to my college. I was having a perpetually great time, was happy, was learning a great deal and felt generally better than ever in my life. I had achieved a state of mind that was comfortable and happy and mellow, but which I knew would be easily lost at home and at college unless I had more time and more practice with it. So I wanted to stay away. Eventually I did come home because I had no more money and I decided it was time to face up to all the decisions I'd been avoiding -- and I felt like my frame of mind was safe. I had planned to apply to other schools because with each year and with each successively more dull freshman class, my college was becoming more intolerable. But I have friends there who will graduate in May and I'd like to see them. The faculty is fine. So if I can get together enough money, I'll go back in January.

> Although I have occasionally had doubts along the way, I am now persuaded that my extended leave of absence has been most beneficial, both personally and academically. After a ten month period studying abroad, I secured an interesting position in journalism which has helped me to choose a plausible career effort and to grow in many other ways. I will return to college with a better idea as to what I want to do and how I can do it.

After two years of my leave, I was not particularly anxious to return to school. I knew that I would at some point but I was not in a hurry. In the course of the next few months I realized that even though I had been fairly successful in a business environment there were limits imposed on my progress by my lack of a college degree. It was then that I started saving so that I would have enough for tuition in the fall of 1976.

Don't want to go back. I feel under social and moral obligations to finish what I start so I will go back. I feel under social and moral pressure to complete college. I don't actively want to go back to academia. I can't feel as though I can give a job a commitment without finishing school. I don't feel school prepares me for a job.

I am currently fulfilling a one-year commitment in the Word Over The World Ambassador Program. We hold forth God's Word to all those who hunger and thirst after righteousness. I have officially withdrawn from college with the understanding that re-entry will be possible when I return in Jan. 1977.

It seems to me that at school as flexible and expensive as this one, I would be silly not to take a leave of absence, enabling me to work in my field. I am working in a low paying/volunteer internship-type position in communications -- especially childrens T.V. I have learned a great deal more than I could have at any academic institution (at least as pertains to my educational interests). I will return to complete work toward my degree.

My interests are in becoming a Neo-Reichian-psychotherapist. The institution I am presently associated with is one of the only institutions involved in this line of psycho-therapy. I have wanted to get my Bachelor's degree, and at the same time do their program. The program does not confer a degree but leads to certification -- which I will be able to apply toward the completion of my Bachelor's degree.

While at college my interests changed from the education of children to psychology to social work. As part of my educational plan I decided to go on leave and volunteer on a full-time basis as a student social worker. Having worked at Boston Childrens Service as a generalist, I decided to concentrate in protective service work. To do so, I received a placement in an agency that works with families in cases of neglect and abuse of children. I never could have learned the "how to" aspects of social work as a full-time student. I am extending my leave to learn more. I then plan to return to school and receive my degree after a semester.

I am presently a student at the Neighborhood Playhouse School of the Theatre in New York City. It is a two-year program, but the student must be invited back for the second year, which shows the school's confidence in one's future as an actor. If I am not invited for the second year of study, I will consider returning to my college.

Some students who transferred directed their comments primarily to dissatisfactions with their social activities and relationships, to the college environment and to the general quality of campus life. Others were dissatisfied with the quality of teaching, with the academic program in their field of interest or with the particular emphasis and requirements of their academic program (e.g., too theoretical, too competitive and pressured). Still others found that specialized areas of instruction, often career related, were not available within the curriculum of their college and that their own desired development required a program of studies that was more centered on their interests and career goals.

> Became also, very oppressed by the cold and barren ambience of the college and by the lack of closeness among students. I found the college I was in to be a totally unacceptable environment in terms of 1) academic pressures, 2) interpersonal distances and 3) cost -- in all categories ridiculously great -- ironic also, is the fact that while the academic pressures are often great, the quality of instruction and the academic standards are by no means consistently high. (Will complete at another college, transfer applications in progress.)

> I took my leave as a prelude to transferring. Most of my reasons were personal -- waning of inspiration and commitment to my formal studies, unsure of my own academic direction, tired of the pressure, dissatisfaction with the environment and the student body at my home school. I found many people unfulfilled, dissatisfied but lacking the energy, creativity or ideas to change their situation or find fulfillment in the present.

> I may not return to this college. I have not found it a friendly place. It is too competitive for me, and not enough fun. I have not been able to make real close friends. I got stuck in a girls' dorm three years in a row, which I hate. I was very dissatisfied with the main teacher in the botany department, who really is a terrible teacher (I'm not the only one who thinks he is a bad teacher) and botany was the field I wanted to pursue at that time. I think I have problems in making close friends, so college was difficult.

> Only implied in g and h: besides not offering my academic requirements, I found I could not cope with the social atmosphere and pressures of my former college. I sincerely felt that it was too small and too homogeneous to allow me to grow inside and mature in the directions I was going. After two years there I felt those around me were against my changing in any way. I knew then that I had to get out.

While on campus I was raped. I felt I would never feel secure in that town again, so I decided not to return. Also soon after beginning my leave, I realized that I wanted to change the direction of my academic program. I have transferred to a university that has a School of Nursing.

I found professors to be without enthusiasm for conveying to students what interested them, i.e., the subjects they were teaching. While I don't believe in spoon-feeding per se, I do believe that for undergraduates who haven't decided the course of their futures, it is essential that teachers present them with what might be more interesting in the field. For an undergraduate without transportation, my college was an incredibly boring prison so far as extracurricular activities were concerned. Friday and Saturday nights in the library is not my idea of keeping myself well-rounded.

My reason for leaving college was that I wanted stronger theater training than I felt any liberal arts college could offer me. I took a leave because my parents wanted me to keep the option of returning open. Transferring has been a good decision for me.

I should have gone to Cooper Union after high school, but was convinced of the need to complete a "liberal" arts education first. I didn't even apply to an art school then, though aside from performing well academically, I was increasingly turned off by "classes"-lectures, assignments, paper writing. Now I am making art and learning what I could not when it was divorced from my driving inspiration. I am a more complete student now, at a specialized school, than I was at college. I did not realize this before my leave -- too caught up in the myth of "college first" -- but I knew I needed to get away to look back and really see.

I am studying classical saxophone, music theory and piano. I have a very competent saxophone instructor and music teacher, and I plan to leave my days free to study. I found this college's atmosphere so overly intellectual and contrived as to be out-landish, strange, and too much removed from the so-called "real world" (the only world). After my leave I will pursue my studies in the School of Music at the University of Michigan.

In order to teach deaf children I needed an elementary teaching certificate and my college has no facilities for or courses in elementary education. I took a leave and spent my senior year at New York University where I completed thirty-four credits of elementary education. I am presently enrolled at NYU in a Masters Program for deaf education. My two years at NYU, although they have allowed me to fulfill all my certification requirements, have been a waste of time educationally. I was educated at my college. I loved it there and hope, eventually to settle in the State.

"Alternatives" of "h" are another University -- Maharishi International University in Fairfield, Iowa -- based on the Science of Creative Intelligence and its practical aspect Transcendental Meditation. I'm not enthusiastic about becoming a statistic through this form, however if it helps you solve some difficulties with education, OK. I'd like to add my basic criticism of the liberal arts education as it stands today by comparing it with my present interest. What the Science of Creative Intelligence (SCI) adds to traditional education is knowledge of the knower. Through the practical aspect of the transcendental meditation technique (TM) the individual is allowed to grow as a human being and grow in the values of creativity, energy, intelligence and happiness, all of which are essential for a successful student and for a successful product of the educational system. Basically, through TM one contacts the source of thought, the field of consciousness, which is experienced as increasing alertness and creativity in activity. As a result, life in general, and studies more specifically, are more enjoyable, easier and more fulfilling. Science of Creative Intelligence is already offered for credit in some universities (Stanford). Worth looking into.

I changed my views of the purposes of college education, i.e., there's more to it than studying all day, every day. One of the major things I liked so much here at the University of Washington (where I am currently working on an M.S.-Civil Engineering, having completed my B.S. here). was the diversity of people, after having spent two years at a college where everyone was middle/upper class, age 18-25, etc. Here there are older people, people on welfare, returning students, and much more, which make the non-academic parts of education so interesting and valuable. I feel although maybe the academics were better at my former school (although I have real doubts about that too), I've grown much more as a person here, which I feel is vastly more important.

My college did not give me the practical education I needed. I found their courses to be too deep and intellectually oriented to be of practical use. Texas A & M is practically oriented, but it is not "easy" -- it is considered to be one of the most demanding schools in Texas. (Transferred to Texas A & M.)

A relatively small number of persons discovered that they did not wish to continue their formal education at the school from which they took leave or at any other traditional college or university. Some wished to be affilliated with an organization that was committed to radically different purposes, values and life styles. Some identified other avenues for pursuing their educational-career development. Still others entertained the idea that eventually they would continue their college studies after they had completed a project or discharged a commitment that for the foreseeable future would occupy most of their time and attention.

> At present date my feelings about college education are as follows: I feel no need for a college education -- my life is my education and is a much more coherent, satisfying and integrated study than the time I've spent in a college atmosphere, regardless of the college. The reason I left college was because my life felt so unbalanced. The education college provides completely stresses the intellect, and does not acknowledge one's emotions, one's spirit. What is the value of knowing facts, philosophies, history, languages, when one does not know oneself? (Transferred to a large state university and subsequently withdrew. Presently self-employed.)
>
> I am a self-employed musician and member of a band which often travels. The benefits which I seek from college are purely personal and cultural, not occupational in any way. Therefore, the most appropriate time to attend college would seem to be after personal, financial and occupational security has been achieved. I think this entire project and survey is an excellent idea. Because of the current lack of knowledge about young people's ambitions, most schools are, I feel, quite unprepared to meet the needs of those such as myself, who desire a broad, quality liberal arts education later in life, and for reasons not associated with choosing or furthering one's occupation. Keep up the good work!
>
> I am living and working and studying in a spiritual community, The Findhorn Foundation, University of Light, Scotland. I do not plan on returning to my college -- the manner of learning is too one-sided for me -- it puts me off balance. My intellect goes racing ahead, but my emotional and spiritual understandings (which for me can only come through experience) lay way behind. Findhorn seems to be a more viable alternative for me educatively, as it can better develop the whole person physically, mentally, spiritually and emotionally. My days are divided between the "work program" (I run the offset printing machine) and "college classes" -- dance; T'ai Chi, an occult perspectives course, "Harmonious Development" -- Gurdjieff and Don Juan; "Journeys to the Self" -- Transpersonal psychology, EST, gestalt, etc., to name a few. They're five week courses that meet three times per week for $1\frac{1}{2}$-2 hours (I also co-teach the dance class). The community atmosphere makes learning on all levels quick and thorough, because so much of it is experiential, and concentrated through relative isolation. The community is all ages. There are 175 people. I think most importantly in so far as Findhorn is "better than" my former college for me, there is spiritual growth and understanding underlying every experience here. I am learning to be "clear and centered," to be able to surrender personal will for divine, for the good of the whole. It's true, I'm not learning a lot about something or one thing, to prepare

me for a specialized career. I am learning to be a better person, a more balanced human being. Perhaps, someday I will want to know something about something, and then I will be able to justify narrowing my learning and awareness (hopefully). Then, I may return to an institution of "higher learning." However, I doubt it will ever be a place as academically pressured, by which I mean as intellectually oriented only, as my college tends to be.

The spirit of the Lord spoke to me in prophecy and to my own heart, that I should not return to school, and that God will direct my path. I intended to finish my college education after working for a year, but during that year I became a Christian and gave my life to the Lord Jesus Christ. He told me not to go back to school, so I am obeying him. To the best of my ability, I will go where and do what the Lord says.

Will not go back to any school till I'm sure of what I'd like to do in the future. Right now I'm a waitress -- have become interested in restaurant management and would like to open my own restaurant.

I am an actor. I will act. I am acting now at the National Theatre Institute. I know what I want and have to do. College is not the right stepping stone. I am never going back to this college. It is a soft extension of high school. How can students be students in a controlled environment? I do not like living in a womb. I resent petty college life existing on petty college principles and discouragement of any form of deviation. The effect is that the college environment propogates consistent mediocrity.

As it stands, I do not plan to return to college. Basically, I was tired of being a student. I am continuing and pursuing a business career in the travel industry. I am now, despite only $1\frac{1}{2}$ years of college, a highly paid executive in New York City. When asked the question why I left, I always answer, "Because I don't feel that a liberal arts education is worth the time or especially the money spent to get a piece of paper which is worth very little or nothing on the professional job market. It is simply not a wise investment. I had an excellent prep school background and did not feel that I was advancing intellectually or socially, in fact, I was bored ninety percent of the time."

As is evident in many of the statements that have been quoted, the decision to return to one's college after an extended leave, or to transfer to another institution, or to discontinue any major efforts toward earning an undergraduate degree, develops out of many considerations. Some of these reinforce one another, serving in their aggregate effect to enforce a decision that might not have been reached had any one of these considerations operated alone. Often the incentives to one solution are opposed and offset by other incentive conditions that urge a different resolution of the matter. Returning to further examination of the responses to Item C, <u>Reasons for extending leave</u>, we find that the differences between the three groups are less striking if they are compared according to the percentages of students who assign any of the codes; 1, <u>Compelling</u>; 2, <u>Important</u>; or 3, <u>Minor</u> to each of the categories of reasons for leave. However, interesting similarities and differences do persist. In table 24, the reasons are listed in order of magnitude of percentage of students who assign to each alternative a code of 1, 2 or 3.

TABLE 24 Item C

<u>Reasons for Extending Leave</u>
Percentage of Respondents Selecting Alternative
"Compelling," "Important" or "Minor"

	Total	Intend to Return	Transferred	No Degree
h. Have discovered alternatives to returning	84%	83%	84%	82%
b. Need more time	70%	80%	60%	82%
f. Does not meet educational needs	70%	54%	78%	72%
g. Dissatisfactions with college	53%	27%	64%	45%
a. Psychologically not ready	42%	57%	32%	45%
d. Financial considerations	42%	37%	44%	45%
c. Relationships with others	40%	40%	40%	36%
e. Health reasons	4%	4%	4%	0%

Earlier reports had indicated that commonly students had engaged in a number of different activities during their leaves, sometimes simultaneously, more often in succession. It seemed probable that persons who had been away from their colleges for a period of twelve to thirty months might have engaged in several patterns of activity in that time. Accordingly Item D which inquires about how time had been spent during the leave, made provision for the respondent to identify different patterns of activity at different times during the leave.

D. How have you spent your time since beginning your leave?
For EACH activity listed below, record the code number of the statement that indicates most accurately the amount of time that you have devoted to it. If your activities have been very different at different time periods, indicate this by recording activity codes for each time period that you list. If essentially the same throughout your leave, use first column only.

Code for Amount of Time:
1. Major amount of time; principal activity
2. Substantial amount of time
3. Moderate amount of time
4. Limited amount of time
5. Little or no time devoted to this activity

TABLE 25

Number of Periods of Distinctive Leave-time Activities

Time Periods	Brown N	Hampshire N	Trinity N	Wesleyan N	Total N	Total %
1	8	7	4	10	29	32
2	5	5	0	4	14	15
3	1	11	3	1	16	17
4	7	16	4	5	32	35
5		1			1	1
Total	21	40	11	20	92	

About one-third of the persons who have not returned "on time" had been involved in a single pattern of activities during their leave. Thirty-five percent reported that during their leave, the pattern of activities in which they were engaged had changed in some significant respect a total of four times. The amount of time that was devoted to the various types of activities at any time during the leave is presented in table 26.

TABLE 26

Classified According to Amount of Time Devoted to Activity

	Major	Substantial	Moderate
Formal Academic Work	42.4%	17.4%	2.8%
Employment	26.1%	17.4%	15.2%
Independent Study	19.6%	23.9%	18.5%
Volunteer Activities	10.9%	4.3%	5.4%
Other	10.9%	4.3%	0.0%
Travel	8.7%	9.8%	14.1%
Personal, Family	5.4%	14.1%	13.0%
Medical Therapy, Convalescence	2.2%	3.3%	4.3%
Recreational, Social	1.1%	15.2%	30.4%

N = 92

The weight of evidence developed in this investigation indicates that persons who take a leave of absence from a liberal arts college, such as those represented in this study, are not "lost" to higher education. The great majority eventually return to their college to receive its degree. Most of those who do not, receive a baccalaureate degree from another college or university. The relative few who choose not to complete the requirements of a degree are engaged in activities that are meaningful and important to themselves and in some cases are involved in work that represents a significant creative achievement.

While it is reasonable and appropriate for each college and university to be concerned with its attrition rate, it is self-defeating to express this concern in the form of sweeping administrative constraints or through various more subtle pressures designed to enforce continuous registration. For some students, taking a leave or transferring to another institution is a courageous and constructive act.

No institution has the resources to be all things to all the people who wish to attend college. Commitment to one education mission may limit or exclude effective participation in the pursuit of other worthy educational goals. It is incumbent upon all colleges and universities to be as forthright and accurate as they can be in representing their educational philosophy and curricular offerings, in describing resources that are actually available to and used by students, in portraying student life as it is experienced by contemporary students, and in identifying educational, extra-curricular and social interests that they may not be equipped to serve well.

With all the help that can be given to them, some applicants will choose to attend institutions that are not appropriate to their personal circumstances, education preparation, and social maturation. When the college's recruiting efforts deceive or misinform or simply by their silences fail to sensitize candidates for admission to characteristics of the institution that are germane to their choice of college, an admittedly difficult problem of choice is compounded. One fundamental step toward reducing attrition at a particular institution can be more effective admissions counseling, from the gloss on the recruiting literature and the "pitch" of the campus tour to the letter of invitation to join the entering class.

However, the most consciencious efforts on the part of colleges to define their "mission" and to help applicants make informed and wise decisions will not result in the elimination of mismatches between persons and institutions. Both the institution and the person are too complex for anyone to anticipate, with certainty, the character of their interaction. What is tolerable incompatability varies considerably from individual to individual, as do capacities for accommodation and for growth. This we do know: that in the hundreds of decisions that finally produce an entering college class, there will be some that prove to be unfortunate.

Beyond admissions mistakes, on the part of institutions and of applicants, there also are those whose development in college brings them to a stage that recommends a temporary absence from college. The very effectiveness of their college program stimulates lines of development in some students that the college is unable to sustain. Their continued growth may require them to pursue their educations in other settings, either temporarily or without expectation of return. These considerations point to the folly of an <u>ipso facto</u> assumption that not to graduate from the admitting college represents personal inadequacy or institutional failure. They also argue for a more active and constructive participation on the part of colleges in facilitating the transitions of their students from their campus to another and from the college into the community.

The institution that serves its students best is not the one that succeeds in binding its students to it for a prescribed period of time. It is the one that has the vision and flexibility and organization to assist its students in taking full advantage of the resources for the kinds of learning that are appropriate for their needs, whether the focus of that learning is centered in the college or in other agencies of the community. In the case of students who find it necessary to leave college for reasons that are unremediable within the context of the college, the institution may participate in the student's leave-taking in ways that can be beneficial to the student and ultimately to the institution as well. Sometimes that contribution may be no more than helping the student to leave with the assurance of the college's continuing interest and its readiness to welcome the student back. Other students might be helped to locate situations away from the college that conform to their requirements and which they will pursue quite independently of the college. In still other situations, the college may take an active role in identifying and/or organizing opportunities for off-campus learning. Agencies of the college may work with students to prepare them for their off-campus experience, to supervise or advise them while engaged in the field situation and to assist them as they relate their experiences in the field to bodies of knowledge and to modes of inquiry that are represented in the various academic disciplines.

A danger of viewing "leaving" as an undesirable situation to be mitigated by various regulatory stratagems, is that it may divert attention from the positive contributions that a leave can make. Numerous students among the respondents commented that if they had not taken a leave, they would have dropped out of college altogether. Taking time to regain perspective, to recover lost enthusiasms and motivation, to cultivate new interests and develop new skills, has proven, in the lives of many of the students who participated in this study, to be an effective counter to discouragement and boredom and directionlessness. For some students, taking a leave may be the "treatment of choice" for the malady of depressed and ineffective participation in the richness of college life. For others it may be the preventive medicine that enlarges self-confidence, sustains intellectual growth and stimulates the development of new interests

"I believe that we give too much time at the wrong times in people's lives to meeting their educational needs. . . . Some international comparisons might lend support to the idea of shorter and more effective exposure to educational institutions." This opinion presented by Harold Howe II in an article titled, The Value of College as Seen by a Non-Economist,[25] is consistent with a viewpoint that emerges from the present research. Anxieties concerning the interruption of college attendance should not divert attention from the more critical issues of the appropriateness and the quality of the college experience. Of greater moment is the contribution that college attendance makes to personal growth and intellectual enrichment of its students. Our concern need not be, "Do they come back?" They do. The more urgent question is, "What happens then?"

TABLE 27 Item C   Reasons for Extending Leave

Percentage of Respondents that Rate Each Alternative

1. "One of the most important or compelling reasons for extending my leave."

Reason	Intend to Return	Transferred	No Degree
a. Psychologically not ready to resume studies	24%	13%	9%
b. Need more time for current interests and activities	38	13	55
c. Obligations to and/or relationships with others (e.g., parents, husband, wife, employer, friend, etc.)	10	12	9
d. Financial considerations	10	10	9
e. Medical, health reasons	3	6	–
f. College from which I took leave does not meet my educational-academic needs	14	62	55
g. Dissatisfactions with the college from which I took leave have not been resolved or remedied	7	37	9
h. Have discovered alternatives to returning that are more attractive or better suited to my requirements	52	67	73
i. Other: Please describe	24	6	27
N	29	52	11

TABLE 28

Colleges and Universities to Which Respondents to Survey 5 Transferred
(or at Which They Were Enrolled at Time of Response)

Private Colleges and Universities (23)	Public Universities (26)	Schools of Fine Art Applied Art (8)
American U.	Framingham State College	Berklee School of Music
Catholic U. of America	Michigan State U.	Boston U., School of Fine Art
Colorado College	San Francisco State U.	Cooper Union (2)
Cornell U. (3)	Southeastern Massachusetts U.	London College of Furniture
Duke U.	SUNY College at Old Westbury	New York U., Dramatic Arts
Manchester College	Texas A. & M. U.	Parson School of Design (2)
Maharischa Internat. U.	U. of Arizona	
Marquette U., Dentistry	U. of California, Berkeley	
Oberlin College	U. of California, Los Angeles	Foreign Universities (3)
Pitzer College	U. of Colorado (2)	
Pomona College	U. of Connecticut	McGill U.
Princeton U. (2)	U. of Kansas	U. de Dakar, Senegal
St. Bonaventure U.	U. of Maryland	U. of Toronto
Stanford U. (2)	U. of Massachusetts (3)	
Springfield College	U. of New Hampshire	
U. of Hartford	U. of Michigan	
U. of Rochester	U. of Oklahoma	
Wheelock College	U. of Pennsylvania	
Yale U.	U. of Virginia	
	U. of Washington (2)	
	U. of Wisconsin	
	Youngstown State U.	

CHAPTER 8

Can Colleges Help Persons Who Leave?

Survey 1 included the question, "Might there have been ways in which the college could have been more helpful to you in thinking about or arranging this leave?" In Survey 2, returnees were asked, "Are there things that you or the college might have done that would have made your leave a more productive experience?" Respondents to Survey 3 were invited to "Suggest ways in which the college might have helped to make your 'leave' more valuable educationally or might have facilitated your return to campus and to formal studies?"

Responses to these questions range from expressions of satisfaction and appreciation for help received, through a variety of complaints, to specific suggestions and recommendations. The great diversity of reactions and opinions reflects the fact that students take leaves for very different reasons. They engage in a great variety of leave-time activities, ranging from formal academic study at another university to full-time employment, or self-directed projects. The judgments that they express reflect their personal experiences and circumstances. Their recommendations often are contradictory and the reader may be tempted to wonder how persons attending the same institution could have such disparate experiences and reactions. The implications of this diversity should be clear, however. Individual students have very different needs related to their own distinctive personal history, developmental status, relationship with their college and the nature of their leave activity and experiences. An institutional policy that assumes that leaves are taken by members of the junior class will assure that many students are poorly served. Excellent facilities for advising students concerning study abroad do little for the student seeking an internship or full-time employment. Some students have influential, knowledgeable family and/or friends who support and facilitate their efforts to arrange a meaningful leave-time experience and need little from their college. Others are totally dependent on their own resources. Some encounter active opposition to their plans.

At every stage of the process of leaving and returning, from the first tentative formulation of plans to re-entry into the life of the school as a returning student, the needs and circumstances of individuals require that institutional policies in regard to leave-taking be both comprehensive and well-differentiated. In consideration of the large number of students who take a leave at some time during their undergraduate career, it is important that the resources for advising and assisting be well-publicized and freely available, that the procedures and conditions for authorizing a leave be clearly stated and efficiently administered, and that the returning student be treated equitably in respect to such matters as sign-up for courses, housing, and financial assistance.

On most campuses it is no longer reasonable to treat leave-taking as an aberration to be ignored or an inconvenience to be tolerated and controlled. Many contemporary students cannot or will not remain in continuous enrollment from the time of their matriculation until their graduation. It is in the best interests of the college and its educational mission to develop more effective ways for integrating campus-based studies and off-campus experiences and for encouraging returning students to retain and share the insights and the enthusiasms that they developed in activities carried out in other places.

It would be presumptuous and grossly inaccurate to suggest that the findings of this study provide a blueprint for improved policies and procedures in respect to leave-taking. The study does identify areas in which some students have been poorly served even though the colleges they attend acknowledge to some degree the personal and educational value of off-campus experiences. The statements of students are here quoted at length to illustrate the diversity of their needs and concerns. They are listed by themes or topics. In some cases, the student's response addresses a single issue. In others, a number of ideas are presented. Although listed under a particular "theme," the entire response to the question concerning the college's contribution is quoted to avoid fragmentation or misrepresentation of the student's thoughts and feelings. Appendix II furnishes further examples of students' comments on their college's contribution or lack of contribution to their leave. In these cases their recommendations appear in the context of their total essay. The statements that make up the greater part of this chapter were made in response to the questions that appear on page 129 in the first paragraph of the chapter.

Theme: Stay out of my life

Some students feel that going to school has dominated their lives. The security and familiarity of college has encouraged them to be passive and dependent. Some feel that the student role has defined them so completely and for so long that they are unsure of any other identity. Some have been so consumed by the demands of their courses, their extra-curricular involvements and the social pressures of peers that they feel out of touch with their own interests and concerns. They feel that they do not have time to pursue or discover what is important to them. Some students are angry that college has not lived up to their expectations or because it has been unresponsive to some important need. For many reasons, there are students who feel the need to put distance, for a time, between themselves and the college. The last thing that they want is for the college to dictate the terms of their leave or to intrude while it is in progress. They need to exercise initiative, to assume responsibility, to demonstrate independence. The institution responds best to these persons when it simply allows them their freedom.

> Fortunately for me, the college had no say in my leave and all I did in the year was self-initiated which obviously has given me a complete feeling of fulfillment in my leave.

> I needed a break from school -- its academic and isolated environment. The college left me alone and I left it alone and that is what we both wanted. I really needed to fend for myself, show myself that I could accomplish what I set out to do and to be totally separated from the college. The experience was one of the best of my life.

> They ignored me and that was fine with me.

> I wanted to get away from college enough that I was perfectly happy with the college's non-participation in my leave.

> They didn't really do anything except send me drivel through the postal system and that was fine with me. I didn't expect or need more.

> No, there are no things that the college or I might have done to make my leave a more productive experience. I know that one of the main reasons that my leave did so much for

me is because I <u>didn't</u> have it planned out in advance, and I <u>didn't</u> have the guidance of people at the college.

I haven't talked to anybody at this school concerning the leave. I consider it to be all my own decision that shouldn't be influenced by anybody.

It would be hard for the college to do anything to make a leave more of a productive experience. Taking a leave is a personal problem and for the college to help counsel people would be difficult.

My college did little for me, which was good; it shifted the burden of responsibility onto my shoulders, where in the end it would do more good.

The most important benefit I have derived from my leave is over-coming a feeling of impotence. To institutionalize leave-taking for everyone might be advantageous, but remember that the real feeling of satisfaction I got is knowing that I left with no guarantees, traveled with no predetermined destinations or accommodations, returned to my studies by choice, and I did it on my own.

The college had nothing to do with what I did except to be cooperative in letting me leave and return on short notice. An involvement on the college's part would have changed the nature of my experience. I suspect it would have been more of a program than an adventure.

Basically, I found my leave to be a personal experience, in which the university could not be of any importance, let alone be involved in what I did. I did it to GET OUT of classrooms, in which I have spent fourteen consecutive years of my life.

Theme: Reduce the "red-tape" associated with taking a leave

Student reports are extremely mixed in regard to the ease or difficulty of taking a leave. Some were able to arrange their leaves and to return without encountering significant problems. Many reported problems in arranging for their leave. There was an even greater variety of complaints associated with their return. Judging from the experiences of many of the students who participated in this study, it would seem highly desirable for colleges to review their policies and procedures in regard to leave-taking. Common complaints concerning the handling of administrative arrangements include: 1) procedures for applying for a leave and for returning are not well-publicized or clearly stated in a single, systematic, comprehensive announcement or publication, 2) the procedures involved in arranging for a leave and for returning appear to be unnecessarily complicated and uncoordinated, 3) the time deadlines for applying for a leave and to a lesser degree for extending a leave are unnecessarily restrictive, 4) the effect of taking a leave upon the student's financial aid is not clearly delineated, 5) in the case of returning students, difficulties with communications concerning their re-enrollment and also with the actual process of registering, enrolling in courses and arranging for housing, and 6) the administration of policies concerning the award of credit for off-campus studies or experiences.

> Perhaps by publishing a brochure giving details on procedure for applying for leave, who to speak to, what forms to fill out, and also what must be done to return after the leave, who to notify, when, etc. Under the current process, the applicant must compile this information bit by bit.

> Only if they could cut out all the red tape concerning leave of absence forms, housing and re-enrollment.

> I remember feeling that trying to get out of the school was more difficult than getting in had been. Apparently there are offices or people that help people transfer, or get into graduate school, or find jobs, but I found everyone uninformed about programs at other schools and unable to give me much advice regarding how to find out where to go and what to do. In almost every aspect I found the college inadequately prepared to help me leave easily. The paper pushing system got unreasonably burdensome.

> People might have been available for signatures.

> I doubt it; only the hassles of application for leave and leave-extension seem undesirable, inefficient and unnecessary.

> All of my help came via my own channels -- the college did nothing but process the papers. The Dean's Office was helpful, but the leave-taking system seems as yet not to be standardized, thus causing some insecurity about procedures, returning, etc.

> Better coordination between the Dean's Office, the Financial Aid Office and the Registrar would help. I did so much running around trying to get things "finalized" for leaving that I was really exasperated.

> The Dean could have been more enthusiastic, helpful and clear about the whole process. He left a lot of red tape tangled and if I hadn't hassled around with a lot of his secretaries, etc., I don't think I would have gotten my leave.

> I had to go through a lot of red tape which is more of a hinderance than a help.

The forms are too involved and can be discouraging as are early deadlines for leave applications.

Not forcing students to decide two months before the semester is over whether to go on leave.

Yes! Financial Aid was an obstacle in my plans. As a needy recipient of the assistance, I was told "Forget about it." It was unfeasible and no attempt was made to suggest how it could be gotten. Only through my own searching was I able to uncover non-affiliated scholarship and loan assistance. I found that for a scholarship, an application had to be in a year and one half prior to the departure. It was too late to meet the deadlines and I settled for a loan.

A little more explicit information about financial arrangements for the leave. More organized in terms of having the forms ready. Have a meeting about leaves and resource ideas earlier in the semester.

I wish the college could have money set away for projects such as mine. I am trying to obtain a grant, which is hard to do.

Easing the cost of off-campus studies.

Yes, by having a more clear-cut policy, regarding the criterion by which one achieves financial independence, and the money available to financially independent students. The university appears to have adopted a policy which implies a lack of trust toward the student; as though the student were scheming to extort funds from the university. For the last six months our energies have been directed toward attempting to convince the university of our sincerity. This has inevitably led to very strong self-doubts (was it all worth it?). It's been so unnecessary.

The Financial Aid Office and the Treasurer's Office are causing me a great headache in getting the project together. The matter is still quite unsettled. The Dean's Office has been somewhat helpful, but at the same time quite unresponsive to my needs as an individual.

The only thing I can think of that you could do to help us is to stop raising the tuition every year so we don't feel economically compelled to rush back and get the whole thing over with.

Returning students get screwed every possible way -- re-enrollment, selection of courses, choice of housing, etc. It is also more difficult to meet people if you returning during the year. Students tend to concentrate on books instead of each other after the first couple of weeks.

Allowing absent students to participate in spring pre-registration.

The Registrar's Office makes the re-admit run around all over campus filling out forms on return. This could be taken care of through mail during the summer as it is with freshmen. The re-admit could better use this time getting reacquainted with the school. We had one meeting with a Dean upon return -- about four or five people at once for about five minutes. No private worries are going to come out in such a session.

My only advice as to how the university could have facilitated my return would be: don't hassle returning students, they've enough new stimuli to handle as it is. Don't treat them as if taking a leave was treason to the institution.

The college is very unclear and not a little hostile to students who desire to spend a year abroad at another academic institution. There is no real system for preparing and advising students for what they will confront during their year and little help is given in coming back. There is an inherent suspicion of the quality of any educational program not conducted by this college.

NO - except to make easier procedure for arranging for credit.

It seemed (despite their alleged liberalness) they did not like the idea of my taking courses from non-Ivy-type professors. They could have been more receptive/liberal about courses taken away from the "home" campus.

Yes -- more specificity about credit.

I would have liked to receive some sort of credit for my work. I believe that I am "learning" more than I could possibly learn on campus about political science, consumerism, legislation, not to mention people, current events. It's too bad that credit equals money -- and that my leave of absence cannot be considered academic with the amount of time and work I am putting into it.

Yes by not having so much red tape involved in obtaining credits for outside work. The possibilities here are liberal but the red tape is a conservative check.

Leave-taking here, especially if the student is planning to study at another university, involves much red-tape, largely because the university is suspicious of the educational quality of any other non-Ivy League situation. The university also makes it extremely difficult for students on financial aid to study elsewhere. In my experience, professors have been uncooperative particularly those who insist upon receiving regular "progress reports" and never acknowledge receipt of the student's reports, much less respond with comments, advice, etc. of their own. A student must arrange, before leaving, to have a faculty member "sponsor" each course credit she/he intends to get from another school. Returning to school generates an equal amount of red tape, wastes a lot of time running from office to office, and also causes much frustration -- an endless series of long, long lines.

Leaves should be encouraged and therefore easy to obtain. Reduce the red-tape involved in getting permission to leave and to return.

Theme: Desire for a more personalized interest and assistance

Many students reported a desire to discuss their plans for a leave of absence with a member of the faculty, their advisor, or some other representative of the college. It was not uncommon for them to find members of the faculty uninterested, uninformed or unavailable. Most schools have procedures for authorizing leaves that require a conference with an advisor or a dean. Often housekeeping matters dominate the session and little attention is given to the student's feelings, his hopes and misgivings about the proposed leave, the circumstances that motivated it and its relationship to his continuing education. To some, this was no problem. One student wrote: "They gave me permission for leave without quarrel -- they didn't give any help but I didn't need any." Another commented: "For myself, the less the college did, the better. For some students it might be beneficial for the University to help with a pool of semi-structured arrangements for the initial period of the leave." Another observed: "This college uses 'intellectual freedom' and 'non-bureaucratic' as excuses for not supplying any direction or assistance. However, this is better than schools that control or inhibit student initiative." More frequently expressed was a desire for personal relationship and for interested adult counsel, illustrated in the following representative quotations:

Yes -- showing more interest -- making it a little easier.

The university personnel were unwilling to step outside their assumed status quo roles in academia and help me think and work out a beneficial schedule for my leave.

It would have been nice if the Dean stayed awake while I informed him of my plans.

The person-to-person contact with the administration, while arranging the leave and during it, is essential. (In my case, it was with the Dean of my class -- at a larger school maybe some counselor could do it.)

Communication with other offices in the administration (Financial Aid, Housing, etc.) could have been better.

The only way the college "helped" me at all was the required ten minute appointment with one of the Deans before a student is allowed to take a leave of absence. I think there should be an office where students who have already decided to take a leave of absence can go and instead of discussing the why's or why not's of dropping out they would pose the question, "Is there anything I can do for you before you leave?" Also there is not a very acceptable way to come back to school. I have had to decide in March whether or not I was going to return in September. People might change their minds in the seven month interim.

No office or organization and only a few friends helped me to make the decision to withdraw. I realized that the decision to leave had to be made on my own, but I would have liked to talk it over with a few professors or a Dean. I did speak with two Deans but both times I felt as if I was one of many students who had rushed in and out of their offices. It would just have been nice if they had the time to consider me as an individual.

Yes -- they just gave me the papers to sign and that was it. I like personal interest but I don't expect it, so I was not disappointed. It merely reinforced my previous beliefs. Perhaps someday. . . .

Advising could have been more conscientious.

My advisor was very cold and abrupt. He could have spent more time discussing alternatives.

Friends who had previously taken leaves encouraged me the most. They had had rewarding experiences. The school encouraged me "zero." My advisors were disinterested in me as a person and a student. They didn't talk to me on an informal basis. They answered quickly and unenthusiastically to any and all questions on academic issues. The placement also is as good as non-existent. Never have they cared what happened to me in the past or will happen to me after I graduate . . . jobless and confused.

The only comment that I can make is that I don't think my academic advisor has been very useful either in my school career, or in relation to my larger plans.

Yes, I might have had a good advisor who is interested in my comings and goings. However that is, I suppose, my own doing. I could have switched advisors but I've never found anyone appropriate. So I've kept this advisor because she is in my field of study.

My advisor was not interested in the least. This bothered me a lot.

No one at this time helped me, which I think is really needed. If there had been more care and personal attention I might not have considered such a drastic change. I felt alienated from the college. My freshmen advisor was not helpful at all.

I would have liked to be given more counseling or concrete help in choosing the kind of volunteer work I will do, or even just more personal consideration and advice or support on what I was going to do.

I only wish the dance teacher here had more specific suggestions for where to study in New York.

I wasn't able to get reading suggestions from my professors before I left. As a result, some of the reading that I did during my leave proved not to be very useful.

I did not find the two faculty members I talked with very articulate about their feelings and ideas on leave-taking.

Strong ties with professors are essential to prevent students from losing their sense of proportion and learning only how to do their jobs and not what their job means.

I have always appreciated the interest my professors have taken in me. Any student needs an older, more experienced and interested advisor/friend. Parents are rarely adequate -- but this is no one's fault. Generally speaking, colleges have too many highly qualified but whimpish, inexperienced or self-centered professors. Some form of liaison between interested faculty and students is a necessity. I believe in this need for "having someone to talk to." But I'm not a loner either. I have good friends my age, but a student-to-student relationship cannot cover all needs -- if I am cynical about any aspect of college, that aspect is the abundance of professors who are career-oriented. They watch themselves instead of becoming involved with students.

That these reactions are not unique to these selected students is evident in the responses of all respondents to related items of the questionnaire. Thirty-three percent of all leave-takers rated themselves as being "dissatisfied" or "highly dissatisfied" with the adequacy of academic advising at their school. One third of the students who did not take leaves also rated themselves as dissatisfied or highly dissatisfied. On all other items related to faculty performance no more than fifteen percent of the students, leave-takers and those not taking a leave, rated themselves as dissatisfied. To the question: <u>Beyond your role as student, how many faculty members of this college respond to you as a person and show a personal interest in you?</u>, sixteen percent of both leave-takers and those who do not take a leave reported <u>none</u> or <u>can't say</u>. Twelve percent thought the number to be one. Sixteen percent of the leave-takers did not discuss the plans for their leave with any member of the faculty. Significantly, twenty-two percent of those taking non-academic leaves did not consult a member of the faculty while only seven percent of those taking academic leaves did not. Seventy percent of the students whose leave activity was a program sponsored by the college reported that the faculty that they consulted concerning their leave were either <u>supportive</u> or <u>helpful</u>. For those involved in academic programs independent of their own college, the comparable percentage was fifty-four. Forty-two percent of those who planned to work or be engaged in some type of volunteer service found the faculty to be supportive or helpful. These results are very understandable, but they also do call attention to the fact that members of the faculty often do not have the time, the interest and/or the expertise to be helpful to students whose needs direct them to off-campus opportunities.

Theme: Don't forget to write

Another expression of the desire for more personalized interest and assistance can be found in statements that students make about communications with their college during their leave. In contrast to those who have a need to separate themselves totally from their college, there are others who wish to retain lines of communication with their school. For some, this need be nothing more than the assurance of receiving official notices that are critical to planning and executing their return to the campus. Others have a particular need to retain their identity with the college during their absence and seek tangible assurances that someone at the college retains a continuing interest in them. Without seeking to assign blame, it is clear that there were many problems with addresses of students on leave and with the handling of their mail. Some student's attempts to communicate with offices or with individuals elicited no response. In consideration of the large numbers of students who are absent from the campus in any given academic term, it has become increasingly important for both students and their colleges to observe procedures that will facilitate communications. To avoid unnecessary misunderstanding both parties should be clear as to the requirements and expectations of the other.

> Do not sever ties with those "birds" who do fly from the nest for a period of time. Keep lines of communication open, to see that all is going well and that the college's help is not needed.

> My close friends kept me in touch with what was going on at the college. The college might have sent me something to acknowledge that I was gone and to show that they had an interest in my coming back.

> Inability to communicate with my advisor led to some very serious misunderstandings. Upon my return, I was virtually forced to take a double load of courses in preparation for a large comprehensive examination which I had not anticipated. This in turn prevented me from pursuing the subjects I really wanted to.

> I felt forgotten while I was gone -- I never heard from the college about senior year activity deadlines -- senior pictures, Psi Chi membership, etc. They didn't mind my leaving and barely acknowledged my return.

> My so-called academic counselor for my independent study received the letter I sent him regarding my activities and pursuit of study along with my request for further suggestions from him. He never bothered to respond.

> Something MUST be done to improve the college's communication with "leave of absence" students. No one bothered to find out if I was returning and as of November of my return (two months after I had registered) my major department had no idea I had returned. Not to mention that the college neglected me in terms of pre-registration, campus housing, etc.

> My college couldn't have done anything to make my leave more productive, but it could definitely have been more helpful in terms of encouragement. I had to do a lot of unnecessary running around to get permission to go, heard next to nothing during the year, which led me to wonder whether they even remembered that I existed and then did a lot more running around upon my return, convincing them of the value of last year.

> I found it difficult to communicate with my supervisor at the college and found she wasn't terribly interested in what I was doing anyway. The school was negligent in sending me relevant materials, such as changes in school policies, timetables and deadlines regarding next semester, course catalogs, etc. Unfortunately the college tends to ignore students that are on leave and makes it that much more difficult to return to the world of full-time students after a leave. I consider myself rather aggressive, determined and confident of what I want educationally. If

I were not, this institutional indifference might have been devastating.

While away my academic advisor did not contact me once although I wrote her four times.

The college could have been more supportive by simply keeping me better informed of administrative and other happenings on campus. Students on leave are more or less forgotten about -- second-class citizens -- although they make up a substantial proportion of the Junior Class population, they are over-looked in all decision making processes.

I lost my sense of belonging to this college when I left. I felt totally divorced from it because no one answered my letters and the college didn't even send me the information and forms that are needed to reregister. Now that I've returned, I feel almost like a stranger in my major department.

The university can tend to be very impersonal. One example: I wrote two letters and waited almost two months for an answer from my "advisor." It turned out that students with whom I corresponded were of more assistance. I don't want to harp on this, but it does seem to me important that the university make a slightly greater effort to keep in touch with its students on leave.

The college might have helped by corresponding more. I would have been interested to know what was going on here. Lack of correspondence made it particularly hard to come back. I didn't realize what was expected of me in terms of bureaucratic business -- necessary forms, etc. The initial period of my return was unnecessarily difficult as a result.

The college didn't seem to give a damn. I was not sent a course catalog, I was not allowed to pre-register. I have been confronted with an amazing administrative hassle over receiving transfer of credit. If only they had sent me an Alumni Monthly occasionally, a housing notification, a college newspaper, a course book -- anything! They seemed to want to resent me for going away.

Theme: Provide more complete, more accessible, better publicized informational resources

Information on programs abroad were not complete at college, nor did they attempt to put me in touch with those who could be of some help.

Yes, notably with respect to the availability of information about organized foreign study programs. My first choice location was Aix-en-Provence, about which no one could speak knowledgeably. Accordingly, I believe that some sort of comprehensive foreign study information library is not only desirable but a virtual necessity in an institution which has no organized study-abroad programs of its own.

Perhaps a more comprehensive "library" in some central location.

I was looking for information on communes, but this was absolutely unavailable.

Provide more information although that could defeat my intention of self-structuring an entire year so that college is not so awesome or merely an extension of high school.

Set up a resource centre which provides information on study, work opportunities outside New England, the country and generally away from the school. As I was thinking about my leave I felt I had to pretty much do everything on my own.

Most of the resources in our Field Study Office relate to political science and social science. I think the office should develop information for students of all disciplines who are thinking of leaves.

Yes - yes - yes - There is a need for much more support and specific advice at it. With regards to leaves -- I probably wouldn't have chosen to participate in a program at this time -- yet I would have appreciated knowing my options -- also information on organizations and collectives of people doing anything and everything is severely lacking. There should be information on nation-wide contacts plus more opportunity to work out independent project ideas in conjunction with time off.

Might have at least some printed matter on college's insights on leaves. Dean's Office was highly inaccessible, providing little guidance on even the red tape and mechanics of taking off.

A good idea would be to publish a pamphlet on students taking leaves; telling what they have done, how they felt about it, giving ideas to students who want to take leaves, yet are afraid to because of lack of definite ideas.

I was pleased with the ease and cooperation with which the college let me leave. Perhaps a pamphlet or booklet which contains various "case histories" or quotes from answers to this questionnaire would be helpful.

Yeah. When you join a college they give you orientation. How about un-orientation. Interviews or get written reports from people who have already taken leaves. Advise, ideas . . . all based on experience. When and if I return I volunteer to give anyone who wants to leave, face-to-face advice. This questionnaire is a start, albeit in a typical print-on-paper approach.

Jesus Christ, Yes! Make leave information more widespread and provide information about people on leave. Have a list of things people have done on leave -- where a person could go to get involved in a particular interest -- perhaps keeping records on these things and making its availability known.

Yes, by having one easily accessible file of programs, activities and addresses of organizations that students could look at when considering what they could do during their leave.

The increasing interest in and popularity of leaves-of-absence from college has stimulated the production of a number of useful guides, directories, manuals and texts. Some of the more recently published volumes are listed in the bibliography. Stopping Out: A Guide to Leaving College and Getting Back In by Judi R. Kesselman[26] provides a more extensive catalog of the relevant literature. For a limited investment, any college can equip an "alternative education library" with basic informational resources.

Student requests for improved counseling and placement services present a more difficult problem. As is evident from the variety of circumstances that motivate leave-taking and from the extensive inventory of situations in which some student wishes to be engaged, no single college could possibly develop and maintain the field resources that would be required to respond adequately to student interest and need. Some colleges already have made considerable progress in developing cooperative arrangements for facilitating a period of study on another campus in the United States or abroad. The Twelve College Exchange is an example of such a consortium. There are many college-sponsored study abroad programs that are recognized and used by students other than those of the sponsoring institution (see U.S. College Sponsored Programs Abroad).[27] The College Venture Program[28] is a counseling and placement service to colleges and to their students who seek opportunities for employment or volunteer service in positions that offer experience relevant to their academic interests and/or career goals. Colleges need to discover how to make better and fuller use of the services of organizations that already exist. They also should identify areas in which their own campus-based services and those of the cooperative arrangements in which they participate do not presently serve well the needs of an identifiable group of students.

The results of this study suggest that students of the fine arts constitute such a group. Some persons who have outstanding talent in one of the arts and who have aspirations for pursuing a career in this field choose for any of a number of reasons to attend a liberal arts college. For them, it is a common experience that, as their program of studies advances, the available faculty are unable to give them the instruction, the stimulation and the guidance that their developing careers require. Few of their peers share their commitment to the arts and the prevailing standards of performance are well below the professional standards to which they aspire. Often the college campus isolates them from the centers of active performance and their broader program of studies makes intensive application to their art difficult or impossible. They need to work in an environment that provides them with a more severe testing of their talents and commitment. Such students commonly report that the agencies of their colleges have been unhelpful, and in some cases antagonistic to their efforts to spend a semester or a year away from the campus in the development of their art.

Clearly, a strong case can be made for the value of the liberal arts in the education of an artist. It is equally clear that some students who wish this broader education would be better served if their college program encouraged a more comprehensive integration of liberal studies and the arts and also facilitated an easier movement between the liberal arts campus and centers of artistic activity and production. In the experience of some of the respondents, their more intensive involvements with their art during their leave helped them to lay to rest an unrealistic career aspiration. They returned to resume their studies with a clearer understanding of themselves and what they wished to accomplish. Some discovered ways in which their liberal studies had the potential to enrich their artistry and returned with new enthusiasm and with a clearer sense of purpose for their remaining academic work. Still others decided that strategies other than continuing their college studies were preferable in advancing their artistic development. It would serve the interests of both students and institutions to develop broader, more accessible bases of cooperation between colleges of the liberal arts and of the fine arts, as well as with field situations in which students could be involved in the active performance of their art or craft.

In an era of tight budgets and limited resources for underwriting new programs or upgrading existing ones, cooperative arrangements appear to offer the best hope for responding to students' needs for off-campus study and employment. However, membership in consortia and participation in programs of college-community cooperation is not enough. To be effectively used by students, such programs must be publicized. Members of the faculty and of the student services staff must be sufficiently aware of these programs to refer interested students to them. Beyond serving as referral agents and informational resources, ideally they also will provide guidance and counseling when appropriate. However, members of the faculty and administrative staff cannot be expected to fulfill this function unless they are supported by ample informational resources that effectively organize and summarize the broad range of options that are available to students today. They are not likely to assign a very high priority to these duties unless the leaders of the University recognize their counseling function as an important contribution to the educational enterprise.

Theme: Provide better counseling, advising, placement assistance

> The whole advising system here needs work, better counseling, more personal interest from faculty, more extensive and better publicized resources and references.
>
> . . . feel that the college needs more counselors and a more active and available counseling service.
>
> Yes. To provide adequate leave counseling. Yes, in giving me some guidance as to who to talk to and what type of things perhaps I should try to pursue.
>
> A definite YES to this question. This leave, I have confidence, will definitely be worth the time involved. However, with the guidance of an organization more experienced with, and knowledgeable of, the opportunities available to me (I'm only sixteen now) I could probably have gained more from this experience.
>
> I was essentially told to go out and do whatever I wanted, it couldn't hurt. Some people might like or need more definite suggestions or specific goals laid out for them.
>
> Providing more job opportunities and placements.

Yes -- job placement, files of good contacts in opportunities (volunteer, if not pay) according to interests. I wish the college could have given some assistance in finding a job.

Yes -- they could have been more helpful in helping me find field work. There should be an office specifically to fulfill this function: A JOB and field work office for regular students, students about to go on leave, and students about to graduate.

A job placement service on campus would have been extremely helpful to me in trying to locate a job -- at least a list of work opportunities which a student could then investigate independently if he/she wished.

Yes -- by having a more extensive, developed placement system that actively informs students of various opportunities available and how to best investigate them.

From the above you will realize that an organization or office which could have given me assistance in job hunting would have been great. It would have saved me countless hours of letterwriting, pacing the sidewalks, and worrying.

Maybe by having a broader field study program which could have many areas of activity and employment in which a student could be placed if that student so chose.

Yes. They could have told me about the arrangement with the Venture Program that helps students on leave find jobs.

Students report the need for counseling, advising, orientation, or some expressions of personal support and recognition at the time of their return to college. They need to be informed about changes in programs and procedures that have occurred during their absence. Some have decided to reorient their studies as a result of their leave experiences and must replan their academic programs. Many report a kind of culture shock in returning to the campus, whether their leave had been spent in study abroad or in the work-a-day world at home. Earlier associations may have been disrupted by their leave and on returning some students feel themselves to be a stranger in what had once been a familiar place. Some suggest that the college organize meetings for returning students or in other ways help them re-establish social relationships and become more quickly and more completely reintegrated into campus life.

At this college, if you're gone for a term, you might as well never have been here. This is hard for a person returning from leave. Discussion groups for people who have been on leave might be nice. Also a listing of leave experiences people have had and who to contact would make people who have been on leave feel useful, better integrated into the school community.

Some kind of arranged social get-together of returnees might have given me access to some people with whom I had something in common -- like when we were freshmen. I don't know anyone here anymore.

There might be some gathering organized for returning students (not necessarily all -- I'm thinking in terms of students who have been abroad) to help ease the transition. There is a culture shock period, a readjustment period when students who are having similar problems might be able to help one another.

One suggestion to the university would be to make more available ways of meeting other students who have also been away in order to facilitate our re-entry into university life. Being able to associate with people in similar circumstances sometimes helps to alleviate a difficult situation.

On returning, I felt a strong sense of disorientation. My first two weeks were lonely and depressing. I do feel that the administration might have shown a greater interest in me -- that I might, for example, have been given the opportunity for a regular consultation with a Dean. My only discussion with a Dean was concerned primarily with the bureaucratic details of my re-enrollment, with only perfunctory mention made of my emotional reactions to returning. The administration should realize that the vast majority of students, in my experience at least, take a leave for personal, not academic reasons.

Some kind of counseling might be helpful. A student could talk with a counselor over how he might get the most out of his leave. I feel it of utmost importance that the student do something constructive with his leave. When a student returns, he often feels out of place. Perhaps even a coffee hour or some kind of get-together could be held for students returning from leaves where they could share their varied experiences.

Before as well as after my leave I would have appreciated academic counseling. I realize that the decisions are my own to make, yet more information could be provided as a basis for these decisions. I know only one professor who even knows my name. My advisor most assuredly does not know my name. She is extremely busy and extremely adept at letting you know that. Since she is so adept, I hardly feel invited to discuss my diffuse interests in the hope of finding a direction to go in. I definitely feel

> that faculty advisors committed to student counseling are
> needed.

> It was difficult to readjust to school. I feel older and
> pressured to catch up. Yet the experiences I have gained
> during my leave are invaluable to my outlook and under-
> standing of life. I do not want to lose them in the busy-
> ness of college life. I feel the college should have some
> counseling services for readmitted students to help them
> sort out the wide variety of feelings they have.

Some respondents added to this theme the recommendation that the college take a more active or aggressive role in advising students, that the college should not merely permit leaves but should promote them.

> The college should take an active role in advocating
> leaves. It should have a special department set up for
> placing people in as many situations as possible.

> I think the academic advisors should advocate more
> strongly that people unsure about their future try to take
> time to work in their field of interest (outside of college
> to see what their job would really be like). They should
> also emphasize that it is easy to take a leave. Some
> students feel that it would be too much trouble, so they
> stay at school, simply because it is easier.

> Too much time before the leave was spent in miserable
> worrying because I didn't know what to do or how to do
> it. I needed someone to ask me, "Are you sure you
> aren't wasting your time here?" No one did which is
> why I indicated great dissatisfaction with advising here.

> A good question for advisors to ask, rather than "Why
> do you want to take a leave?", is to ask of all students,
> personally, every year, "Why do you want to stay in
> school?" I think persons with a positive answer do
> better in their studies by having their answer in mind.
> People without an answer would benefit from some time
> off to relax, clear their heads and think things over.

> I would recommend a leave to almost anyone. Eight
> semesters at one school is ridiculously limiting. The
> benefits of a leave far outweigh the costs, in my opin-
> ion. I believe that colleges should voice the benefits
> of taking a leave more than they do. It might make the
> "home" school more vibrant and exciting to have more
> active students doing new things. Students should be
> pushed to be more active and creative. Educate students
> about leave programs and do it early. Give them greater
> value and recognition and more faculty support.

> More active advocacy of leave-taking. My college offers
> no unasked for information or advice on leaves of absence
> or exchange programs or any of the innumerable possibilities

available. There should be encouragement and administrative acceptance of such activities.

In this chapter we have reviewed some of the most frequently stated suggestions concerning ways in which students felt that their colleges might have been more helpful to them in preparing for their leave of absence and in returning to the college. However, in concentrating attention on problems that students have experienced and on institutional deficiencies that ask for remedy, we must not ignore the fact that more than half of the respondents either did not offer suggestions as to how their college might have been more helpful to them, or they stated that they had no criticism of the performance of their college in regard to their leave. The reality at each of the participating colleges seemed to be that the needs of some students were met to their satisfaction while other students were less well served. Individual colleges and all of American higher education today face the challenge, not only of working more effectively with the larger numbers of students who take a leave of absence, but of discovering more effective ways to articulate and integrate the resources for learning that exist on the campus and in the larger community.

CHAPTER 9

Will Colleges Give Leadership and Direction?

The number of persons who take a leave from college has become sufficiently large that it is only prudent for colleges to re-examine and, where necessary, to revise their policies and procedures that relate to leave-taking. Some of the issues that deserve attention are regulations that define the timing and continuity of college attendance, the procedures for securing permission for a leave, and criteria for the award of academic credit for work that is done outside of the classroom. They include also the adequacy of academic advising, counseling and informational resources that are available to students and regulations governing registration, housing and financial aid. These topics are discussed in chapter 8.

Of greater concern is the number of students who are unable to find personal meaning and value in their academic work and for whom the college environment has become a sterile and inhibiting place. To a degree that is striking and deserving of critical attention, students use adjectives like "confining," "stale," "stifling," and "suffocating" in describing the atmosphere of their colleges. A Wesleyan student wrote:

> I dislike college and its limiting ways of experiencing life. Not only is one sealed off from many classes, ages and types of people, but the nature of the institution even seals those at the college off from one another. I felt suffocated and needed to breathe.

Another offered the opinion:

> It would be a good idea if more people took a year off. Staleness is a dominant factor around here. A little interruption in carefully planned lives helps reveal how transitory such plans are.

The following are the observations of two Brown students:

> The bureaucratic and preprofessional, achievement oriented atmosphere of Brown has succeeded in stifling much of my academic enthusiasm.

> The most important aspect of the leave was the fresh perspective on myself and of my capabilities offered by a "breather" from the organized and cushioned life on a college campus. During my leave I was inspired and excited by what I was doing.

In evaluating her year-long leave spent at University College, London, a Tufts student wrote:

> The profitability of the entire experience derived largely from the fact that I was able to completely free myself from American students, lifestyles, attitudes, biases. Separated from the worn out and stifling situation which seems to prevail in American universities, new ideas began happening, new energy, new frameworks, new analyses all sought to arise.

Another student expressed similar feelings in these words:

> I left sheltered, stifling Tufts and became exposed to a small part of the world. It got to the point at college where I would say: "I can't be depressed today for I must study for an exam." I now can look back and say, "If college does that, I don't want it." I enjoy being human again: loving, feeling, socializing, caring -- it's human. My leave of absence was the best move I ever made.

The following are quoted from statements of students from Hampshire and Wheaton Colleges:

> I had an incredibly happy and fulfilling year. I grew and realized many new things about myself and the people around me. This was not without its frustrations, but the rewards far outweighed them. I found thoughts and capabilities within me that I feel had been stifled at Wheaton.

> I thought it important that I not stagnate for four years in one environment. I worked with new groups of people, encountered different social expectations, and experienced a less isolated style of living. I enjoyed the change but will return to Hampshire to graduate.

A Trinity student expressed some of the same serious concerns in a delightfully humorous way:

> College can suffocate you. With glamorous gasses. But it is still suffocation. It is so enclosed. While there are provisions for expansion, there are few provisions for change of atmosphere or attitude. The heaviness of college air seems to stem from: a) the fact that there is too much work to even consider doing

anything else seriously, b) the Santa Claus fallacy, where students feel that everything they do now will affect their whole future -- so they grab and grab and act under this mistaken, unhappy notion and hence lose their sense of humor -- and a sense of humor is essential to good air, and c) over-analysis or the inability to call a dog a dog.

Clearly these perceptions of the impact of college cannot be attributed to the climate created by a particular faculty and administration, or to the unique conditions of a specific college campus. Expressed in many different ways, there exists a feeling, common to students at each of the colleges, that there is a substantial disharmony between the institutional press and the readiness of many students to meet the motivational and emotional demands of their present college environment. Contributing to this situation are the lack of clarity and agreement as to the appropriate purposes and goals of colleges and universities; a too constricted vision of the conditions under which learning takes place; and a failure to give adequate regard to the needs and circumstances of individuals involved in the learning process, teachers and students alike.

Some attribute this oppressive atmosphere to the heavy demands of their academic work. It is oppressive and anxiety-producing whether students actually fulfill their academic assignments or not. Others cite the competition between students for grades and for academic recognition which the academic pressures foster and the currently depressed job market intensifies. Still others cite the immaturity of peers and their myopic preoccupations with collegiate activities and values. Comments quoted in earlier chapters and statements appearing in the appendix are laced with one or more of these themes. A few additional illustrations are listed here for the reader's immediate consideration.

> I think everyone should get away from their home institution sometime. Anywhere, doing anything, as long as they avoid blase acceptance of their situation, apathy, ruts of indifference and boredom. It's unhealthy not to adventure, get out and make changes. I had to do it or I would have gone crazy.

> I suppose that my idea of college is too idealistic. I hoped that it would be a community of mature people engaged in a process of self-development through study and the cultivation of relationships with people who had an eager attitude toward life. Unfortunately, I found a fractured community of immature teenagers going to college for the purpose of getting good grades from an Ivy League college so that they could land a status-giving job with a high salary, meanwhile passing their time drinking beer and watching football games.

> I feel I have personally developed beyond the "college scene." I feel a lot more mature and tend to criticize (to myself mostly) many of my fellow students for lack of maturity and limited appreciation of that which is different from oneself. All the conformism I see around me has never bothered me more. Since my return I feel like an adult among children.

Many students emphasized their unreadiness for the college experience. For some this was an unreadiness to assume responsibility for the management of their time, the direction of their efforts and the consequences of their actions. Others discovered that their professors assumed an educational preparation that their earlier schooling had not furnished. There were still others who, although they had developed the needed study skills and the intellectual groundwork for the learning required in college, felt unprepared in terms of the experiential backgrounds that transform the abstractions of text and classroom into knowledge that is infused with meaning and vitality.

> My leave was one of the best things that ever happened to me. Through it, I took myself out of my perfectly regulated and controlled, practically homogeneous university environment. Stimulating as college can be at times, four straight years of academic abstractions can get to be stifling. Everything is out of context. We learn about "human beings" and "experiences," especially in literature classes. We learn the theories of Freud and Jung when we don't yet have the experience, or the maturity to know our own minds. How can I evaluate Freud or any other theory when I have seen so little of life, of people, of suffering? How can I judge people and society when I don't even know what it is like to support and be responsible for myself. In such a situation, prolonged intellectual study can become very baffling.

Many writers have addressed various facets of the issue of personality development in college.[29] It is beyond the scope of this report to discuss this topic in detail. However, the evidence of the study is consistent with much of what has been written in calling attention to ways in which colleges and universities do not address the critical needs of some of their students and do in fact offer an environment that is unsupportive of and even frustrating to these needs. It is by no means clear that the remedy is to be found in colleges assuming a more active role in serving these needs. It is possible that colleges might become less effective in their central educational mission were they to devote their limited resources to functions that other agencies of society are better equipped to perform. However, it is incumbent upon colleges to develop a greater sensitivity to the needs of their students, to remove from their organizational structure and operating procedures those elements that frustrate personal growth and inhibit full participation in the educational process. It also is their responsibility to seek out more effective ways to relate the learning that takes place on their own campus to the educational opportunities that exist in other academic communities and in the many agencies of the larger society.

The first Report of the Assembly on University Goals and Governance called for a comprehensive re-examination of policies and practices as they relate to the goals of higher education in contemporary society and in the decades ahead. Sections of the report that recommend more imaginative and creative uses of off-campus learning will be cited here in summarizing some of the major implications of the present study.

> Any arrangement that seems to enforce attendance, that causes some to believe that they are coerced into attending, violates the spirit that ought to prevail in these situations.[30] . . . For students from certain favored backgrounds, going to college from high school is automatic; many, though not all, proceed then to graduate or professional school. Some insist that their choice is not a free one; the employment (and social) situation compels them to be students from the time they are six until they are in their twenties. This "involuntary servitude" -- it is seen as such by some -- is wasteful and ought to be eliminated. It ought to be possible for more students to interrupt their studies, work for a time and return with this regarded as a natural educational sequence.[31]

Many students who participated in this study have experienced college as involuntary servitude.

> I think a leave is a good idea for anybody. When one attends school for 12 years, it is hard to know anything else, hard to look at college as anything else but the next step in a process that you had almost no choice in entering. This was my experience.
>
> Taking "leave" is taking temporary liberation from a routine plan which has been created for four of a student's years. I believe that the encouragement of such alternate programs would have the final effect of raising the educational-social level of the college campus by applying the pressure of a competitive alternative. A combination of college life and an alternative life could only widen the student's and professor's horizons.
>
> My parents zealously prepared me for kindergarten, which prepared me for elementary school. This prepared me for prep school, which prepared me for college, which is preparing me for grad school, to prepare for a career, so that

> I can prepare for retirement. I felt totally locked into
> this rigid pattern. Taking a semester off proves that
> it is possible to interrupt "the straight line." On the
> strength of this flexibility alone, it is one of the most
> valuable things I have ever done.

College is perceived by students as a societally enforced means to the ends that they wish to achieve. Many feel exploited by the educational system, for they consider the rapidly escalating costs to be excessive, particularly in consideration of the discouraging job prospects of college graduates. The academic program makes demands upon their time and psychological resources that they are unable or unwilling to fulfill, or that they can meet only at the sacrifice of other significant personal objectives and concerns. Many persons who eagerly sought admission to college discover that their motivations for college attendance were externally derived and that they lack the resources within themselves to define personally meaningful educational goals. Neither do they find that their college experience gives meaning and purpose to their academic program. Some who function effectively and happily for a period of time find that the pace, the pressure, and the very intensity and concentration of their college life eventually become enervating and destructive of motivation. They feel the need for change, for fresh perspectives, for a renewal that often cannot be generated without detachment and temporary withdrawal.

Professional scholars need a sabbatical to renew their enthusiasm for learning and to permit explorations that may add new dimensions or give new directions to their scholarship. They require time for sustained attention to a project that cannot be pursued productively in the fragments of time available in the normal schedule of the academic year. Students also develop needs that can be served best by taking the time to engage in activities that present new challenges, fresh initiatives in and responsibilities for their personal and intellectual development.

> The tradition that a bachelor's degree is awarded at the
> end of four years of formal study should be challenged.
> . . . The incentives to intersperse long work periods
> with periods of full-time or part-time study would be
> able to defer or interrupt college, graduate or professional school, precisely because there is no rhythm or
> pattern of intellectual curiosity or social maturity that
> is common to all. . . . Students ought to be permitted
> to intermingle study and work in ways that are now uncommon. This is not simply a plea for an extension of

> what now passes for cooperative work and study programs, where the student spends one or more terms away from a college campus. Rather, it is an assertion that significant employment opportunities for students may be provided in term-time if the university recognizes the value of such experience and is prepared to admit its educational importance. New counseling and instructional techniques will be needed for such educational combinations.[32] . . . New alternative paths to intellectual and professional development are in order. . . . In the last few years undergraduate requirements have been reduced, but few major curricular innovations have been instituted. Few alternatives for a liberal education have been conceptualized, let alone implemented. . . . Faculties ought to devise new options to achieve a liberal education; they need to infuse work and apprenticeship experiences with intellectual content.[33]

Even in colleges and universities that take pride in being innovative and progressive in their educational policies, such as those participating in this study, many students report that their institutions accept or accommodate grudgingly to students' desires-needs to work or study away from the campus for a period of time. Little is done to encourage students to explore the possibilities and the potential advantages of various off-campus activities and involvements. Informational resources are limited, counseling is inadequate or not available to them. Their reports on faculty reactions are mixed. Some students received help and encouragement from their faculty advisors; others encountered disinterested, uncooperative attitudes and some felt an open hostility. With the exception of their participation in the Venture Program, colleges are doing little in a systematic or programmatic way to assist students who wish to integrate off-campus activities with their campus-based studies. Only scattered interest has been shown in utilizing the experience of returning students in the educational programs of the colleges. Students see leave-taking regulations as parochial and serving institutional interests. They are not perceived as having been formulated out of a well-articulated educational philosophy.

> A variety of calendar reforms would give students opportunities to work off-campus in ways that are not now possible. The classroom need not be the only setting for teaching; residence halls, museums, hospitals, courthouses, factories, school houses and other public and private facilities offer appropriate sites for education. Where they can be useful, the college or university has an interest in gaining access to them.[34]

The present reality is an institutional commitment to calendars and schedules and an organization of the curriculum that offers administrative convenience and serves the interests of the faculty. It is not apparent that these arrangements have a logic that is based upon how people learn. They do constitute barriers to the participation in higher education to those persons who lack the leisure to conform to these structural requirements and present problems to students who wish to pursue their interests for a time through off-campus activities.

Students frequently reported that they encountered difficulties in coordinating the timing and scheduling of their leaves with the semester patterns of their colleges. They had problems in securing satisfactory field placements, in obtaining interested and competent field supervision, and in receiving recognition of the educational value of their leave-time experiences.

Piece-meal administrative responses to these problems fail to address the interests and needs of some students and totally miss the opportunities that might be developed to involve a more diverse group of people in the educational venture. These problems and opportunities will receive a satisfactory response only when they are approached in the context of a serious commitment to a student body that includes a broader age spectrum than the years of late adolescence and a conception of learning that is less centered in the classroom and defined in terms other than semester-hours of academic credit.

As the Newman Reports recognize and as is obvious in the comprehensive recommendations of the Assembly on University Goals and Governance, redirections of this magnitude cannot be accomplished by individual institutions acting alone, but will require the cooperation and support of large segments of society. Colleges and universities, foundations, accrediting agencies, scholarly and professional associations, business, industry, and government will have roles to play in implementing a conception of higher education that provides for greater flexibility in the processes of higher education and in developing a broader involvement of the resources of the community in life-long learning that encourages a continuing interplay between study and application, between knowledge and craft.

The history of American higher education is strewn with the litter of sound ideas that have been overgeneralized and indiscriminately put into use. This report is not an invitation to ride yet another bandwagon.

Leave-taking is not a miracle-cure for student discontents nor is it a nostrum for institutional ills. The study does provide evidence that leave-taking is a symptom of inadequacies in our present campus-bound conceptions of education. The leave experiences of more than a thousand students testify to the values that they received from expanding the locus of their educational endeavors and suggests the importance of enlarging and enriching these opportunities for students to come. The book will have fulfilled its purpose if it helps students and their advisors to be more keenly aware of alternatives that are available in their pursuit of intellectual and personal growth, and if it challenges them to exercise these options to the greatest personal benefit of students.

Notes

1. Summerskill, John. Dropouts from College, pp. 627-28.

2. Pervin, Lawrence A., ed. The College Dropout, p. 4.

3. Shriver, R. S. Wesleyan University News, p. 1.

4. Carnegie Commission on Higher Education. Less Time, More Options: Education Beyond the High School, p. 1.

5. Ibid., p. 13.

6. Newman, Frank. A Preview of the Second Newman Report, p. 34.

7. $x^2 = 20.97$. For 1 and 5 degrees of freedom, $p = 0.001$.

8. Office of Research, American Council on Education. National Norms for Entering College Freshmen, Fall 1970.

9. Lindsay, Nancy S. Where Did You Go? Out!
Yartz, Larry J. Student Attrition at Allegheny University.

10. See appendix II, protocols 39, 40, 44, 48, 86-90.

11. See appendix II, protocols 7, 8, 28, 68-85.

12. See appendix II, protocols 3, 12, 27, 34, 38, 42, 44, 50, 53, 55, 61, 63, 66, 72, 81, 82, 93, 94.

13. See appendix II, protocols 12, 20, 27, 38, 51, 54, 56, 57, 77.

14. See appendix II, protocols 5, 6, 10, 30, 36, 53, 75, 76.

15. See appendix II, protocols 1, 2, 4, 11, 19, 25, 26, 29, 41, 45, 84.

16. See chapter 8, p. 144, and appendix II, protocols 27-33, 78.

17. Pervin, Lawrence A., ed. The College Dropout, p. 238.

18. Cohen, Gail A., ed. U.S. College-Sponsored Programs Abroad.

19. Bolles, Richard Nelson. What Color is Your Parachute? A Practical Manual for Job-Hunters and Career-Changers. 1976 Edition. Berkeley: Ten Speed Press, 1976.

20. Lindsay, Nancy S. Where Did You Go? Out!, pages unnumbered, see inside rear cover.

21. See appendix II, protocols 27, 30, 42, 66, 69.

22. Pervin, Lawrence A., ed. The College Dropout, pp. 9, 10, 14, 16, 18.

23. Astin, Alexander. Preventing Students from Dropping Out, p. 1.

24. See appendix I, page 192.

25. Howe, Harold, II. *The Value of College as Seen by a Non-Economist*, p. 13.

26. Kesselman, Judi R. *Stopping Out: A Guide to Leaving College and Getting Back In*. See especially pp. 123-34; also in this text, page 74.

27. Cohen, Gail A., ed. *U.S. College-Sponsored Programs Abroad Academic Year*.

28. Pamphlets titled *College Venture Program, Student Guidelines*, and *Discover College Venture* may be obtained from the College Venture Program, Northeastern University, 360 Huntington Avenue, Boston, Massachusetts, 02115.

29. See especially: Freedman, Mervin B. *The College Experience*.
    Heath, Douglas H. *Growing Up in College*.
    Katz, Joseph, and Associates. *No Time for Youth*.
    Madison, Peter. *Personality Development in College*.
    Minter, W. John, ed. *The Individual and the System*.
    Sanford, Nevitt. *Where Colleges Fail*.

30. Meyerson, Martin, and Graubard, Stephen R. *The Assembly on University Goals and Governance*, p. 323.

31. Ibid., p. 327.

32. Ibid., p. 330.

33. Ibid., p. 324.

34. Ibid., p. 337.

35. See appendix II, protocols 58, 79.

Bibliography

Adinolfi, Allen A. "Characteristics of Highly Accepted, Highly Rejected, and Relatively Unknown University Freshmen." Journal of Counseling Psychology, 1972, 17:456-64.

Astin, Alexander W. Preventing Students from Dropping Out. San Francisco: Jossey-Bass, 1975.

Babbott, Edward F. "Postponing college: alternatives for an interim year." The College Board Review 80:21-29.

Berdie, Ralph F. "The Study of University Students: Analyses and Recommendations." Journal of College Student Personnel, 1972, 13:4-11.

Butts, R. Freeman. "The Search for Purpose in American Education." The College Board Review, 1975, 98:3-19.

Carnegie Commission on Higher Education. Less Time, More Options: Education Beyond High School. New York: McGraw-Hill, 1971.

―――――――――――. Priorities for Action. New York: McGraw-Hill, 1973.

Cohen, Gail E., ed. U.S. College-Sponsored Programs Abroad: Academic Year. New York: Institute of International Education, 1976.

Cope, Robert G., and Hannah, William. Revolving College Doors: The Causes and Consequences of Dropping Out, Stopping Out, and Transferring. New York: John Wiley & Sons, 1975.

Cramer, Stanley H., and Stevic, Richard R. "A review of the 1970-71 literature: Research on the transition from high school to college." The College Board Review, 1971, 81:32-38.

Dennis, Lawrence E., and Kauffman, Joseph F., eds. The College and the Student. Washington, D.C.: American Council on Education, 1966.

Freeman, Mervin B. The College Experience. San Francisco: Jossey-Bass, 1967.

Fry, P. S. "Changes in Youth's Attitudes Toward Authority: The Transition from University to Employment." Journal of Counseling Psychology, 1976, 23:66-74.

Garraty, John A., Kemperer, Lily Von., and Cyril, J. H. The New Guide to Study Abroad. 5th edition. New York: Harper & Row, 1976.

Heath, Douglas H. Growing Up in College: Liberal Education and Maturity. San Francisco: Jossey-Bass, 1968.

Hecklinger, Fred J. "The Undecided Student--Is He Less Satisfied with College?" Journal of College Student Personnel, 1972, 13:247-51.

Howe, Harold, II. "The Value of College as Seen by a Non-Economist." *The College Board Review*, 1976, 100:6-13.

Katz, Joseph and Associates. *No Time for Youth: Growth and Constraint in College Students*. San Francisco: Jossey-Bass, 1968.

Kesselman, Judi R. *Stopping Out, A Guide to Leaving College and Getting Back In*. New York: M. Evans and Company, 1976.

Lewchuk, Ross C., ed. *National Register of Internships and Experiential Education*. Washington, D.C.: Acropolis Books Ltd. 1973.

Lindsay, Nancy S. *Where Did You Go? Out!* Cambridge: Harvard University, 1974.

London, Herbert I. "The Case for Nontraditional Learning." *Change*, 1976, 8:25-37.

MacMitchell, T. Leslie. "New Perspectives on Admissions." *The College Board Review*, 1972, 86:23-33.

Madison, Peter. *Personality Development in College*. Reading, Massachusetts: Addison-Wesley, 1969.

Meyerson, Martin, and Graubard, Stephen R. "The Assembly on University Goals and Governance." in American Higher Education: Toward an Uncertain Future, Volume II. *Daedalus*, 1975, 104:322-46.

Minter, W. John, ed. *The Individual and the System*. Boulder: Western Interstate Commission for Higher Education, 1967.

Mondale, Walter F. "The Next Step: Lifelong Learning." *Change*, 1976, 8:42-45.

Newman, Frank, et. al. *Report on Higher Education*. Washington, D.C.: Office of Education, U.S. Department of Health, Education and Welfare, 1971.

Newman, Frank. "A Preview of the Second Newman Report." *Change*, 1972, 4:28-34.

Nosow, Sigmund. "Students' Perceptions of Field Experience Education." *Journal of College Student Personnel*, 1975, 16:508-13.

Office of Research, American Council on Education. "National Norms for Entering College Freshmen, Fall 1970." *ACE Research Reports*, 1970, 5:1-100.

Pandey, R. E. "Personality Characteristics of Successful, Dropout, and Probationary Black and White University Students." *Journal of Counseling Psychology*, 1972, 5:382-86.

Perkins, David S. "Aspects of Student Discontent, 1975." *Journal of Higher Education*, 1975, 46:471-77.

Pervin, Lawrence A., Reik, Louis E., and Dalrymple, Willard, eds., *The College Dropout and the Utilization of Talent*. Princeton: Princeton University Press, 1966.

Renetzky, Alvin, ed. <u>Directory of Internships, Work Experience Programs, and On-the-Job Training Opportunities</u>. Thousand Oaks, California: Ready Reference Press, 1976.

Report of a Special Task Force to the Secretary of Health, Education, and Welfare. <u>The Second Newman Report: National Policy and Higher Education</u>. Cambridge: The MIT Press, 1973.

Ritterbush, Philip C., ed. <u>Let the Entire Community Become Our University</u>. Washington, D.C.: Acropolis Books Ltd., 1973.

Rossman, Jack E., and Kirk, Barbara A. "Factors Related to Persistence and Withdrawal among University Students." <u>Journal of Counseling Psychology</u>, 1970, 17:56-62.

Rowland, Howard S., and Rowland, Beatrice L. <u>The New York Times Guide to Student Adventures and Studies Abroad</u>. New York: Quadrangle Press, New York Times Book Co., 1974.

Sanford, Nevitt. <u>Where Colleges Fail: A Study of the Student as a Person</u>. San Francisco: Jossey-Bass, 1967.

Schmidt, Du Mont K., and Sedlacek, William E. "Variables Related to University Student Satisfaction." <u>Journal of College Student Personnel</u>, 1972, 13:233-238.

Sherman, Margaret, E., ed. <u>Whole World Handbook: A student guide to work, study and travel abroad</u>. New York: Council on International Educational Exchange, 1976.

Shriver, R. J. <u>Wesleyan University News</u>, 1964, 2:1.

Smith, G. Kerry, ed. <u>Stress and Campus Response</u>. San Francisco: Jossey-Bass, 1968.

Starr, Ann, Betz, Ellen L., and Menne, John. "Differences in College Student Satisfaction: Academic Dropouts, Nonacademic Dropouts, and Nondropouts." <u>Journal of Counseling Psychology</u>, 1972, 19:318-22.

Summerskill, John. "Dropouts from college." in <u>The American College</u>. Nevitt Sanford, ed. New York: John Wiley & Sons, 1962.

UNESCO <u>World Guide to Higher Education</u>. Epping, Essex, England: Bowker, 1976.

Wright, Eric. "A Study of Student Leaves of Absence." <u>Journal of Higher Education</u>, 1973, 44:235-47.

Yankelovich, Daniel, and Clark, Ruth. "College and Noncollege Youth Values." <u>Change</u>, 1974, 6:45-46.

Yartz, Larry J. <u>Student Attrition at Allegheny University</u>. Meadville, Pennsylvania: Allegheny College, 1974.

APPENDIX I

Survey Instruments

The text of the several surveys used in this study are reproduced here for those who may wish to examine them in detail. The full text may clarify the design of the research and facilitate relating the findings to the survey instruments from which they are derived. Cross-references are given in the text of Survey 1 that identify items in the other surveys that are similar or identical in wording. The response alternatives of reported items are reproduced in the first survey only. Thereafter, only the stem of the item is listed. The number and letter in the parenthesis at the end of the question refers to the survey and item that includes the response alternative.

A potential use for the surveys beyond their possible utility in further research was suggested by comments volunteered by some of the respondents. They stated that completing the surveys had helped them to organize and clarify their own thoughts and feelings about their leaves. The following are illustrative: [35]

> Taking a leave was a very difficult decision for me to make. This questionnaire has helped me look objectively at exactly what I'm doing.

> Just filling out the questions on my reasons for taking a leave and rating my satisfactions with college were more helpful in letting me see my motivations than any of the Dean bullshit where your're both playing roles.

Students differ greatly in the amount of guidance that they seek or are willing to accept. Some decried the prefunctory nature of the handling of their leaves. Others expressed the wish that they had received more personalized attention in their leaving and returning. Still others who had received helpful attention from faculty or other advisors expressed appreciation for the assistance. Questionnaires might prove to be a useful adjunct to "exit" interviews and to "debriefing" or "reorienting" sessions conducted for returnees.

Collating Number: _____

"LEAVE-TAKING" SURVEY 1

Cooperative Research Project of Brown, Hampshire, Trinity and Wesleyan

Instructions: Except for those items in which other instructions are given, write the number of the alternative that you select in the appropriate space in the left-hand margin. Work quickly through the questions; your first reaction to the question is generally a good one to record. We invite you to make any comments or to furnish additional information that you consider to be relevant to this study. Thank you for your participation.

____ A. Type of Leave: Although individual institutions use different terminology, for the purposes of this survey we will use the term "leave" to refer to that period of time in which a person is involved in activities other than those of a full-time student enroled in a program of academic studies at the main campus of the institution from which the person expects to receive a degree. Please indicate which of the following categories of "leave" most accurately describes the type of activity in which you will be engaged. Select the most accurate alternative and write its number on the line in the left-hand margin.

1A, A

1. Enrolment in a program of study conducted by this college at a location other than its main campus.
2. "Education in the Field" or "Work-Study" activity to be supervised or evaluated by the college for possible academic credit.
3. Enrolment in a program of study at an institution of higher learning other than the one from which you expect to receive a baccalaurate degree.
4. Full-time employment or volunteer service.
5. Self-directed reading, research, work in the creative or performing arts, travel, etc.
6. Other--please mark number and describe

____ B. Reasons for taking a leave of absence: Each student has his or her own very personal reasons for attending college and in some instances for choosing to interrupt or terminate college work. The following are some broad categories of reasons that students give for taking a leave. Please indicate the importance to you of each reason by writing the code number of the most descriptive statement. Add any reasons that are important in your case but which are not included in the list which follows.

1A, B

166

Code for Degree of Importance
1. A precipitating factor, one of the most important or crucial reasons for my taking a leave at this time.
2. A contributing factor. Although not decisive, was an important consideration in decision to take a leave.
3. A minor factor, may have influenced my decision to take a leave but only in limited or peripheral ways.
4. Not a factor in my decision to take a leave, although it may be present in my personal history.
5. Does not apply in my case.

Code each item

a. A recommended or required part of my college program.
b. To obtain course work or experiences not available to me at this campus.
c. Lack of sufficiently well-defined purposes for being in college to justify the time, effort and/or expense involved.
d. The seeming irrelevancy of college to issues that are important to me.
e. My need for a change; desire for different kinds of experiences and/or associations.
f. Lack of interest in my course of studies.
g. Lack of success in my course of studies.
h. Personal need for experiences that might give a perspective on myself, to college, my relations to society, etc.
i. Failure to find satisfying personal and/or social relationships at this college.
j. Personal medical, health reasons.
k. Financial considerations.
l. Personal circumstances not related to college.
m. Family circumstances.
n. Other – code importance and describe _____
o. Other – code importance and describe _____

1A, C

C. How do each of the following persons feel about your plans to take a leave? For each, write the number of the statement that reflects their attitude most accurately.

Code for attitude toward your leave

1. Took the initiative in suggesting a leave and/or in helping with plans.
2. Encouraged me and supported my plans.
3. Initially unenthusiastic or opposed but now accepting or supportive.
4. Willing to accept whatever I decide to do.
5. Disinterested or indifferent.
6. Doesn't think it is a good idea, tried to disuade me.
7. Have not discussed plans with this (these person(s).
8. Question not appropriate to my situation.

Code each item

a. Father
b. Mother
c. Best friend(s)
d. Faculty member(s) who know you best
e. Others - code attitude and indicate relationship _____

D. Which of the following statements describes most accurately your feelings about taking a leave? (Write number of best alternative.)

1. I anticipate my leave with eagerness and enthusiasm.
2. I accept a leave as the best thing for me at this time.
3. I am ambivalent in my feelings. Although I believe a leave is desirable, I am reluctant to take it.
4. If circumstances did not require it, I would not take a leave at this time.

3, C

E. In general, are you enjoying your studies this term as much as you had expected to? (If not presently enroled, during the last term in which you were enroled.)

1. No, I am definitely enjoying them less than I had expected.
2. No, but I am only mildly disappointed.
3. My expectations for this term are reasonably well satisfied.
4. I am enjoying my studies this term much more than I had expected.

F. In terms of your own personal satisfaction, how much importance do you attach to getting good grades or favorable faculty evaluations and reports?
   1. None or not much.
   2. A moderate amount.
   3. Quite a bit.
   4. A great deal.
   5. Does not apply to my situation.

3, D
4, D

G. What proportion of the faculty members who have taught you during the past year would you say are superior teachers?
   1. Very few.
   2. Less than half.
   3. More than half.
   4. Almost all.
   5. Have not been enroled during past year.

3, E
4, E

H. What proportion of the faculty members that you have observed at this college would you say are genuinely interested in students and their problems?
   1. Very few.
   2. Less than half.
   3. More than half.
   4. Almost all.
   5. Have not been enroled during past year.

3, F
4, F

I. Beyond your role as student, how many faculty members of this college respond to you as a person and show a personal interest in you?
   1. One.   2. Two or three.   3. Four or more.   4. None.   5. Can't say.

3, G
4, G

J. In your dealings with members of the college administration and staff, have you been made to feel that they have an interest in you as a person?
   1. To them, I exist only as a name or an enrolment statistic, not as a person.
   2. Very seldom am I aware of any interest in me as an individual.
   3. Occasionally I am aware of a personal interest in me.
   4. Frequently I am aware of a personal interest in me.
   5. In most of my relationships I am aware of a personal interest.
   6. Personal contacts have been so infrequent that I have no basis for judgment.
   7. This varies greatly from person to person and from one office to another.

3, H
4, H

169

K. During the present term or the last in which you were enroled, how much time per week, on an average, have you devoted to activities directly related to your program of studies (include class and laboratory time, reading, papers, problem sets, field or studio work, etc.)?
   1. Less than 20 hours per week.
   2. 20 to 29 hours per week.
   3. 30 to 39 hours per week.
   4. 40 to 49 hours per week.
   5. 50 or more hours per week.
   6. So variable from week to week that an average is meaningless.
   7. Don't really know.

L. During the present term or the last in which you were enroled, how much time per week, on the average, have you devoted to activities that you pursued with some degree of regularity and commitment (e.g., organized extracurricular or community activities, personal projects such as writing, music, personal exercise, etc.)?
   1. Practically none.
   2. Less than 5 hours per week.
   3. 5 to 9 hours per week.
   4. 10 to 19 hours per week.
   5. 20 or more hours per week.
   6. So variable from week to week that an average is meaningless.
   7. Don't really know.

M. During the present term or the last in which you were enroled, how much time, on the average, have you spent in gainful employment or in a work-study (bursary) program?
   1. None
   2. Less than 5 hours per week.
   3. 5 to 9 hours per week.
   4. 10 to 14 hours per week.
   5. 15 or more hours per week.
   6. Worked irregularly or for very short time.

N. Which of the following statements best describes your relationships with other students during the present term, or the last in which you were enroled? They have been:
   1. A relatively inconsequential part of my college experience.
   2. A significant but less important aspect of my college experience.
   3. One of the more important aspects of my college experience.
   4. The single most important feature of my college experience.

O. How many close friends do you have among the students of this college?
   1. None that I consider a close friend.
   2. One.
   3. Two or three.
   4. Four or five.
   5. Six or more.
   6. Don't really know.

P. Where are you living (or where did you live during the last term in which you were enroled)?
   1. College dormitory.
   2. College apartment.
   3. College controlled off-campus housing.
   4. Non-college off-campus housing.
   5. Home of parents, relatives or family friends.
   6. Other: please specify _____

Q. What kind of social relationships and opportunities do (did) your living arrangements provide?
   1. Little or none.
   2. Uncongenial. I keep my social contacts to a minimum.
   3. Superficial. We get along but share few significant interests.
   4. Rewarding. People in my living unit are congenial and sharing.
   5. People in my living unit are some of my best friends.
   6. Mixed. Some good relationships, some not so good.
   7. Can't say.

R. Generally speaking, how do you feel about competing with other people for grades or for academic recognition?
   1. I enjoy competing and prefer situations that provide opportunities to compete with others.
   2. For me, competition adds motivation and interest to learning.
   3. I am relatively uninfluenced by the presence or absence of competition.
   4. For me, competition in learning is distracting and undesirable.
   5. I avoid or reject competition in learning situations if at all possible.
   6. Can't say.

S. With how many persons do (did) you share your living arrangements? Write the number.

T. How important is it to you that you obtain a college degree?
   1. It is essential to my development and to my future.
   2. It is extremely important to me.
   3. It is fairly important to me.
   4. It is not very important to me.
   5. I would not attend college if a college degree were not a social and vocational necessity.

U. After obtaining your bachelor's degree, do you expect to continue your education in a graduate or a professional school?

1A, F   1. Definitely yes.   4. Definitely not.
2 , J   2. Probably yes.   5. Do not intend to complete bachelor's degree.
3 , R   3. Probably not.   6. Haven't thought enough about this matter to say.
4 , Q

V. How important is it to your parents that you obtain a college degree?

   1. Not very important to them.   4. Extremely important.
2 , J   2. Fairly important.   5. Not certain of their attitude.
4 , R   3. Quite important.

W. How important is it to your parents that you graduate from this particular college?

   1. Not very important.   4. Extremely important.
4 , S   2. Fairly important.   5. Not certain of their attitude.
   3. Quite important.

X. In thinking about your occupational future, do you feel that in the long run you will have a preference for:

1A, E   1. I have been unable to decide.
2 , K   2. I have not given sufficient thought to this matter to say.
3 , S   3. An academic life (teaching, research, other scholarly work).
4 , T   4. A business life.
   5. A professional life (physician, lawyer, engineer, etc.).
   6. A life of a trained technician or craftsman.
   7. A life centering upon some aspect of the creative arts.
   8. A life centering upon a home and a family.
   9. Other: please specify _____

Y. Judging from the amount of time, effort and attention that you have given to each during the present term (or the last in which enroled), what relative degree of importance do (did) you attach to the activities listed below? Mark the most important, 1; the second most important, 2; etc. Mark any in which you have not been engaged with an X.

2 , L
3 , T
4 , U

Make each item

_____ 1. Course work in my major field.
_____ 2. Course work in general.
_____ 3. Individual study, research, writing, art work, etc.
_____ 4. Organized extracurricular activities: student government, athletics, clubs, etc.
_____ 5. Concerts, exhibits, seminars, lectures, etc.
_____ 6. Social life and social relationships.
_____ 7. Self-discovery, self-insight, discovery of new interests, talents, life-style, etc.
_____ 8. Active involvement in community and/or political affairs.
_____ 9. Gainful employment.

Z. Rate the degree of difficulty that you have experienced in each of the following problem areas during the present term (or the last in which enroled). Assign to each one of the following codes:

Code for degree of difficulty
1. A serious problem.   4. A trivial problem.
2. A moderate problem.   5. Not a problem.
3. A minor problem.   6. Uncertain, little way of knowing at this time.

2, M
3, U
4, V

Code each item

_____ a. Managing my time.
_____ b. Handling the content of my courses
_____ c. Trying to "find" myself in the sense of personal meaning and identity; where I am headed, what I am seeking in life, etc.
_____ d. Making decisions concerning my career.
_____ e. Some aspect of parent and/or family relations.
_____ f. Social relationships.
_____ g. My relationships with particular person(s) of the opposite sex.
_____ h. Finances.
_____ i. Health-medical.
_____ j. Other: please specify _____

1 A, D
3, V
4, W

AA. Please rate your degree of satisfaction with EACH of the following aspects of college life as you have experienced them this term or during the last term in which you were enroled. Write the appropriate code number for each item.

Code for Degree of Satisfaction
1. Highly satisfied. As well as resonably could be expected.
2. Basically satisfied. Dissatisfactions are minor or apply to limited situations.
3. Ambivalent. Mixed feelings, both of satisfaction and dissatisfaction, related to specific situations.
4. Basically dissatisfied. Discontents and inadequacies are greater than any satisfaction.
5. High dissatisfied. Unsatisfactory to a degree or with a frequency that is unacceptable to me.
6. Does not apply, can't say.

Code each item
a. The quality of instruction.
b. The intellectual leadership and stimulation provided by members of the faculty.
c. The relevance of your coursework to your own interests and concerns.
d. Opportunities to pursue your own intellectual, cultural and/or artistic interests.
e. Availability of courses, seminars, laboratories, independent study, etc. in fields of your principal interests.
f. The recognition that your academic efforts and abilities have received from your instructors.
g. Accessibility of faculty for consultation and academic assistance.
h. Responsiveness of the administration to students and to issues of student well-being.
i. The adequacy of academic advising.
j. The adequacy of professional counseling.
k. The adequacy of health services.
l. Academic regulations and requirements.
m. The level of academic motivation and commitment that characterizes students at your college.
n. The amount of academic competitiveness among students.
o. The level of political and social awareness of students.
p. Opportunities to know students who hold ideas, values and interests different from your own.
q. Opportunities to know students from socio-economic backgrounds different from your own.
r. Opportunities to participate in extracurricular activities that are of interest to you.
s. Degree of personal freedom permitted by the college.
t. Opportunity to form friendships and to experience satisfying personal relationships.
u. The help with academic or personal problems that students give to one another.
v. Your living arrangements.

174

BB. From the list that follows, select the five adjectives or phrases that in your judgment describe most accurately the atmosphere of this college and relationships. For each of the five words that you select, write an "X" over the printed M to indicate that they are most descriptive of the atmosphere of this college. Examine the list again and place an "X" over the L before each of the five words that you think are most descriptive of the college. Words that are neither "most" or "least" descriptive but which do apply to your college may be marked on the A to indicate that they are descriptive to a degree. Leave all other words unmarked.

M L A Achievement oriented
M L A Bureaucratic
M L A Competitive
M L A Conservative
M L A Cooperative
M L A Creative
M L A Disorganized
M L A Friendly
M L A Happy
M L A Individualistic
M L A Innovative
M L A Intellectual
M L A Joyless
M L A Liberal
M L A Lonely

M L A Permissive
M L A Pleasure-seeking
M L A Pressured
M L A Radical
M L A Regulative
M L A Relaxed
M L A Self-centered
M L A Socially aware
M L A Status-conscious
M L A Stressful
M L A Stimulating
M L A Strong sense of community
M L A Supportive
M L A Traditional
M L A Unfriendly

Add any adjectives or phrases not included in the list above that you feel are especially characteristic of this college.

_____ _____ _____

_____ _____ _____

Please make any additional comments concerning your college experiences and/or your proposed "leave". We would be particularly interested in your reactions to the following questions:

1. What are your objectives in taking this leave of absence? What do you hope to accomplish during the time that you are away from college?

2. What will you be doing during your leave? How do you propose to pursue the objectives that you outlined above?

3. What persons, offices, or organizations were most helpful to you in thinking through your decision to take a leave and/or in arranging for the program of activities in which you will be engaged during your leave? Please be as specific as possible.

4. Might there have been any ways in which the college could have been more helpful to you in thinking about or arranging for this leave?

5. Additional comments:

"LEAVE-TAKING" SURVEY -- BACKGROUND INFORMATION
Cooperative Research Project of Brown, Hampshire, Trinity and Wesleyan

Collating Number: _____ This number will be used to correlate your answers with other elements of the research project. It will NOT be used to associate your name with any of your responses. As indicated in the letter, you may be assured of confidential handling of your answers.

Instructions: The following information is needed to provide categories for the analysis of data derived from the leave-taking study. Please answer all questions to the best of your ability by writing the number of the most accurate or descriptive alternative on the lines to the left of the question. This information will be used for statistical analysis of the data of this study only and will not be shared with any other office or agency.

____ 1. From what kind of secondary school did you graduate?
    1. Public school   4. Non-public, Catholic
    2. Federal Government school   5. Non-public, other religious affiliation
    3. An alternative school   6. Non-public, not religiously affiliated
       7. Other: _____

____ 2. Are you (write numbers of all that apply)
    1. White/Caucasian   5. Puerto Rican-American
    2. Black/Negro/Afro-American   6. Chinese-American/Japanese-American/Oriental
    3. American Indian/Native American 7. Other: _____
    4. Mexican-American/Chicano

____ 3. Are You
    1. An only child 2. The oldest child 3. The youngest child 4. An in-between child

____ 4. How old will you be on December 31 of this year?
    1. 16 or younger   5. 20
    2. 17   6. 21
    3. 18   7. 22-25
    4. 19   8. 26 or older

____ 5. Your sex: 1. Female 2. Male

6. Which of the following is currently true about your parents?
   1. Both alive and married to each other.
   2. Both alive and divorced or separated.
   3. One or both parents deceased.

7. Which of the following categories comes closest to your parents' occupations? If either is retired, deceased or unemployed, indicate the former or customary occupation.
   1. Unskilled worker, laborer, farm worker.
   2. Semiskilled worker (e.g. machine operator).
   3. Service worker (policeman, fireman, barber, military noncommissioned office, etc.).
   4. Skilled worker or craftsman (carpenter, electrician, plumber, etc.).
   5. Salesman, bookkeeper, secretary, office worker, etc.
   6. Owner, manager, partner of a small business; lower level govt. official; military commissioned officer.
   7. Profession requiring a bachelor's degree (engineer, elementary or secondary teacher, etc.).
   8. Owner, high-level executive -- large business or high-level government agency.
   9. Professional requiring an advanced college degree (doctor, lawyer, college professor, etc.).

   Father ___
   Mother ___

8. How much formal education does (did) your parents have? Indicate only the highest level (i.e. mark only one of the nine alternatives).
   1. Grammar school or less.
   2. Some high (secondary) school.
   3. Finished high school.
   4. Business or trade school.
   5. Some college.
   6. Finished college, received Bachelor's Degree.
   7. Attended graduate or professional school (e.g., law or medical school) but did not attain a graduate or professional degree.
   8. Attained a Masters Degree.
   9. Attained highest graduate or professional degree (e.g., Ph.D., M.D., J.D., D.D.S., etc.).

   Father ___
   Mother ___

9. What is your best estimate of the total income last year of your parental family (not your own family if you are married)? Consider annual income for all sources before taxes.
   1. Less than $5,000.   4. $15,000 to $19,999.   7. $30,000 to $39,999.
   2. $ 5,000 to $ 9,999.   5. $20,000 to $24,999.   8. $40,000 to $49,999.
   3. $10,000 to $14,999.   6. $25,000 to $29,999.   9. $50,000 and above.

10. What is your best estimate of when you will return to this college from your leave? If you have returned from a leave, what was it's duration?
   1. One term.
   2. Two terms.
   3. Three terms.
   4. Four or more terms.
   5. The duration of my leave cannot be decided at this time.
   6. My present expectation is that I will not return to this college.
   7. Other, please explain: _____

11. Since your graduation from secondary school and before your taking this leave, have there been any times other than summers when you have not been enrolled in a college level program?
   1. No.
   2. Yes, please give particulars. When? For how long? Type of activity. _____

12. Have you ever lived or traveled outside the limits of the continental United States?
   1. No.
   2. Yes. If yes, please indicate time and place and for how long a period of time.

Additional comments:

Please return with the accompanying Survey in the self-addressed envelope to Wesleyan University, Office of Institutional Research, Middletown, CT. 06457. Thank you.

"LEAVE-TAKING" SURVEY 2

Cooperative Research Project of Brown, Hampshire, Trinity, Tufts, Wesleyan and Wheaton

Collating Number: _____ This number will be used to correlate your answers with other elements of the research project. It will NOT be used to associate your name with any of your responses. As indicated in the letter, you may be assured of confidential handling of your answers.

Definition of "Leave": Although individual institutions use different terminology, for the purposes of this survey we will use the term "leave" to refer to that period of time in which a person is involved in activities other than those of a full-time student enroled in a program of academic studies at the main campus of the institution from which the person expects to receive a degree.

Instructions: Except for those items in which other instructions are given, write the number of the alternative that you select in the appropriate space in the left-hand margin. Work quickly through the questions; your first reaction to the question is generally a good one to record. We invite you to make any comments or to furnish additional information that you consider to be relevant to this study. Thank you for your participation.

A. During the period that you were not in residence at this college, how much time did you spend in the following types of activities? For EACH activity record the code number of the most descriptive statement.
   Code
   1. Major amount of time. The principal activity during a significant portion of my leave.
   2. A substantial amount of time.
   3. A moderate amount of time.
   4. A limited amount of time.
   5. Little or no time devoted to this activity.

   Activity: Code each item
   a. Formal academic work
   b. Individual study, reading, research, writing, studio work, field work, etc.
   c. Volunteer social service, political activity, community action, etc.
   d. Employment
   e. Travel
   f. Recreational-social activities
   g. Personal-family matters
   h. Medical-psychiatric treatment, convalescence, etc.
   i. Other: please describe _____

B. Which of the following best describes the community in which you spent the greater amount of time during your leave? White number of alternative that you select on line at the left.
   1. In the central city of a metropolitan area of more than 2,000,000 population.
   2. In the central city of a metropolitan area of less than 2,000,000 population.
   3. In a suburb of a metropolitan area.
   4. In a smaller city (less than 100,000 population).
   5. In a town of less than 10,000.
   6. Farm, ranch or other open country.
   7. Remained in the college community.

C. Which of the following most accurately describes the nature of your living arrangements during the greater part of your leave?
   1. Lived with parents, relatives or close family friends.
   2. Lived in accommodations provided or arranged for by program or organization through which leave was taken.
   3. Worked out my own living arrangements with person(s) I knew through previous associations.
   4. Worked out my own living arrangements with person(s) not previously known.
   5. Made my own arrangements to live alone.
   6. Had several different living arrangements during leave, all of which were provided for me.
   7. Had several different living arrangements, all of which I negotiated myself.
   8. Had several arrangements, some provided for me, others that I worked out myself.
   9. Other, please describe:

D. Considering your objectives in taking a leave, how valuable were the experiences associated with your leave from college?
   1. They exceeded my highest hopes and expectations.
   2. They fully justified my taking a leave.
   3. They were satisfactory although disappointing in some respects.
   4. They were not nearly as satisfactory as I had hoped they would be.
   5. For most intents and purposes, my leave was time poorly spent.

E. What would be your most probable reaction to students who sought your advice concerning the desirability of their taking a leave similar to yours?
   1. Would recommend it to almost any student.
   2. Would be selective in the students to whom I would recommend it.
   3. Would caution student concerning conditions that might counter-indicate this type of leave.
   4. Would actively discourage most students from considering this type of leave.
   5. Can't say.

F. Which of the following most closely describes your feelings in turning from these activities to a program of formal education?
1. I am anticipating my studies with great eagerness and enthusiasm.
2. I feel ready to undertake collegiate studies.
3. I am ambivalent. Some things attract me to college but others are not very appealing.
4. I recognize the importance of college but would prefer to be doing other things.
5. I would not be enroling in college if it were not for external pressures (career, social, family).

G. Select the one statement that most accurately describes your situation.
1. To this time, I have been unable to decide kpon a major field of concentration.
2. I am no longer interested in my "pre-leave" major (or intended major) but have been unable to select a new field of concentration.
3. Although different, my present major is related to the one that I had selected (or was intending) before my leave.
4. I have changed my field of concentration to a completely different area.
5. My present major (or intended major) is the same as before my leave.

H. How confident are you of your present choice of a major or field of concentration?
1. I am confident that I have the interest and ability to complete the program of studies that I have chosen.
2. I am fairly confident that I will complete a program of studies in this or a closely related field.
3. My choice is tentative and exploratory. I very well may change field.
4. My choice is more a response to a college requirement than an expression of a personal preference.
5. I have not reached a decision.

I. How important is it to you that you obtain a college degree? (See also Survey 1, T.)

J. After obtaining your bachelor's degree, do you expect to continue your education in a graduate or professional school? (1, U.)

K. In thinking about your occupational future, do you feel that in the long run you will have a preference for: (1, X.)

182

L. During this academic year, what relative degree of importance do you expect to give to each of the following areas? (1, Y.)

M. Listed below are types of problems that college students frequently encounter. Indicate the degree to which you think that EACH problem area might pose difficulties for you during this academic year. (1, Z.)

N. How much communication have you had with persons (faculty, staff, students, etc.) at the college (University) during the time of your leave? List ALL numbers that apply on line(s) to the left.
   1. None.
   2. Official correspondence with offices or officials of the college (University).
   3. Occasional personal communications, written or telephonic.
   4. Frequent personal communications, written or telephonic.
   5. Visited the campus occasionally.
   6. Visited the campus frequently.
   7. Although on leave, I continued to live in the immediate vicinity of the college (University).

O. How would you characterize (in respect to age, socio-economic status, educational level, and ethnic background) the persons with whom you had the greatest amount of association during your working hours?

P. How would you characterize (in respect to the same characteristics) the persons with whom you associated during your leisure or "off-duty" times?

Q. PLEASE DESCRIBE AND EVALUATE YOUR LEAVE. We would be particularly interested in the following: (1) What did you do during your leave? (2) What values or benefits did you receive from this involvement? (3) What difficulties or disappointments did you experience? (4) Are there things that you or the college might have done that would have made your leave a more productive experience? This outline is only a suggestion. Feel free to organize your response in any way that you prefer.

"LEAVE-TAKING SURVEY 3
Cooperative Research Project of Brown, Hampshire, Trinity and Wesleyan

Collating Number: _____ This number will be used to correlate your answers with other elements of the research project. It will NOT be used to associate your name with any of your responses. As indicated in the letter, you may be assured of confidential handling of your answers.

Definition of "Leave": Although individual institutions use different terminology, for the purposes of this survey we will use the term "leave" to refer to that period of time in which a person is involved in activities other than those of a full-time student enroled in a program of academic studies at the main campus of the institution from which the person expects to receive a degree.

Instructions: Except for those items in which other instructions are given, write the number of the alternative that you select in the appropriate space in the left-hand margin. Work quickly through the questions; your first reaction to the question is generally a good one to record. We invite you to make any comments or to furnish additional information that you consider to be relevant to this study. Thank you for your participation.

_____ A. With the wisdom of hindsight and the opportunity to choose again whether to continue your program of studies at this college, would you:
1. Definitely choose the same type of "leave".
2. Definitely choose to take a "leave" but one involving some other activity.
3. Probably choose the same type of "leave".
4. Probably choose to take a "leave" but one involving some other activity.
5. Uncertain.
6. Probably would continue my program of studies at this college.
7. Definitely would continue my program of studies at this college.

_____ B. In comparing your college experiences since returning to the campus with those of the period immediately before your "leave", which statement describes your feelings most accurately?
1. This past year has been much more satisfactory.
2. This past year has been somewhat more satisfactory.
3. I am aware of little difference.
4. The year before my leave was somewhat more satisfactory.
5. The year before my leave was much more satisfactory.

____ C. In General, are you enjoying your studies this term as much as you had expected to?
    1. No, I am definitely enjoying them less than I had expected.
    2. No, but I am only mildly disappointed.
    3. My expectations for this term are reasonably well satisfied.

____ D. In terms of your own personal satisfaction, how much importance do you attach to getting good grades or favorable faculty evaluations and reports? (See Survey 1, F.)

____ E. What proportion of the faculty members who have taught you during the past year would you say are superior teachers? (1, G.)

____ F. What proportion of the faculty members that you have observed would you say are genuinely interested in students and their problems? (1, H.)

____ G. Beyond your role as student, how many faculty members of this college respond to you as a person and show a personal interest in you? (1, I.)

____ H. In your dealings with members of the college administration and staff, have you been made to feel that they have an interest in you as a person? (1, J.)

____ I. Since your return from your leave, how much time per week, on the average, have you devoted to activities directly related to your program of studies? (1, K.)

____ J. Since your return from your leave, how much time perweek, on the average, have you devoted to activities that you have pursued with some degree of regularity and commitment? (1, L.)

____ K. Have you been employed for wages or in a work-study (bursary) program during the last academic term? (1, M.)

____ L. Which of the following statements best describes your relationships with other students since your return to this college? (1, N.)

____ M. How many close friends do you have among the students of this college? (1, O.)

____ N. Where are you living this term? (1, P.)

185

____ O. What kind of social relationships and opportunities do your living arrangements provide? (See also Survey 1, Q.)

____ P. Generally speaking, how do you feel about competing with other people for grades or for academic recognition? (1, R.)

____ Q. How important is it to you that you obtain a college degree? (1, T.)

____ R. After obtaining your bachelor's degree, do you expect to continue your education in a graduate or a professional school? (1, U.)

____ S. In thinking about your occupational future, do you feel that in the long run you will have a preference for: (1, X.)

T. Judging by the amount of time, effort and attention that you have given to each since your return to this campus, what relative degree of importance have you assigned to the activities listed below? (1, Y.)

U. Rate the degree of difficulty that you have experienced in each of the following problem areas since your return to this college. (1, Z.)

V. Please rate your degree of satisfaction with EACH of the following aspects of college life as you have experienced them during the past academic term. (1, AA.)

W. From the list that follows, select the five adjectives or phrases that in your judgment describe most accurately the atmosphere of this college as you have experienced it in your associations and relationships of the past year. (1, BB.)

X. Please write a statement about your experiences while "on leave" and in resuming your studies. Organize your comments in any way that is appropriate to your situation. We would be particularly interested in observations that you might have concerning the following:

 1. In what ways did the experiences of your "leave" contribute to (a) your personal development, (b) your motivations for and attitudes toward your continuing education?
 2. Have there been ways in which you have been handicapped or disadvantaged for having taken a "leave"? Please describe or discuss.

3. Can you suggest ways in which the college (University) might have helped to make your "leave" more valuable educationally or might have facilitated your return to the campus and to formal studies.

"LEAVE-TAKING" SURVEY 4
Cooperative Research Project of Brown, Hampshire, Trinity and Wesleyan

Collating Number: _____ This number will be used to correlate your answers with other elements of the research project. It will NOT be used to associate your name with any of your responses. As indicated in the letter, you may be assured of confidential handling of your answers.

Definition of "Leave": Although individual institutions use different terminology, for the purposes of this survey we will use the term "leave" to refer to that period of time in which a person is involved in activities other than those of a full-time student enrolled in a program of academic studies at the main campus of the institution from which the person expects to receive a degree.

Instructions: Except for those items in which other instructions are given, write the number of the alternative that you select in the appropriate space in the left-hand margin. Work quickly through the questions; your first reactions to the question is generally a good one to record. We invite you to make any comments or to furnish additional information that you consider to be relevant to this study. Thank you for your participation.

_____ A. Select the alternative that describes most accurately the greatest degree of consideration that you have given to taking a leave from college. (See definition above).
   1. Have never given serious consideration to the possibility of taking a leave.
   2. Have thought about taking a leave but never to the point of active investigation or planning.
   3. Investigated one or more leave-taking possibilities, but didn't pursue them.
   4. Arranged for a leave, but decided against taking it.
   5. Was committed to taking a leave but was unable to make satisfactory arrangements.
   6. Can't say.

B. Reasons for not taking a leave of absence: Students who have pursued their collegiate studies without interruption at a single campus have mentioned one or more of the considerations listed below as having influenced their decision. Please rate the degree in which EACH influenced your own thinking on this matter.
   Code for Degree of Importance
   1. A determining consideration.   4. A minor consideration.
   2. An important consideration.   5. Not a consideration.
   3. A moderate consideration.   6. Does not apply.

Code each item by writing the number of the alternative that is most applicable.
a. Wanted to complete undergraduate studies as promptly as possible.
b. Being away might produce undesirable discontinuities in program of studies.
c. Anticipated difficulties in resuming academic work at my college.
d. Faculty advisor(s) recommended against taking a leave.
e. Loss of association with particular member(s) of the faculty.
f. Loss of association with college friends.
g. Inability to participate in college activities that were important to me (e.g., performing arts groups, athletics or other extra-curricular, cultural, social, activities).
h. Available leave activities were not sufficiently attractive.
i. Difficulties in arranging for a suitable leave.
j. Financial considerations.
k. Unsatisfactory leave experience of other students.
l. Opposition of parent(s).
m. Friends advised against taking a leave.
n. College regulations made taking a leave difficult or unattractive.
o. Other: code and describe

C. With the wisdom of hindsight and the opportunity to choose again whether to continue your program of studies at this college without taking a leave, would you:
1. Definitely NOT take a leave.
2. Probably NOT take a leave.
3. Uncertain.
4. Probably would take a leave.
5. Definitely would take a leave.
6. The assumption that I would study at this college cannot be made.

D. In terms of your own personal satisfaction, how much importance do you attach to getting good grades or favorable faculty evaluations and reports? (See also Survey 1, F.)

E. What proportion of the faculty members who have taught you during the past year would you say are superior teachers? (See also Survey 1, G.)

F. What proportion of the faculty members that you have observed would you say are genuinely interested in students and their problems? (See also Survey 1, H.)

____ G. Beyond your role as student, how many faculty members of this college respond to you as a person and show a personal interest in you? (See also Survey 1, I.)

____ H. In your dealings with members of the college administration and staff, have you been made to feel that they have an interest in you as a person? (1, J.)

____ I. During the last academic term, how much time per week, on the average, have you devoted to activities directly related to your program of studies (include class and laboratory time, reading, papers, problem sets, field or studio work, etc.)? (1, K.)

____ J. During the last academic term, how much time per week, on the average, have you devoted to activities that you have pursued with some degree of regularity and commitment (e.g., organized extracurricular or community activities, personal projects such as writing, music, personal exercises, etc.)? (1, L.)

____ K. Have you been employed for wages or in a work-study (bursary) program during the last academic term? (1, M.)

____ L. Which of the following statements best describes your relationships with other students during the last academic term? They have been: (1, N.)

____ M. How many close friends do you have among the students of this college? (1, O.)

____ N. What kind of social relationships and opportunities do your living arrangements provide? (1, Q.)

____ O. Generally speaking, how do you feel about competing with other people for grades or for academic recognition? (1, R.)

____ P. How important is it to you that you obtain a college degree? (1, T.)

____ Q. After obtaining your bachelor's degree, do you expect to continue your education in a graduate or a professional school? (1, U.)

____ R. How important is it to your parents that you obtain a college degree? (1, V.)

190

_____ S. How important is it to your parents that you graduate from this particular college? (Also see Survey 1, W.)

_____ T. In thinking about your occupational future, do you feel that in the long run you will have a preference for: (1, X.)

_____ U. Judging by the amount of time, effort and attention that you have given to each during the last academic term, what relative degree of importance have you assigned to the activities listed below? . . . (1, Y.)

_____ V. Rate the degree of difficulty that you have experienced in each of the following problem areas during the last academic term. (1, Z.)

_____ W. Please rate your degree of satisfaction with EACH of the following aspects of college life as you have experienced them during the past academic term. (1, AA.)

_____ X. From the list that follows, select the FIVE adjectives or phrases that in your judgment describe most accurately the atmosphere of this college as you have experienced it in your associations and relationships of the past year. . . . (1, BB.)

Use this space for any additional information or comments that might represent your situation or attitudes more accurately and completely than the items of the survey gave opportunity to express.

"LEAVE-TAKING" SURVEY 5

Greetings: Six New England colleges and universities, Brown, Hampshire, Trinity, Tufts, Wesleyan and Wheaton currently are engaged in a cooperative investigation of leave-taking. The research is designed to determine the characteristics of students who go on leaves, why leaves are taken, and what benefits and difficulties are experienced. One objective of the study is to determine what proportion of leave-takers eventually return to their college, what percentage transfer to another institution, and how many do not continue in any program of higher education.

It is our understanding that you took a leave from your college and that to this time you have not reregistered there as a student in residence. If this indeed is the case, we request your cooperation in completing and returning this brief questionnaire. The short-answer portion will require just a few minutes to complete. If you wish to describe the circumstances of your leave in greater detail, we would be most interested in your observations and comments. You may be assured of responsible, confidential treatment of all information that you furnish.

Definition of "Leave": For the purposes of this survey, we use the term "leave" to refer to that period of time in which a person is involved in activities other than those of a full-time student enroled in a program of academic studies at the main campus of the institution from which the person expects to receive a degree.

Instructions: Except for those items in which other instructions are given, write the number of the alternative that you select in the appropriate space in the left-hand margin. Work quickly, your first reaction to the question is generally a good one to record. Thank you for your participation.

(C. Hess Haagen)
Project Coordinator

_____ A. Originally, how long did you expect to be away from the institution from which you took "leave"?
    1. One semester or academic term
    2. Two semesters or academic terms
    3. Three semesters or academic terms
    4. Four or more semesters or academic terms
    5. Duration of leave was uncertain
    6. Did not intend to return

_____ B. Is it your intention eventually to return to the institution from which you took leave?
    1. Yes
        Estimate date of return: _____
    2. No. Will complete work at another institution
    3. No. Do not plan to take an undergraduate degree

C. Reasons for extending leave: The timing of an individual's leave reflects highly individual and personal considerations. The following are some broad categories of reasons that students have given for extending their leaves. Please indicate the importance to you of EACH reason by writing the code number of the statement that best describes your situation. Add any reasons that are important in your case but which are not included in the list which follows:

Code for Degree of Importance
1. One of the most important or compelling reasons for extending my leave
2. An important, although not decisive consideration in extending my leave
3. A minor consideration that may have influenced my decision in limited or peripheral ways
4. Did not influence my decision, although it may be present in my personal situation
5. Does not apply in my case.

a. Psychologically not ready to resume studies
b. Need more time for current interests and activities
c. Obligations to and/or relationships with others (e.g. parents, husband, wife, employer, friend, etc.)
d. Financial considerations
e. Medical, health reasons
f. College from which I took leave does not meet my educational-academic needs
g. Dissatisfactions with the college from which I took leave have not been resolved or remedied
h. Have discovered alternatives to returning that are more attractive or better suited to my requirements
i. Other: Please describe _____

D. How have you spent your time since beginning your leave? For EACH activity listed below, record the code number of the statement that indicates most accurately the amount of time that you have devoted to it. If your activities have been very different at different time periods, indicate this by recording activity codes for each time period that you list. If essentially the same throughout your leave, use 1st column only.

193

Code for Amount of time
1. Major amount of time; principal activity
2. Substantial amount of time
3. Moderate amount of time
4. Limited amount of time
5. Little or no time devoted to this activity

Time Periods During Leave
1st   2nd   3rd   4th

____ ____ ____ ____   a. Formal academic work

____ ____ ____ ____   b. Individual study, reading, research, field work, studio work, writing, etc.

____ ____ ____ ____   c. Volunteer social service, political activity, community action, etc.

____ ____ ____ ____   d. Employment

____ ____ ____ ____   e. Travel

____ ____ ____ ____   f. Recreational, social activities

____ ____ ____ ____   g. Personal, family matters

____ ____ ____ ____   h. Medical, psychiatric treatment, convalescence, etc.

____ ____ ____ ____   i. Other: please describe _____

Record the duration of each time period that is reported.

The following information is needed to provide categories for statistical analysis:

E. Sex: 1. Female   2. Male

F. From what kind of secondary school did you graduate?   1. Public   2. Private

____ G. Field of your declared or intended undergraduate major or concentration:
1. Performing arts (e.g., art, music, theater arts, dance, etc.)
2. Ancient, modern languages and literatures, including English, linguistics, comparative literature
3. History, Area Studies (e.g., American, Latin-American, European, African, Far Eastern)
4. Philosophy, Religion
5. Social Science (e.g., Economic, Government, Sociology, Urban Studies, International Affairs)
6. Behavioral Science (e.g., Anthropology, Psychology, etc.)
7. Mathematics
8. Biological and Physical Sciences
9. Undecided

____ H. How many semesters or academic terms had you completed before taking this leave?

____ I. Record the beginning date of your leave (month and year)

____ J. Since going on leave, have you applied to any other college or university for acceptance as a degree candidate? (i.e., as a transfer student with advanced standing)
1. No   2. Yes   If yes, name of school(s) _____

Observations, comments, explanations, queries:

Append additional pages if needed. Return in self-addressed envelope to Wesleyan University, Office of Institutional Research, Middletown, CT. 06457. Thank you.

Collating Number: _____ This number will be used to correlate your answers with other elements of the research project. It will NOT be used to associate your name with any of your responses.

APPENDIX II

Student Protocols

On each of the Surveys, respondents were invited to make any comments about their leaves that they were willing to share. Topics of particular relevance to the study were listed. The "open-ended" questions of Survey 1 are reproduced in appendix I, page 166, Survey 2 on page 180 and Survey 3, page 184.

One thousand three hundred and twenty-five of the persons who returned Survey 1 wrote additional comments, 1,045 respondents wrote additional comments on Survey 2 and 552 on Survey 3. From these records we have selected for quotation statements that illustrate the range of activities in which leave-takers engaged and their attitudes toward leave-taking as an important option in higher education. When available, we have selected those statements which provide a fuller evaluation of the personal and academic consequences of the leave.

The statements are reproduced as they were written except for the deletion of names that would be identifying, the addition of words or phrases when required to clarify meaning or reference, and the omission of material that is repetitive in those cases in which responses to two or three surveys are available. Some persons responded briefly, in outline form or in telegraphic style. Others wrote at considerable length. The Survey that is being quoted is always identified: 1, 2, or 3. The number of the topic is listed as a subscript only in those cases in which this identification seems necessary for an understanding of the statement. For easier reference, statements are grouped according to principal leave activity.

MEDICAL - HEALTH CARE

1. Male - Employed: Small Country Hospital in Appalachia - One Year

1: 1_1. My objectives have been reasonably identified in the multiple choice section of this survey. To expound upon those; (a) to gain experience in the field away from the "ivory-tower," so to speak, (b) to gain insight into whether my educational direction is, in fact, consistent with what I would like to devote my life to, (c) to have time to think through alternatives, (d) to not allow my college years to slip by without a more complete perspective of interests and direction.

1_2. My plans are to go to Tennessee to work in a small Appalachian country hospital and to do a doctor's aid position with a new country physician. My career interest is medicine; hopefully the experience close to a medical practice will furnish a more accurate image of what the field of medical practice can, in fact, be like.

1_3. No organization was consulted regarding my decision to take a leave, nor arranging my activities during that period of time. Close friends gave advice; mostly it was personal initiative. One physician, a friend for some time, was instrumental in arranging an interview with a colleague who will be taking me on as an aide in Tennessee.

1_4. Perhaps, counselling was and is readily available for those who do need it. I think concentration advisors should be consulted if leaves are for pursuit of academic related purposes; perhaps suggestions from these advisors could provide viable options for activities during the leave period. Perhaps concentration advisors could be so informed to deal with students in this regard.

1_5. The lack of "red tape" involved in taking a leave from the institution I attend was greatly appreciated. This is the way, I believe, it should be.

2: During my year of leave I was situated in a small Appalachian Mountain community in upper Tennessee, employed simultaneously at a small country hospital and at a two physician clinic. At the hospital my position was that of an orderly-nurse's aid. At the clinic my duties were varied, from nurse, dispenser of pills and medicine, receptionist, insurance clerk, technician, and so on. I worked closely under one physician who provided a vivid picture of medicine from the standpoint of the doctor. Both physicians were extremely helpful, informative, and patient, explaining medical procedures, modes of thought on patient encounters, drugs and therapies and many other aspects of medicine that I would confront in pursuing a career in the field. I was afforded a good deal of responsibilities at the clinic for one of my academic and medical training, due to the dearth of qualified medical personnel in the isolated rural mountain community. In terms of assessing the value of my leave, I just cannot imagine a more full or rewarding experience. My exposure to medicine was fantastic which has been of enormous importance in determining and finalizing my desire to pursue a doctorate in medicine. In terms of personal development, I feel that my experience has fostered a more realistic approach and appraisal of my life in relation to confidence in social interactions, academic relevancy and direction, and career aspirations. So basically I am eagerly anticipating resuming academics with some sort of unprecedented lucidity and perspective.

Concerning whether academic institutions should encourage leave-taking, I would recommend a more definitive stand in favor of such a practice as a viable and integral part of one's education. The added perspective away from the ivory tower of academia would be justification enough to warrant a policy of active encouragement rather than the passive sort that institutions seem to adopt toward leaves. Ultimately I hope such a policy will be instituted for I assume I am not alone in saying that a leave could be a pleasurable and enlightening period of development.

3: The task of writing about my leave from academia seems at this point to be a large undertaking due mostly to the feeling that it was probably the most enlightening experience in some time. At the risk of sounding rather trite, I believe I could say, in comparison, my years at college have not been nearly as rewarding. On campus there is a propensity toward intellectual seclusion from events in the real world. For myself, I choose not to rush through four straight years of college without a definitive direction. Two years of college studies left me rather confused. I needed time to sort and integrate things. My activities on leave were guided by a desire to stick my nose, so to speak, into the field that tentatively I had chosen, namely medicine. To say the very least, I found it stimulating and challenging. In returning to academia, there is no question in my mind that I have developed a more positive attitude toward my studies. It seems to be a case of knowledge of the end, being a physician, justifying the means, difficult and at times seemingly irrelevant pre-med work, etc. No serious problems have arisen. For me there have been no significant disadvantages.

2. Male - Employed: University of Connecticut Health Center,
   Computer Assisted Instruction - One Semester

1: I want to get an idea of what it's like to be a part of the real world, dealing with people, and the stresses of the outside. I also will get a tremendous opportunity to work in my field, medicine, which college doesn't supply.

2: I spent my leave working full time at the University of Connecticut Health Center. In addition, I spent a significant amount of time visiting clinics and taking medical school courses. In the very least, I learned something about my capabilities due to the leave. I learned that I could adapt to a heavy pressure environment and that I could hack medical school, an important confidence builder since I am a pre-med. The clinical experience just reinforced my belief that I do want to be a physician. The greatest thing I found was that I could be mentally stimulated, something college has not done for me, and when motivated by this stimulant I can conquer any problem put before me. My work involved Computer Assisted Instruction, a new field. My exposure here has given me insight in what the term expert means. Essentially, beneath the role of expert, (or even doctor), is just another person, who likes to joke, laugh, cry and who makes mistakes. I know now that I can remain "human" and still do my job as a professional.

3. Female - Employed: Physical Therapy Aide, Massachusetts Rehabilitation Hospital, Boston - One Semester

1: To do a lot of reading I couldn't do in college. Figure out what I want to concentrate in. Working and living in Cambridge, Massachusetts and taking a dance course. Leaving myself time to read and enjoy doing certain things.

2: I was a physical therapy aide in the Massachusetts Rehabilitation Hospital in Boston. I was there for six months. During this time I was trained, as I had no experience in the field. I was very much on my own in my treatment of patients. I learned a lot about this field just from listening to the nurses and doctors. I also attended weekly classes (for the aides) and many lectures and movies about strokes, different diseases, etc. I enjoy working in a hospital -- my relationships with my patients (and co-workers) were very important to me. I made many good friends, I was exposed to many things -- terrible things -- that saddened me and disgusted me, i.e., quadruplegic adolescents, double amputees, people with active minds who couldn't express themselves. My patients' rehabilitations, though, were enough to make the work experience positive. Nothing made me happier than to finally see one of my patients walking without my assistance.

The Institute for Off-Campus Experience got me this job. I am indebted to them forever. Not only did I make good money ($105 for a 35 hour week), but I learned so much about medicine, the sick, the dying, and the rehabilitation experience. I do not plan to become a physical therapist, but my dealings with the social workers and psychologists have inspired me to go into the field of rehabilitation counseling.

3: My leave contributed to personal development in several ways -- I grew from looking for a job and not being able to find one for quite awhile, from living on my own in a city (Cambridge, Massachusetts), and from being a member of the working class and not that of the elite student from a private college. The job I found as a physical therapy aide had nothing to do with my major in psychology, but I was exposed to different roles and areas psychology can play in a hospital setting. My education is now towards psychology and mental health of physically disabled people as a direct result of my work experience while on leave. I have not been handicapped at all for my leave. I had no problem returning from my leave. I'm not sure there is any necessary role for the college to take.

4. Male - Employed: Orderly, Inner City Hospital - One Year

2: I would describe my period of absence from college as having two purposes: (a) clarification of academic and career aims and (b) social adjustment.

Due to the fact that I was very unsure of my pre-med major, I chose to work in an inner city hospital in order to view all aspects of the medical profession. After working there for one year, I decided that the medical profession was not for me. In addition to helping me make this important decision, I believe that an even greater benefit was derived by simply being part of the workaday world, learning where the average person puts emphasis on which values, what things are really important in life. This was invaluable. As far as social adjustment goes, I was hoping that being out of school would spur me to make more meaningful social contacts. This did not prove to be the case, and I led a rather insular life.

Therefore, my advice to students thinking about taking time off would be: If you are unsure of your academic or career goals, take some time off, and get out there in the "real" world and work! It really helps you put things in perspective. BUT, if you are having trouble feeling comfortable in a social setting, stay in school. The opportunity for contact and understanding is far greater in school. Finally, I think it should be emphasized that freshman year should be a time of unpressured exploration. Career aims and academic commitments should not be worried about at this time. School is a place to learn and grow.

5. Female - Employed: Hematology Technician - One Semester

1: Mostly my leave came about because I was frustrated by my lack of achievement and growing disenchantment with my own capabilities. I need to know my desires and objectives more clearly and realize a better focused motivation toward them. I need to have time to live and make decisions without pressure of classwork and the academic timetable.

2: During leave I worked as a Hematology Technician - related to my pre-med studies. The experience was stimulating and enjoyable intellectually and personally with much patient contact. I needed time away from school. I find the same problems upon my return to school as before, though I've more energy to deal with them. I don't enjoy my University but was unsuccessful at transfer, so I plan to finish up at my original school. I don't like the atmosphere (pseudo-intellectual, unfriendly tunnel-visioned students) and just feel like I don't belong. I can immerse myself in my studies, though, to successfully finish my B.S. and hopefully choose a more successful pathway from that point on.

3: My leave allowed time away from a program in which I was miserable and underachieving. This time away gave me a better look at myself. I gained back some self-confidence, reasoned out why I was unhappy at this school, and decided what some essentials of my life were. I think I gained in every way except longer time now to finish. I don't think the University could have done much. I would have found administration concern too stilted. I found "friends" amongst the faculty who performed the capacity of advising and supporting me.

RESEARCH

6. Female - Employed: Research Assistant in Bacteriology and Chemistry - One Year

1: I want to learn to relax, how to accept my feelings and emotions as something valid and positive, have a little time away from academics to look objectively at what it is I really want to accomplish in college and gain some practical experience in the field I think I'm interested in. I will be working in a research position in bacteriology and chemistry for the National Marine Fisheries Service in Gloucester, Massachusetts. I just want to live a quiet, normal, realistic life for a while. Probably the two most influential factors in my decision to take a leave were several friends who had previously taken time off and my Dean, who is a most understanding and wonderful advisor. I feel that my leave is coming at just the right time. My two previous years of college were necessary to introduce me to many of my own latent thoughts, but now I feel that I need some time away from college.

2: Taking time off from college was the best thing I have ever done in my whole life. I didn't leave with the expectation of "finding myself" or getting any definite answers as to what I wanted to "do" with my life. I just wanted to live outside of academics for awhile, to see what the real world was like and to get some practical experience in my field, biology and chemistry. I was tired of living the safe, protected life of a student. I worked in a technology laboratory doing research in chemistry and bacteriology. I had to learn, as a woman, to deal with middle aged white men and their perception of me and my capabilities. I had to struggle often, but gained confidence in myself and my capabilities in the sciences. That is probably one of the most important happenings during my leave. I also did many things that I never had time to do because I always had to work at strict academics. I joined a modern dance troupe, a children's theatre, learned to play the guitar and in general had the best times of my life. I met many wonderful people and could relax and be myself because I didn't have to worry about ridiculous, frantic academic pressure. Academe is often inflated with its own self-importance. I am having somewhat of a hard time readjusting to institution life, but I am determined to get a college degree and will probably get another advanced degree.

7. Female - Employed: Developmental Psychological Research - One Semester

2: I did a field study in cognitive develop research, co-designing and carrying out an experiment on the non-egocentricity of preschoolers communicative competence. It was a great learning experience for psychological methodology. Also, I gained real insight on the actualities of researchers of big names.

Difficulties I encountered were not having enough guidance and disagreeing with my supervisor when we did get down to work together. I greatly appreciate the experience I had living alone with myself and living in New York City for a limited period of time. Returning to school I had a hard time getting back into a rhythm of studying. I'm not sure if this was because of returning from leave or because the field of my investigation is hard to define and developing a program of specific relevant things to read and write is difficult.

3: Actually now that I think about it, the leave experience was well worthwhile for my studies (research apprentice in cognitive development), but perhaps it was ill timed. I feel I've gained a lot methodologically in experimental developmental psychology but have missed out on the theoretical, which I could have gotten from courses. Also taking leave hampered even more the little academic advising I was getting at college.

8. Female - Employed: Psychological Research, Head Start Center in New York City - One Semester

1: I will be doing field research for my final major course work. I hope to gain from interacting with people in a graduate research university and with people in the field of education -- to gain in ways not possible in a classroom or seminar. I will be doing educational/psychological research at a university in New York City and will work with teachers, parents and children in Harlem and with four black psychologists doing related research. The college is very supportive and helpful to students interested in off-campus experiences. It is dependent on the student taking the initiative to explore and make known his interests and needs, but then the resources of people and programs get discovered and possibilities seem endless.

2: I worked with a group of five black and two white psychologists who are concerned with issues of culture, education and the development of cognitive processes, with a particular focus on the problems faced by the Black Child in school. Psychological research on language and memory was being carried out with black children to adults in different school/social settings; I was responsible for the research with preschool children inside and outside of school. I designed and evolved a procedure to study language and memory in a formal and informal situation, I transcribed hours of tapes, analyzed the data into quantitative units, applied statistical correlations and am now writing up the research project formally.

This experience was invaluable to me in every way. I gained insights into many aspects of experimental psychology, learned how to work out procedural problems that arose day to day, and in working with the other researchers and with the teachers and children in Harlem, I learned a lot about how to establish relationships of respect and trust through a process of mutual learning and sharing as we worked together to understand how the children learn, and what one could do to best facilitate their learning.

EDUCATION

9. Female - Employed: Teacher's Aide, Title I - One Semester

2: I worked as a teacher's aide under a Title I program at Somerville high school (outside Boston). My job was to tutor students with learning disabilities. I lived in Somerville while I was working there and I think that that made the experience more meaningful than it might otherwise have been. I got to know many of the students well, and developed good relationships with them. My position did not involve as much responsibility as I would have liked, but I did feel that I had the respect of the students, which was what I cared about most.

Probably the most significant part of my experience was that I was closely involved with people very different from myself in terms of background but especially in terms of values. It was definitely a challenge and I think the most rewarding aspect of my job was being able to establish communication on a common level that certainly existed but that might not have been readily apparent. By the end of the semester I felt very comfortable with all the students, although I think there was still some amount of tension with the administration and some of the teachers. Because of this there were times when I occasionally felt resented or out of place.

The other thing that I found invaluable was getting away from my own academic world and being able to live independently, organizing my own life and my free time. I think there are times when college life and academics can become a crutch, and it felt satisfying to be able to get along well, if not better, without it. The main drawback was that I found it hard to meet people without the aid of a college environment, but I think that might have been inevitable because of the limited amount of time I spent there.

10. Female - Employed: Transitional Aide, Elementary School - One Semester

1: I want to experience many of the realities that are never learned in college, not even during "observation" phases of education classes. I also want to help at home, to rest and to give myself perspective to view my college career. Mainly, to step off the treadmill. My college seems to have a very unbending stance, under a thin veneer of innovation. Innovative programs here often demand more work, they ask that you "prove your commitment" more than regular courses. I've found less ideal learning or learning for knowledge's sake, rather than requirements, here than in high school. I was very upset to find many college decisions bureaucratic and pragmatic. My high school perhaps led me to expect too much.

2: During my leave I worked as a transitional aide, in a Roxbury elementary school effected by busing. I was responsible for discipline within the school and also schedule, personal problems with the students. Because of my education major I expanded this to include working with a reading group and tutoring some slower students. I also counselled high school students in a part-time job. As an education major it was an invaluable look at the system from the inside.

My major difficulty was in accepting all the structure within the Boston Public School system. It was disappointing occasionally because I saw students with glaring educational disabilities whose problems were not being met. I also realized that many education courses at my school were esoteric and not going to prepare me for the reality of urban teaching. This just reinforced my feeling that my college was basically a middle-upper class oriented school, very caught up in its image. This university, in my opinion, encourages isolationism and has little or no commitment to life outside.

3: Reasons for my leave were largely financial, I worked in a school, closely related to my education major. It convinced me that I had chosen the right field and helped me to continue with my goals. I will probably graduate late due to my leave and other mistakes (academic) I have made. I also feel more alienated (if it's possible) towards the school than I did before I left. Quite often I feel as if I were visiting. As I did not plan to take my leave until conditions forced it, it is hard for me to say whether there are ways in which the college could have been more helpful. I would have appreciated having someone (administration) to keep in touch with to advise me. Unlike the condoned "Venture Program" I was not made aware of options. Due to my lack of knowledge about protocol, I received no credit for my leave although I worked in a school.

SOCIAL SERVICE

11. Female - Employed: Community Organizer - One Year

1: 1_1. Wider experience, especially in areas more relevant to living in present day society. Growth. Gain more definite knowledge of direction "career-wise." Clearer idea of what I want educationally.

1_2. Working as a community organizer -- gaining experience in dealing with people, political experience, dealing with people from different backgrounds, constructive approach to socio-economic problems of inner-city. Experience in the working world. Wider, different experience -- knowledge of choices.

2: Worked for seven months as community organizer in small Italian neighborhood. Beneficial experience with cities, city neighborhoods, ethnic neighborhood, city covernment, working class people, approaches to problems created when all these interact. Satisfied a need to see/experience the "real" world and deal with its problems. Good personal experience in realizing my politics, limits to my dedication to reform, my ability to get beyond my socio-economic background and deal with people from different backgrounds.

Disappointed when my dedication petered out after seven months of long hours, tough work, and limited social life. Disappointed in myself that, what people described as my "radical phase," did turn out to be only a phase. (I think primarily because of the concentrated effort and stamina required not because of a change in my desire to see things change.) I also hoped a leave of absence would help me formulate a career goal but it only helped me realize that I don't want to organize.

3: During my leave, I worked as a community organizer in a working-class Italian neighborhood. Two things about this I think really contributed to a greater maturity, a greater self-confidence and self-reliance and a greater sensitivity in myself. One was just the fact of working hard, for a long period, for long hours, and for little pay. Summer jobs I've never taken very seriously and they only last three months anyway. The second factor was working and living with people who have different lives, backgrounds, experiences than myself. After spending years going to school with people of basically the same economic and social background, working and living in an ethnic working class neighborhood was an eye-opener and also refreshing in a way. It made it difficult to come back to a situation that seems unreal and ivory-towered at times.

The experience has helped in classes, particularly political science and urban studies courses, because I have something concrete to draw on. I know now that I want an education on my own terms. Sometimes course content makes no sense, becomes too distant, and I wonder if it's realistic to expect students to grasp and understand things when they have so little experience with which to personalize concepts, ideas, etc.

12. Male - Employed: Human Resources Center, University of Pennsylvania - One Year

2: I worked full time at the Human Resources Center, University of Pennsylvania, Philadelphia and lived in another part of the city. I was part of the professional staff there and worked on several projects ranging from the production of a book by the Director of my involvement in a program designed to alleviate some racial problems at a Philadelphia suburban school. I sought this employment because of my developing interest in Urban Affairs (changed from pre-med to urban studies prior to leaving) and because of the opportunities available at a large urban university. I was able to communicate with many of the leaders in some of the fields that I thought I might be interested in and find out what they were up to. Plus my living arrangements afforded me the opportunity to have to set up some kind of inner city housing where I'd have to do things myself or they wouldn't get done. I lived in a not very fashionable part of town and was able to experience a type of existance that my suburban upbringing had not exposed me to. Other than some slow stretches on the job, I had no major disappointments. My college was encouraging and made things easy and was helpful as much as they could be.

3: Taking a leave of absence has been the best thing that has happened to me as far as my intellectual, academic, personal development is concerned. My first two years were spent floundering in pre-med and I took the leave to explore my interests -- Urban Studies -- which were greatly fostered and expanded during my leave. As I spent the year with graduate school professors, I was introduced to many concepts I would not have normally come in contact with for several years (if at all) and they gave me a greater appreciation for my previous work and helped develop in me a philosophy -- an outlook, perspective -- which I have taken with me back to school and applied -- if grades are any indication -- with some success.

I feel I'm more mature in my approach to my work and as my interests have become defined, more serious in trying to produce significant results. I am more critical of my own work and have much higher standards than two years ago. In short, my time off increased my knowledge and my ability to work and made me ready and willing to continue my work. The whole experience was very beneficial, and in no way damaging. Fortunately my courses (upon my return) stressed individual projects and I had much opportunity to apply and expand my off-campus work..

The student has got to want to come back him- (her-) self and realize that a lot of things -- especially some of the drudgery -- remain the same and have to be put up with. With luck, the leave should make you ready to want to continue your studies. I found that most of my teachers were interested in my time off, and they encouraged me to follow-up on what I had gained from it, which was quite helpful. Having so much work to do that I had no time to sulk or complain was good for me but I don't know how useful it would be for others. Coming back is, in someways, starting again. You've got to get busy doing things and try to relax and enjoy yourself. Take a course that is a bit far out but one that you've always wanted to. You've got to explore possibilities and commit yourself to what you're doing. The college can be sympathetic and encouraging, but the student has got to want to do it.

13. Female - Employed: Emergency Financial Assistance Program, Syracuse, New York - One Year

2: Tutored eight girls in math, science, social studies. Lived in a house with them and a resident family and communally we ran the house. I also cooked meals for the fourteen of us for about six months. At the Social Service Agency I worked for the Emergency Financial Assistance Program in Syracuse, New York (PEACE, Inc.). I interviewed clients and had the power to decide whether they should receive a voucher for food, housing, clothing, etc. We were a referral agency and so I had to learn a lot about the other agencies in the city. Worked on project HEAT - which meant I negotiated with credit managers at Niagara Mohawk to stop people from getting their heat turned off or by allotting them $50 from PEACE to apply to their bill. Also did some money-management counselling.

I felt the tutoring was extremely valuable in that I built up some very strong relationships with the girls, and I think I also helped the program run fairly smoothly in its first year. It gave me a different view of the school system and an interesting view of suburbia and minorities from a low socio-economic status. The experience reinforced my ideas of going into education, and further confirmed my feelings of how drastically the schools have to be changed. My work at PEACE made me realize that I was capable of making consequential decisions (something I never have felt in my educational career). It made me realize the need for more programs for the poor. It helped me break down stereotypes I had, coming from a small all-white town. I also built some very strong relationships there. Much of my work was difficult though I really enjoyed the challenge. I think my biggest disappointment was having to leave.

3: My experiences while on leave involved mainly working with adolescent girls aged 15 and 16, disadvantaged economically. They were away from home in a house in a suburb where we all lived as a "family." I was a tutor and counselor to them. I also worked in a social service agency during the day, interviewing people who needed emergency food help.

I feel the experiences added to my personal development in that it gave me time to do what I wanted to do, and pursue reading I wanted to do in a more relaxed manner. I gained much confidence in myself because I did very well in both my jobs and enjoyed the challenges they offered me. My work convinced me of the need for a college education and I have been very motivated in my school work this year. My self-confidence has shown through in my work and I find myself much less pressured, and my work more enjoyable. One of the purposes of my leave was to get away from school -- there is nothing the school could have done that would have effected me either way, I don't think.

14. Male - Employed: Community Organizer in Atlanta, Georgia - One Semester

1: An opportunity to experience something new. I will be working at a settlement house in a black ghetto in Atlanta. I also hope to work on a ranch and perhaps bike cross-country before returning to school.

3: On my return to school this past September I found myself frightened and overwhelmed by the atmosphere of academia. Everything was so forced; school work, relationships, classroom discussions. Nothing and nobody was relaxed. I tried to rationalize my reasons for having returned but it all came down to the same thing -- that degree was going to be a necessity. And so I threw myself into my work full steam.

My experience while on leave was a turning point in my life -- because of its importance to me I could not and would not begin to describe my experience here. Suffice it to say that I was involved in community organizing in Atlanta, Georgia. The college could not have done anything to facilitate my return, but -- quite frankly -- there was only but one teacher who expressed any interest in my work and experience in Atlanta. It was upsetting to find all these teachers well -- so uncaring. It was as if the only meaningful education one could receive is that in the classroom and we all know (don't we?) what bullshit that is.

So now where am I? Back in school, taking an unbelievable course load so that I may graduate with my class, escaping into my books and playing with the kids in the neighborhood. Three more semesters and I'm restless, itch'n for adventure -- and I'm stuck. Stuck in a little utopia where I keep on futilely clawing to escape.

15. Male - Employed: Child Care Worker, School for Delinquents - One Year

2: During my leave from school I worked as a Child Care Worker at a school for delinquents in Cincinnati, Ohio. I was responsible for the running of one particular cottage on the school grounds. I value this experience quite a bit. I was considering a major in juvenile corrections but I was not sure that I wanted to and this working experience helped to confirm my interest. I enjoyed the kids very much and the work was something that I would very much like to be doing right now while pursuing my academic studies. Working with the kids helped me to discover some very important things about myself and they became very important to me.

The difficulties and disappointments that I received concerned the rehabilitation that I was supposed to be giving to the kids. I had quite a few kids and simply not enough time to devote to all of my kids. Some of them got out of the institution and continued in their same delinquent pattern and I experienced quite a few disappointments thinking that I might have been able to help them. These difficulties and disappointments are job related and will probably always exist.

I don't think that there is anything that I could have done to make my leave more productive. It turned out to be much more than I ever imagined it could be. It was so attractive to me that I almost didn't make it back to college. The school could have made some arrangements for me to do some independent study projects while on leave that would have helped to further my education. In spite of this I enjoyed my leave tremendously and I am glad that I had the opportunity to do it.

GOVERNMENT - POLITICAL

16. Male - Employed: Several Governmental Internships and Positions in Political Campaigns - One Semester

1: In the winter study period 1970 I worked in Washington for my congressman and in January 1971 I worked in the State House. In the fall of 1972 I took a leave to work on the campaign staff of Senator McGovern. On my present leave I will work for Senator Gary Hart of Colorado and for the Democratic National Committee at the Party Conference in Kansas City.

3: My major is political science, and I have a deep interest in government and politics. I have taken two "leaves." I should like to point out that I have not had academic problems. I have taken "leaves" because my political science courses have not satisfied my interests and career goals. My leaves provided experience in political campaigns and government work. They were important to my personal development. Combining "leaves" with my regular education made my college experience more relevant.

I do not feel handicapped for having taken a "leave." Upon returning I perhaps felt a little out of touch -- at first. Semester "leaves" and on-campus internships can be an important part of a college education. They provide experience in the real world which the classroom cannot. I have been active in Massachusetts government and politics for years and so I am able to set up my leaves myself. But I know many people who wanted to do what I did but didn't know how to set it up. There should be a college office to help people with "leaves" and internships for course credit. Not everyone is suited for a "leave," but almost everyone could benefit from an internship in their field.

17. Female - Employed: Intern, Environmental Lobbying Group, Washington, D.C. - One Semester

2: I worked at an Environmental Lobbying Group in Washington, D.C. Environmental Action is a very small (staff of eight) non-profit organization that was born after Earth Day, 1970, since then, the group has developed a strong reputation for being the leaders in several environmental legislation fights on the national level. The job of college intern is informal, and unstructured. My situation was peculiar, because the staff person with whom I was to work quit three weeks into the semester. I had chosen a special field of interest and began to study corporate agriculture, and the effects of agricultural business, energy in agriculture, and the mono-operation of the food industry "independently."

Perhaps I "wasted" a lot of time groping around for my niche, but once I found it I really fell into place. The greatest satisfaction of the job was in my own ability to independently find the critical issues within the "corporate agriculture" question, and work on the legislation that pertained to the issue. I was able to combine academic research with practical application of the knowledge to the legislative process.

It was especially hard, though, to continually be "alone" with my work. No one was around to explain the next step, and my organizing efforts probably suffered because of inexperience. But, in this way I found the most effective method of organizing consumer, environmental groups and the like and got experience "lobbying."

Washington is a unique environment, of course, especially well suited to someone with political interests. Working in a non-government group, I think, is just as "revealing" of the legislative process as working inside the government. I've done both and felt much less stiffled at Environment Action. I enjoyed my leave very much.

18. Female - Employed: Office of Neighborhood Government, New York City - One Semester

3: My leave was spent working as a coordinator of two district service cabinets in the Office of Neighborhood Government, Mayor's Office (Lindsay), New York City. The job gave me a great ego boost -- I left feeling I was more than competent as an organizer, administrator, problem solver person. I related well with most everyone I came in contact with. Hence, personally I had the sense I could "make it" in the "real world" -- earn enough money to support myself as well as doing a job that gave me and others satisfaction.

Now that I'm back at school I have thought a lot about going into public administration -- hence the job gave me a focus. However, the most important aspect of my leave was my own feeling of confidence and competence. In addition, my own studies became focused around the questions my job raised concerning decentralization, power, and making government more responsive. I'm now getting the theoretical base from which I can more easily evaluate my field work.

After my job I tried to write an analysis of my experience. Unfortunately, I lacked the necessary reading from which I could create a framework. I'm now getting that base. It might have been more valuable to have done the reading first. But I didn't. My studies, though, since my return, have been more fruitful and stimulating. And I feel I can be more critical of the authors' opinions. The leave was successful from any perspective.

Living off campus, upon return was absolutely necessary for maintaining my sanity as a student. Returning to school wasn't extraordinarily difficult -- except that I had to reorient myself from a pragmatic approach to a very abstract thought process. This took several months to accomplish. But this semester (second since return) has been more valuable!!! The college couldn't have quickened this judgment process, however, digesting the experience with professors who were familiar with city problems would have been a good thing to do.

19. Female - Employed: Congressional Intern - One Semester

1: I wanted some time away from school to decide what type of career I wanted, to see if I really wanted to get involved in government. I will be working on the staff of Representative Toby Moffett in Washington, D.C. It will give me a chance to work on a professional basis and hopefully will give me an accurate picture of a career on Capitol Hill. I basically did it by myself. My faculty advisor was very encouraging. There should be available somewhere a list of programs or suggestions -- perhaps an education-in-the-field coordinator.

Students should be <u>encouraged</u> to take leaves by giving them full credit for semesters spent away from school.

2: From January 1975 to August 1975, I was working in the Washington Office of the U.S. Representative Toby Moffett (Dem. - 6th, Connecticut). I was on a leave of absence from college during that time. My primary responsibilities were in the transportation area. In time, I became the person responsible for transportation in the office including the regional rail reorganization legislation. I also took care of transportation correspondance and acted as a liasion with local rail groups and the U.S. Railway Association. My other responsibilities included some press work, helping arrange a conference of freshmen members of Congress and monitoring various issues. The position was partially salaried. During the 75-76 school year, I hope to continue working with the local office of Rep. Moffett in conjunction with my thesis.

20. Female - Employed: Policy Advisor to High Elected Official - Currently on Leave

1: I want to find out whether I really need a college education in order to be productive in a challenging full-time job. I hope to find out what, if anything, I am missing in the way of social, intellectual, or academic background. Also, how will other people evaluate my experiences if they're not documented by a diploma? I have been working as a Policy Advisor to a high elected official. It is a full-time, challenging, yet frustrating position. Basically, I'm finding out what my limits are in terms of my capabilities and ability to deal with political and social situations.

No one could give me an unbiased viewpoint, and no one could help me put the decision into a more long-term framework. The university's interests are basically contrary to the notion that all of life is an education and they don't have a monopoly on learning. Although I feel that most of my academic work has been mediocre, it is usually highly rated by the university. I have rarely received constructive and/or extensive criticism. Opportunities outside the university are much more challenging, and people don't stand for any bullshit.

LAW

21. Female - Employed: Assistant in a Private Law Firm - One Semester

2: During my leave I worked in a law firm as an assistant to an attorney. My duties included everything from doing research and writing correspondence to secretarial work and running errands. My decision to take a leave was made more or less without forethought. When I took the job at the beginning of the summer I said that I would be able to stay for at least six months. I made that statement with the knowledge that it would be possible for me to take a leave of absence and still graduate on schedule the following June. I was not at all certain, however, that that is what I would do. I wanted to work in a private law firm, as I had already made the decision to study law and I wanted as much prior exposure to the field as possible. I had done several volunteer internships during my college years; including one with the Consumer Protection Division and one with a legal assistance project. I thought that a job with a private firm would be a good experience, as well as provide a good summer income.

At the end of the summer my employer told me that he realized that my education was my number one priority and that he would understand if I decided to leave. At that time I had made tentative plans with my school to take a leave. I decided to confirm those plans, to work full time through the semester, and to take two evening courses at another local university in order to be able to complete both of my majors. I made that decision because I was enjoying my job, learning a great deal, and wanted to earn as much money as possible.

Working in the firm gave me many valuable insights into the life of an attorney -- both on a professional and a social level. Although I already felt confident in my decision to pursue a career in law before I worked in the firm, my experiences there served to confirm and intensify my desire to study law. I was given a substantial amount of responsibility, was treated with respect, and allowed to do a good deal of work on my own. I found that my judgment was trusted and my opinions were sought. I also had the opportunity to improve my secretarial skills and to learn how to use a computerized typewriter, abilities on which I definitely place a positive value.

I did find it difficult to work all day and to attend classes and study at night. My schedule was very hectic and I had very little "free" time for social activities. I more or less felt, however, that I could survive the routine for the length of time I had undertaken it. The college had virtually nothing to do with my leave of absence and I do not know what role, if any, it could have or should have played. I do appreciate the fact that they made my taking a leave a relatively uncomplicated and easy procedure.

Being half in and half out of the academic community certainly had its effects. I found that although I missed being a full-time student and having the majority of my time available to put into my studies, I did not miss the academic environment. I think that this feeling evolved from being outside of that very secure world and into the real world of employment, and having the responsibility of an apartment, a car, and my own finances. I felt that, in a sense, I had already "graduated" and gone on to another stage, and that going back into the world of pure academia would be a regression.

I hasten to point out that it is not academia itself that I wished to avoid (for I was truly looking forward to full-time studies), but the academic environment which I found too care-free for my taste at this point in my life. (I might also add that before my leave I had thoroughly enjoyed this secure environment of relative carefreeness and no responsibility.) Now, although I appreciate the value of having had the opportunity to experience an academic environment and I think I will always look at those years as the best because of the above-mentioned characteristics, I feel that I have the responsibility of being a member of the "real" world, as well as of being as economically self-sufficient as a student can. For those reasons, this semester I am carrying a full course load and working part time (20 hours a week). I find it extremely difficult but not impossible. At this time I cannot imagine being a student and not work at least part time. However, my studies do have priority, and I would not jeopardize them for that concern.

22. Female - Employed: Intern, Boston Legal Assistance Project - One Semester

1: I hope to be able to obtain a better definition of my interests so that I will be able to return to college with more concrete ideas about what academic program to follow. I also see my leave as being a possible determinant in my decision concerning my career choice, or at least influencing graduate plans. I will be working for the Boston Legal Assistance Project in East Boston on a number of different projects. This experience will hopefully provide insight into the legal profession or some aspects of it. My reactions and the knowledge I will gain should influence my plans significantly upon returning to college in terms of the course of study I will pursue.

I feel that I did most of my own thinking and deciding, as no one was actively encouraging me. I was interviewed by the Massachusetts Internship Office in Boston who referred me to a few places, but it was my responsibility from there to call them and arrange interviews, etc. So actually I was almost my own coordinator, but not without some help and reassurance from the people at the college.

2: I went on leave to do an internship at the Boston Legal Assistance Project in East Boston because I was uncertain about my interest in legal studies. I arranged the internship independent of the college. The experience was both rewarding and disappointing. My supervisor was too busy to devote the time to me that I felt was necessary to make it a really educationally worthwhile experience. My activities included some pre-client interviewing work with the welfare department, errand running, researching of land titles and corporation deeds. I also went to court a few times to observe.

This experience was rewarding in that I got to work with people from different backgrounds and of different ages. I also learned what actually goes on in a legal aid office and something about what the life of this kind of lawyer is like. The disadvantages were that I was not given enough to do at times and at other times I was not told how to do whatever it was they wanted me to do (!). I was not getting paid, which was one of the primary reasons why I left my internship after two months to get a paying job.

COMMUNICATIONS - JOURNALISM

23. Female - Employed: Writer and Production Manager, Nationally Syndicated Magazine

2: During my leave I was production manager and author of a monthly column for WomenSports, a nationally syndicated magazine published by Billie Jean King, and I served as editor of TennisWomen, an official publication of the Women's Tennis Association. This was a most educational and enjoyable experience in terms of the material worked with, the people encountered and the opportunities for future employment. On the condition of dropping out of school, I was assured a permanent position with WomenSports in addition to being offered the position of production manager for San Francisco Magazine, but at this point in my life I felt it imperative to obtain a college degree.

I feel it is important to note that this was a totally self-initiated project and I am receiving no college credit for my work, thus, I am taking an overload of courses in order to graduate with my class. The time value of my semester off lies in the ability to evaluate my education with an increased awareness of the opportunities available.

24. Male - Employed: Printing, Publishing - Currently on Leave

1: I hope to gain some experience in printing and graphic design. I hope to get a job with a printer/publisher who is producing materials of the kind I would like to produce. (From a communication two years after the start of the leave.)

5: When I first went on leave (time period one), I worked for a small poetry publisher/printer in Ithaca, New York. The quality of work produced there was not extremely high but it did serve as an introduction to the problems facing the producers of books in small editions. And while working there I continued studying the history of printing. Hoping to work for a better quality press, I left there and sent applications to most of the good small presses in the East. While awaiting their responses, all negative, I was able to use the Rare Books Collection at the Boston Public Library in continuing my study of the history of fine presses and printing.

After exhausting all possibilities of an apprenticeship with a fine printer in the East, I decided to try my luck in the San Francisco Bay area, that being a hotbed of fine press activity. Again, I met with little luck in securing my hope, though, I quite easily got a job in a small printshop as a letterpress printer. I wanted to remain in San Francisco mainly because of the fine press activity there as well as the availability of some very fine rare book collections in the local libraries, chiefly the San Francisco Public and the University of California at Berkeley Bancroft Libraries. So even though I was not practicing fine press techniques, I was at least becoming more knowledgeable in the history of the craft. A month or so ago I finally achieved my long hoped for wish and started work with a fine press, the Plantin Press in Los Angeles. And while I cannot even begin to predict my future, its probably safe to say that I'll remain here for at least a few more months.

Whether or not I return to college at that time will, assuming that they'll have me back, be determined by my decision to open a small press (hopefully, combining job work of a high caliber with the production of finely made children's books), or instead return to further my knowledge of the history of printing. That is a decision some months away, however.

The one thing which I feel definitely sure of in regards to my further higher education, is that it will not take place in a more traditional school. Three semesters of a traditionally stifling program at Cornell were more than enough for me. This is to say that if I should decide to return to college, it would most probably be a return to the one from which I took my leave. It has the flexibility, the program and facilities (well-stocked rare book rooms) for the study of fine printing from a historical perspective.

25. Male - Employed: Television News - Two Years

1: I would not have taken a leave if I had not been offered a job that had a very real future in it. In addition, I was aware that if I did not act on this chance in the present, there was a strong possibility that the job would not be available in the future. I was also aware that it was possible for me to continue my education should my plans go awry. Of minor significance, yet nevertheless a factor, I also had a desire for greater financial independence from my parents. In addition, I was slightly distressed by the job market for individuals with a college degree. I knew several seniors who did not know what they would do when they graduated in June. I will continue my education by registering for courses at a metropolitan university. Hopefully, I will receive a degree within a year of my class and at the same time will be able to pursue a career in television journalism. I will be on the staff of a local news program.

2: I spent two years in New York working in television news and going to a metropolitan university as a part-time student. Certainly many of my initial concerns and fears about taking a first job have been mitigated; and I now have a better understanding of the working experience in general. You learn the personal ups and downs of working week in and week out, you become involved in office politics, and can't help become aware of ego conflicts and the like. In addition, I picked up skills I had never had to use before -- job interviewing, developing working relations with my colleagues, and resume writing.

I certainly have returned to college with more self-confidence and fewer concerns about what I'll do after college. I may have been overly ambitious by trying to work and go to school simultaneously. In order to get my academic studies completed it was necessary to live a very highly planned and ordered life. As a result, much of the fun of living in New York City was lost and I never really discovered the school's social activities. My decision to return to college full time was based on the belief that it would take me too long to complete school if I continued working. Thus, if I was going to complete college, I had better go back full time.

26. Male - Employed: Reporter, Daily Newspaper - Two Years

2: My objective in taking a leave was to gain experience in a specific field -- journalism. From May 1972 to July 1974 I was employed as a reporter on the county staff of the Berkshire Eagle, a daily newspaper of 30,000 circulation published in Pittsfield, Massachusetts. I worked in the paper's bureau in Great Barrington, and for the last seven months I was bureau chief. I received the most help in arranging for this job from the New England Press Association and persons in journalism not connected to my college.

During my leave I became proficient in the writing and reporting skills used by a daily newspaper reporter. The Eagle is recognized as a newspaper with a good reputation which serves as a training ground for young reporters. I believe that my experience will serve as a solid base for continuing a career in journalism. My two-year leave was the most enjoyable and vocationally instructive period of my life. My experience during my leave convinced me that I will probably center my career in journalism. I decided to finish my college education and obtain a BA degree so as not to limit my options in the future.

ARTS AND CRAFTS

27. Female - Employed: Experimental Theater, London - One Semester

2: On January 1, 1974, I flew to London, England, never having been off the East Coast in my life. I had arranged to work as an apprentice for the D'Oyly Carte Opera Company, hopefully working with costumes. I arrived at Heathrowe Airport knowing no one, and took a cab to a hotel that someone had recommended. Well, the hotel had very little heat because of the miner's strike and the energy crisis combined. I couldn't wait to move out. For the next week, I look for flats, answering advertisements in newspapers and magazines.

Ten days after my arrival in London, I moved into a flat of seven people (although there were usually eight to ten occupants at any given time). There were two Australians, one Ecquadorian, one Brazilian, one Kenyan, one Englishman, and myself. I wasn't as lucky with work. Because of the three-day work week imposed on Britain, D'Oyly Carte was not too keen about taking on extra help, even unpaid. There was nothing for me to do. So for the month of January, I wandered around the city by myself feeling cold and miserable by myself, knowing no one, and not knowing what to do.

Since I had never travelled in my life, I didn't know where to begin in getting to know such a huge and complex city. Looking back, I can't believe how I wasted that month. Finally, after trying innumerable places (mostly museums and theatres), I found another job. A small, experimental theater and arts workshop, run by the Inner London Education Authority who gladly welcomed my unpaid help. I was to work with costumes. I had only one co-worker, a young girl who had trained in fashion design. The center, known as the Cockpit Theater and Arts Workshop, was an ideal place to work. It housed several experimental music groups, primarily the National Youth Jazz Ensemble. It housed several art workshops, mostly geared towards discovering art in many forms. It housed poetry workshops and creative writing groups. It housed several theater workshops for the community, from workshops at the local old-age home (they put on a Victorian melodrama with all of the old ladies) to story telling for local children on Saturdays, drama classes for children, resident actors performed medieval marketcart theater in the market street near the theater, a drama group for young adults (age 15-25) -- they performed plays for a two-week span for the community, etc.

But the most important aspect of the center was a group known as the Theater in Education (T.I.E.) team. It was because of this team that the I.L.E.A. sponsored the Cockpit. T.I.E. is the process of teaching children (usually inner-city children), who are not usually very receptive to standard methods of education, through theater. A team has a theater as a home base and the groups of children come to the theater for one day. A team usually works out approximately four projects in a year, each project geared towards a different set of students. For example, a project on King Lear will be geared towards students taking A-levels (going on to higher education), a project on trade unions will be geared towards students who will quit school at age 15 to go to work in the mines or on the railroad. A given group of students will come in on one day, see presentations, play games that pertain to the subject, discuss in small groups, participate in the acting, etc.

It was the T.I.E. team that interested me most in my work. I was providing anyone in the Cockpit who wanted costumes with them, so I had contact with all of the groups. The experience was invaluable. Not only did I learn a lot technically -- the girl that I worked with was very willing to teach me all that she knew about costumes and sewing -- I also learned an incredible amount about the way in which theater can be used, and the powerful tool that it can become. Outside of work, I used my time in different ways. I got to know various parts of London well, I travelled a bit outside of London, I saw art exhibitions, theater productions, joined the London dance center, read, made friends, etc.

The first three months were very hard. Always, I had had close friends around me. Always, I had had family near me. I was terribly lonely and unhappy for a long time. I seemed to have difficulty meeting and getting to know people. I had never had this problem. I was frustrated because I am fascinated by other people and different ways of life, but I seemed to be leading the life of a social hermit. I felt degraded by the fact that I was always alone. I thought that it reflected on my personality. Finally, one of my sisters wrote to me, "You have spent all of your life getting to know others, doing things for others. You know yourself only through others. Take the time to get to know yourself by yourself." It was the best advice I'd received in my life.

The last month, no longer desperate for friends, they seemed to come out of the woodwork. There were not enough hours in the day to do all that I wanted to do. In that time, I learned to respect myself as an individual much more, to value friendship much more, and to enjoy what others had to offer much more than I ever had before. I could enjoy others without worrying about whether or not we would become good friends, without worrying always about the impression I was making, etc. Because I respected myself more, I could respect others more.

I'm sure my difficulties and disappointments were great, but I remember few of them. I was disappointed that my first job did not turn out, but I was lucky that it didn't since my second job was so much better. My biggest difficulty was in learning to be alone. Since I have returned, many people have expressed astonishment that I felt no fear before going, and sheer amazement that I didn't return home when my original job fell through. I attribute this willpower to my parents, who never once questioned my decision about going, who never pitied me when things went wrong, and who always gave me positive encouragement from the other side of the Atlantic.

I know that both of them were always worried about me, and many times stopped short of asking if I wouldn't like to come home. But they never did and I will be eternally grateful, because if they had ever expressed their doubts to me when I was unhappy, I probably would have been on the next plane home. I think that the most important thing that any college or university can do is to guide parents towards this kind of attitude, to make parents realize what kinds of opportunities their children can have and to encourage them in every conceivable way.

3: For four months I worked for an experimental, educational theatre in London, England. It was the first time I had been away from any kind of security. Even when I came to college, the entire freshman class was in the same boat I was in -- not knowing anyone, the surroundings, being away from home.

This leave was the best thing I ever could have done for my personal development. I was forced to be totally independent; I couldn't even call my parents. I knew no one in London. I learned to respect being "along" -- not as a bad position to be in, but a natural one. I had always been surrounded by people all of my life. I got to know myself by myself, instead of in relation to other people. I learned how to carve a niche for myself, how to meet people, how to organize my time without the "guidance" of extra-curricular activities. All of London was open to me. I had to decide exactly what my time warranted. I had to find a job, an apartment, and friends by myself. The most striking effect this had on me was to respect a person's right to be alone, and to value friendship much more highly than I ever had in the past.

The leave also affected my education. The job that I had opened up an entirely new field for me, and that's what I'm going into now. I intend to receive a master's degree in it. I'm not sure if I would have reached this stage without a leave, but I found myself choosing my courses much more carefully for what they had to offer to me in my field. I continue to take some more "broad liberal arts basic" courses, but the rest of them now seem to center around my career.

I think I came back taking school much more seriously, and yet less seriously at the same time. I became more objective about it and was able to put it into perspective with relation to all learning. I began to value activities outside of the classroom just as much, if not more than, the cut and dried learning that the university offers. At no time did I ever feel that I was hindered or hurt by taking a leave of absence, that is from my point of view. Since I returned, I haven't killed myself to work on academics. I simply give them the time that I feel they are worth. Some professors may think that is wrong. For a time, I felt a bit set back socially. I was very used to being alone and when I returned I had to work in a theatre where 45 people were living in two houses. It took me a long time to readjust.

The school facilitated my leave simply by granting it to me. A positive attitude on the part of the University towards leave-taking has a great effect on many parents. The University's approach should be broadly publicized with parents so that a student finds more support from both sides rather than being in the center of a conflict between the two. I think that each university should keep tabs on its "leave of absence" students and at least the advisors should take an active interest in what the student is doing. I think that every student should write up a paper on what he/she did and they should be kept on file for future reference.

28. Female - Employed: French National Television as Apprentice and Interpreter, O'Neill Theatre Institute While Exchange Student at Trinity College - Two Years

1: Objectives: To leave school-academic environment and be on my own; to learn French fluently; to be an apprentice in theater or television. After being in France, I will seek a wider exposure to and work in theater by studying at the National Theatre Institute.

2: During the first year of my leave I worked for the French National Television as an apprentice and interpreter. I also took some acting and mime courses. It was a thoroughly worthwhile experience to be working with professionals and to be living on my own. Living in a foreign country and reaching a point of fluency in the language gave insight into the culture. I feel I understand France in a way that has little to do with academic study yet is, to me, infinitely important for not only awareness and understanding of myself and my cultural background but also in a way, applicable to other understanding situations in which I have not lived; understanding the elements which contribute.

My basic disappointment came from wishing I knew more or had a specific skill but that was, on the whole a very minor problem. I feel especially positive about the leave. The second year is in two parts in my mind. The first part being the semester I spent at the O'Neill Theatre Institute, the second being my semester as a visiting student at Trinity College.

The National Theatre Institute (NTI) provided me with an exploration into all aspects of theatre which was exactly what I wanted. The experience was a full, integrated one and one which a normal school cannot possibly provide. I learned a tremendous amount, experienced many challenges, frustrations, failures. I feel it normal and right that the college accept my experience there, with my evaluation of it as a large part of my education-exploration process.

After that semester I had many reasons for not wishing to return to this college (reasons I have only put aside in favor of completing work towards a degree). At Trinity I was able to study several rather common subjects within the academic structure (while experiencing that!). I lived at home and enjoyed that. I also became involved in work in theatre outside of the school, in a hired amateur production -- an experience which taught me plenty about organization and running of such a group as well as what it is like to perform the same show for three and a half months to varied audiences.

In summary then, I would say that my two years on leave were highly productive, full years. They were disconnected from the college, therefore, I cannot critique the colleges' role in their process.

29. Male - Employed: Singer, Zaitchik Brothers Band - One Semester

1: I hope to go somewhere with my singing career. We are, at the moment, very close to a recording contract and I feel that if I give all my time to it perhaps it will happen. I will be performing a good deal more than I was able to while enrolled. I will also have time to write more music and take care of more of the business aspects of running and being part of a band. (I'll also work days to help with band and family finances.)

My father and oldest brother (both college professors) were most helpful, as well as the rest of my family, my friends, roommates, and my Dean. The Housing Office could have given me more time to move out of my dorm. Actually, they were the only people that were not warm and friendly during my final hectic week.

So far I am enjoying my leave tremendously, but I do miss my friends, and the classes (and even the old college town). It is great to participate in and contribute to the "real" world again.

2: I sang with a band (Zaitchik Brothers Band) in the Northeast Region. We toured with the James Cotton Band and also performed with Earl Hines, Koko Taylor, Cold Blood, John Hammond, and Chris Rhodes.

we also did several demonstrator recordings, one with Cat Anderson as guest artist.

Financially, I did not do as well in helping with school costs as I had hoped but as an artist I received incredible exposure and learned a great deal from my close proximity to such gifted performers. I also made many contacts with record executives and agents which may eventually be productive. I have been performing since the age of ten, but while many experiences were not new, I had, for the first time, a chance to "live the life" and experience being on the road.

Any disappointments I experienced were related directly to the frustrations and the demand physically of being on the road. Also, being so close to the "big time" and having a "taste," but not being able to follow through, due to my desire to finish school, was extremely difficult.

If I did not enjoy school as much as I do, and if I did not find my experiences here so rewarding, I would have been tempted to have remained working. However, since I do feel these things, and since I do not yet know which of two careers I will choose (entertainment vs. clinical psychology), I hope to at least finish my undergraduate work before persuing my "alter-career" further. I feel that I experienced more during those months because of the knowledge I have gained at school, and, conversely, I believe that my leave will help me to get more out of my studies. I am very glad that I took the step to take a leave.

3: I still think of my leave as an educative and valuable experience. I would not hesitate to tell others to do similar things or, at least to take some time away from pure academics.

30. Male - Employed: Singer and Dancer - One Semester

1: I didn't hope to accomplish anything. I was just leaving a situation that I didn't like and hoping to find one that I did like. I was looking for a simpler existence. My life at college was cluttered with too many things going on. My energies were not focused. During my leave I was a singer in a puppet show and a dancer in a local dance group. This was a good situation. My activities were limited in terms of number of different ones.

2: Although I took my leave during the spring term of 1972, I first wanted to leave in the fall of 1971. (My parents convinced me to wait one term for financial and practical reasons.) It seems that my trip to Israel that summer precipitated the feelings about what I was doing in college that led me to my wanting to leave. A combination of the directedness of the lives of Israeli's and my contrasting non-directed tripping through the country made me dissatisfied with the non-directed playing I was doing in college. I wanted some sort of feeling of home, which I wasn't getting with my friends in the dorm, and a feeling of doing something and knowing exactly what that something was, which I wasn't getting from my college activities.

I returned to college in the fall of 1972 with the goal of becoming a performer (probably a dancer). Having this goal helped me. I took all academic courses in Spring, 1973, and I did well in them because having a goal allowed me to have the attitude that these courses weren't all that important. I should just get as much enjoyment from them as I could. I was never interested in academic courses. I never wanted to put in the effort. Before my leave, this bothered me. I said to myself, "If I don't like academics, I shouldn't be in college." After the leave I realized that it would be a good idea to get my degree, and that the college could offer me some things (singing lessons, independent studies in dance).

31. Male - Employed: Intern, Architectural Office - One Semester

1: My leave will permit me to meet new people, learn about <u>real</u> architecture, to experience a different life-style from that of student. I will be working for an architect during weekdays as draftsman, studying in seminar format with city planner and discussing with students and staff personnel. A student who formerly attended the program, the academic dean and my concentration advisor were all helpful.

2: The semester leave consisted (formally) of an internship-work placement in an architect's office as an all-around apprentice-student, a discussion class with fellow student interns concerning our work and city travel experiences, and a seminar taught by a city planner on planning and ecology. On my own, I spent a great deal of time reading books of my own choice on architecture from the city library, living near and meeting hundreds of students at the University of Pennsylvania, and working on my art work.

The primary gain came from the architecture office work experience both on a technical-pragmatic level and as well as a theoretical-philosophical one. I know more about architecture than ever before and am firmly convinced of the value of attending a professional school. Socially, the many new friends made at Penn and those on the internship program were valuable and rewarding, giving me added confidence this year at college.

The major drawbacks were that the program was not fully ready to handle pre-architecture students, several personality conflicts with one of the teachers of the program, and the lack of experienced Urban Studies students enrolled in the program. The college helped me adequately and admirably.

3: My semester "on leave" was spent enrolled in a work-study program called the Philadelphia Urban Semester. I lived, worked, and studied from 1/75 - 5/75 in Philadelphia, Pennsylvania. I consider the two principal learning experiences garnered during last semester to be: a) personal-social development and b) the volunteer work-study placement.

I gained immensely from the environment in which I lived and socialized at nights and on weekends and, as well, the professional cultural situations of the workdays at the office. The former renewed my personal confidence and eagerness to meet new and different people, and the latter evidenced for me the true workings of an architect's office and confirmed my interest in continuing my education in order to accrue a professional degree. I approached architecture with as much enthusiasm as ever, but it is now tempered with a fair level of practical realism and rational taste. I have not been hampered in any way.

32. Male - Conservator of Musical Instruments - Two Leaves of One Semester Each

   2: First leave - '74. I worked independently at the Library of Congress, and in a private (borrowed) workshop redesigning and building a hurdy-gurdy (organistrum). I became well versed in doing obscure research and had a lot of fun -- I had no one to teach me woodworking, so my craft suffered. My school did nothing to help me with the project. Some interest expressed would have been nice, but too much to expect.

   My second leave was spring term last year, which I spent in the restoration shop in the Department of Musical Instruments at the Smithsonian -- I learned some workworking and did drafting for them in return, working under Scot O'Dell, Bob Sheldon, and Tom Wolf. This was an extraordinary experience and I enjoyed it

33. Female - Employed: Museum Work - One Semester

   2: I was employed as curator of biology, Dartmouth College Museum, Hanover, New Hampshire. My jobs included: preparing animals for display - skinning, mounting, stuffing, etc.; field work in Vermont and New Hampshire taking wildflower photographs, exhibits on edible plants and rare wildflowers; slide and tape shows, research exhibit on bats and rabies in Vermont and New Hampshire; helped organize collections to move to new building; other small jobs and painted fish; did secretarial and carpentry jobs.

   I gained experience in museum work and had great individual responsibility. Valuable relationship with director -- taught me a great deal -- earned money to pay for final semester of college. Leave couldn't have been better. College had nothing to do with it.

CONSERVATION, FORESTRY, AGRICULTURE

34. Female - Employed: Intern, Environmental Action - One Semester

   1: Get off my ass, and take some responsibility. Work in a field I may want to enter after law school. Live on my own in Washington, D.C. I arranged the leave myself with the help of one faculty member (not my advisor), the Whole Woman's Center and my support group.

   2: I worked at Environmental Action, a lobbying and magazine group in Washington as an intern. I researched environmental issues, political issues, wrote and published an article on occupational health in their magazine, wrote copy for a radio announcement advocating the stoppage of defense department appropriations in light of environmental concerns, and lobbied on a solid waste bill in the Senate. I also kept up with the political scene on my own while there (visits to Sirica's court, impeachment hearings, House and Senate galleries, and other public interest groups).

35. Male - Employed: Logging in Washington and Alaska - One Year

2: Taking a year off, probably between sophomore and junior year, is something I've planned on since high school. Partly at the urging of my family and partly of my own desires; it's difficult to distinguish. I've always felt that it would be a good time to do exactly what I want without any worries concerning an impending future. I've always enjoyed working -- I find it more fulfilling and less a strain on me psychologically than school. Logging sounded cool, so I thought I'd check it out. I got a job at home, bought a car and drove to Washington. Finding a job was just a matter of time. I worked for two outfits in Washington between October and May. The work is hard and rather dangerous, but I enjoyed it a lot. Being an Easterner, with long hair, etc., sometimes created problems, but I found that as long as I worked hard things were all right. In May I went to Alaska and worked there. This was different in that I was living in a camp, forty minutes by plane to town, no women, etc. But I earned $450 a week and intend on going back next summer and in the future.

The leave was very satisfying. I enjoyed the independence and freedom. It has given me much more confidence in my own abilities and possibilities for the future. I returned to school rather alienated from the very strange and bizarre social scene it is. This, though, I see as a positive force. Being alienated, I think, enhances my chances of getting something out of school.

3: I greatly appreciate the fact that the college made it so easy for me to leave and to return. I experienced only minimal problems -- "handicaps" - upon returning, i.e., registering for courses already full. This, however, seems an unavoidable problem involved in leave-taking and not all that crucial.

There have been larger problems for this year. Before my year off I often felt alienated and deeply dissatisfied with school. These feelings have been increased this year. This is not coincidental; my experiences last year certainly have contributed. However, I in no way regret taking the leave nor do I view my dissatisfactions as somehow produced by correctable and superficial mechanisms.

My values and life styles, for whatever reasons, just don't fit into a college atmosphere -- especially a private, conservative school like my college. I value education and would like to teach school, so I stay -- this is just something I have to deal with. Even in this context I believe taking the leave was a good idea. Although it did not (it could not) solve any problems for me, and, although it prolonged an experience I anxiously look forward to terminating, it still was a very valuable event. The leave has served to further develop my critical framework, to give me additional confidence in myself and my ability to approach and define institutions, events, and processes. This is why I go to college and why I value education. This is also what I had hoped to attain through a leave of absence; I think it worked out quite well.

36. Male - Employed: Farm Laborer

2: The first semester of my sophomore year was the low point of four years of intensive educational training. After two years of high pressure education at a prestigious eastern prep school, I entered college with great expectations. My freshman year passed quickly although as I look back at it now, it was all pretty much in a daze. My life freshman year was centered solely around my studies and crew, with very little time given to other activities. By the time sophomore year started, I realized that I needed something different. I no longer felt that my life should be so dull and routine as it had been the previous three years. My discontent grew as the semester passed and I began to question the relevance of my work.

Seriously thinking about taking a year off, I decided to try farming, remembering the good times I had on my uncle's farm during the summer before college. In November the opportunity presented itself and I got a job working on a small dairy farm situated ten miles west of Ithaca, New York. Starting in February, I began working at the farm. As the one and only hired hand, it was my job to do much of the hard labor. While Jim milked the cows, I would feed all the animals: 75 dairy cattle, 6 pigs and 2 horses. When the milking was done I would clean both barns and bed the animals. Between milkings and while the grounds were still too cold or wet to work, we repaired the stalls in the barns, the barns themselves, and got machinery ready for the spring field work. When spring arrived I did much of the field work: plowing, fitting fence, mending, etc.

As pertinent to the question of values and benefits that I received from working on the farm, I think that I can make the general statement that it reorganized my outlook on life. I left the protected environment of college and went out to find what the real world was like. It can be argued, I suppose, that living on a farm is in its own right a socially, culturally protected environment, but it at least gave me a basic view as to how the real world worked.

I also left to find out who I am. I did not know what I really wanted out of life and I needed to find out. I could see no relevance to my existence at college, why I was working or what I was working for. The leave was intended to give me time to think about these matters, to see if I could come to some conclusion about the relation of myself to the workings of the world. While I did not find out what I wanted out of life, I did find what I did not want.

As to the difficulties or disappointments encountered on my leave of absence, the greatest encountered was the monotony. Working upward of fourteen hours a day left me so tired that when I wanted to go to town for a beer, I could not get motivated to do it. Looking at the same 40 cows, 4 walls, and 3 silos, day in and day out, just finally drove me out. Why I picked farming when I wanted a little excitement in my life, I will never figure out.

3: I worked on a dairy farm and was, therefore, about as far from an academic environment as one could possibly get. Because of certain personal experiences, which I prefer not to delineate, I have become more wary, in a sense, of the way people think and, therefore, how and why they act as they do. I used to be naive with regard to the actions of people and often felt that the wool had been pulled over my eyes. That is, I felt that on several occasions I was being used as the brunt of jokes. Now I feel that I have matured to the point where these things either don't occur, or no longer bother me.

The environment with which I was associated on my leave was such that I now realize the value of my college education. Because of this, I have become far more motivated with regard to my studies and am better able to apply myself.

I was handicapped, though, by doing no "academic work" (the only reading I ever did was from two farming magazines oriented obviously to the less well-educated farmer). Coming back to the academic environment, the difficult adjustment to the pressured, study-oriented life was quite noticeable. I ascertained a distinct mental block when it came around to writing papers and tests, a very important part of my major, American History which entails a great deal of critical research and writing. I feel, however, that I have regained and improved my ability in the necessary skills to a degree where it is of only a minor concern.

I can really think of no process or device, at this time, through which the university might make the assimilation process easier. However, if the deans might print up a list of those students who have been back on campus for at least a semester (after taking a leave of absence) and make it available to new returnees, it might prove helpful to those students who encounter problems after readmission.

37. Female - Leave Activities Include Farm Experiences

2: First Half: Lived in Maine with a small community of very highly skilled craftspeople. I lived on a "farm" and led a very "close-to-the earth" life style while working in a small local business that handled farming and construction equipment. This experience has had a great importance in deciding how I want my life to be, what my priorities are, etc.

Second Half: I went to France all alone, but not speaking French, had a lonely but good time for two months, then I went to Scotland and found myself a job in the Hebrides taking peat out of the bogs for a local distillery. A friend then met me (three months later) and we travelled through Britain and Norway.

I have some disappointments about my European trip, especially my time in France. I missed my close friends, etc. But my time in Scotland alone was great and I'm sure has made me a stronger person. Both my leave experiences (Maine and Europe) have made me decide that farming and husbandry are very important to me, not just being a natural historian.

CONSTRUCTION

38. Male - Employed: Laborer on Construction - One Year

1: I am interrupting my formal education in order to gain a wider experience, different from the social and academic environment of school. I will be working at hard, outdoor physical labor in a situation where I am living with other workers. I want to experience the reality of living on a wage, working at a full-time job. I think this will give me a new perspective on school -- more motivation and appreciation when I return. My father helped me arrange the job. I had one meeting with the Dean of Freshmen but this was more formal than helpful. I hope this year works out. I feel somewhat apprehensive about being out of school.

2: Worked for the Bechtel Construction Corporation in Rock Springs/ Green River, Wyoming on the construction of a soda ash refining plant for Food Machinery and Chemical Corporation (FMC). Lived in a work camp provided by Bechtel in Rock Springs.

The primary value of the experience was living and working in an environment totally foreign to me and from working and supporting myself as a manual laborer. It helped me to realize that college is a rare luxury which should not be taken for granted.

The greatest disappointment has manifested itself in the last few weeks. Since returning to school, I find the experience of last year subordinated by the continuity between school now and two years ago. College has changed very little -- the same people, same routine, same activities. I find myself forgetting that I ever left. The year in Rock Springs was such a different experience than life at college, that increasingly it seems like a distant memory, almost a dream -- there being virtually no relationship between it and school. I feel like I never left, have to force myself to think about Rock Springs to maintain an awareness of the things I learned there.

3: My leave was personally valuable in that I gained a new perspectime on my life and opportunities. I saw the world from the point of view of a ditch digger. I worked with people who have no other prospect for the duration of their lives but manual labor. Consequently, I appreciate and value the opportunities before me, and the experience of college more keenly than before. Knowing the alternative, I see more clearly the luxury, challenge, excitment of college and a professional occupation. Still, my college experience this year has been ambivilant. As a result of this new awareness, I enjoy college -- appreciate it -- more thoroughly than I did my first year. It is a totally self-centered experience dedicated to personal gratification and I savor it as such. While this is true, paradoxically, I do not feel much more motivated academically than I did as a freshman. My pursuit and interest in my classes has been lukewarm.

My leave was an experience of isolation from my peers, and indeed from much of humanity -- working with a handful of construction men in the wasteland of southwest Wyoming. If I was handicapped at all by it -- or at least if normal development was stifled in anyway -- it would be with regard to social life, relations with the opposite sex, and general sense of easiness and compatibility with students and their interests and orientations.

The college participated in my experience on the most minimal level. The Dean I corresponded with did no more than prepare papers needed for taking the leave and returning to school; purely logistics. This is not to condemn the administration, though, because I'm not sure there was much room for their involvement anyway. Perhaps some counselling might have helped. . . . But leave-taking is generally a very individualistic endeavor. Nevertheless, I wonder if I could have spent the year in a more productive way. If the Dean had talked with me extensively and stimulated some critical thinking on my part, I might have seen that an alternative to what I planned would have possibly been more valuable and productive. To this extent, input from a counsellor would have been helpful. As far as my return to campus, the only aspect of life disrupted by the leave was social -- friends changed, relationships altered, etc., -- and these matters are purely personal and must be worked out on a personal level where the administration can be of little assistance.

39. Male - Employed: Alaska Pipeline Construction - Currently on Leave

1: To bring into focus, through the broadening of scope, (a paradox?) my ambitions as (a) a person, (b) a student. Thus, lending direction to my "career objective(s)" and allowing for an academic experience that will have applied to it the necessary "sense of responsibility" -- the end of which, hopefully, being a unique self-satisfaction. Economic self-sustenance would allow my parents, who are both at retirement age, to, at long last, waylay the arduous task of supporting my educational needs and relax. Hopefully, through emersion in a 40 hour (or as in my case 70-80 hour) work system I will be able to incorporate a greater degree of diligence and responsibility to my ultimate task. Exposure to other perspectives (or non-perspectives) through travel will also, I believe, enhance my sense of self-purpose.

I will, in all probability, be on Alaska's "north slope" as a pipeline worker by May. The concept was originally proposed by a professor last year and again by another professor in much greater depth this year. A few people in my living quarters were taking a leave and I discussed the proposition with them. My close friends at this school, and other schools, concurred with what had become my idea and added their beliefs, mostly supportive. Finally, and most significantly, I discussed at great length the idea with my parents who, though originally in firm opposition, in the end realized its potential merit and arranged through a business contact for my departure to the Arctic.

I am presently living in Alaska as a member of the local (and disgustingly powerful) teamsters union. I think it is very important to note that I am, aside from the rest of my "condition," in a state of considerable debt -- a debt incurred for my education (after only three terms). The possibility of relieving myself of this burden before leaving school was tremendously appealing. Finally, I have enjoyed thoroughly any opportunities I have had to travel. In this light, the seemingly "once-in-a-lifetime opportunity" to come to Alaska and work on its pipeline was, when uncovered, irresistable.

TRANSPORTATION

40. Male - Employed: Retail Delivery Driver - One Year

2: I worked as a retail delivery driver for a small local dairy. The job paid reasonably well and allowed a good part of the afternoon to be spent at my own pursuits. The early starting hour (5:30 a.m.) made evening social activities more difficult to participate in, but the afternoon time compensated for it. I worked six days a week so travel was out of the question. I managed to save $4,500 which I sorely needed to continue my education and convince several parties of my worthiness.

I also had a good deal of time to myself which I had longed for throughout high school and the first two years of college. Some of this time was taken up in coping with the family situation, which at that time was rather unstable. The remainder was spent in as much leisure activity as my job and budget allowed (hiking, bicycling, reading). This time was most valuable in that it provided a "time-out" from the responsibilities of academic life and a chance to try on different ones.

The major problem with my year off was built-in from the start. The necessity to save as much money as possible restricted my options in enough ways so that any benefits I received came from the people around me or within myself, rather than travelling, participating in educational programs, or having money to spend on recreation. I think I got around it pretty well, within the limits I was working in.

In response to the last question, a hearty "yes." They could have given me financial aid! Actually, there wasn't much, given the reason for my leave-taking, that the college could have done to make it a better experience. As for my own part, I think I did as well as possible within my limits.

41. Male - Employed: Cab Driver - One Semester

2: The purpose of my leave was to decide if I wanted to go on with a pre-med curriculum and if I didn't, what would I do instead. During that time I drove a cab and lived at my fraternity house. Cab-driving exposed me to a working-class kind of existence. I also changed my thinking away from pre-med to possibly engineering or a math related field in business, such as actuary. My leave gave me an extra year to decide on my future after college instead of rushing to a decision at the end of this year. Actually, I would have had to decide by now what I wanted to do so I could apply to graduate schools and/or for jobs.

3: My leave gave me a chance to change my priorities from pre-med to a math oriented career in either engineering or business. My only disadvantage was getting back into the practice of studying when I first got back.

MANUFACTURING

42. Male - Employed: Factory Worker - One Year

1: It was my hope to have some sort of experiences which would counter the insidious world view that tends to permeate college life, that world view tending to be characteristically overly analytic, cerebral, intellectual. I hoped my experiences would put me in closer physical, spiritual, emotional contact with the world and that I would be able to integrate various parts of myself and discover some of my strengths and weaknesses by throwing myself alone into the world and trying to survive there.

One person, a friend, influenced my decision to leave. He and I spent many nights drinking beer in a small Italian restaurant. Many times I violently expressed the desire to go to California and he said I should go if I wanted to and that he would go with me. Otherwise, I did not test my inner turmoil against any more sober, external agency and, so, the final decision was arrived at purely in my own head, in a vacuum, as it were. If I had felt confortable enough to go to any member of the college community to discuss my situation, I probably would not have left school to begin with.

43. Male – Employed: Factory Worker – One Semester

3: I worked in a textile factory (knit goods) for six months as a nylon processor. I bought a car and saved some money. This was my first opportunity to experience a totally new situation in terms of: a) the people I worked with (race, class, age, etc.), b) the workplace as an institution and c) my own political, social, economic relations with the first two.

My reaction was: a) the workplace was an institution that made people sick (mentally and physically), b) going to school was easier and a more enjoyable way to spend time and c) that I would go back to school and base my studies in this area. I saw a cancer that had to be snuffed out.

I was not disadvantaged or handicapped for having taken a leave. I was my own instigator with the help of my friends who thought it was the best thing for me to do. Nobody at the college (employees) gave me any advice. The college should take an active role in advocating leaves and should have a special department set up for placing people in as many situations as possible.

BUSINESS: SUPERVISORY – MANAGERIAL

44. Male – Employed: Supervisor Position in Major Corporation – Five Semesters

2: I left college to take my leave in February 1973. I returned this September after two and a half years. During the first eighteen months of my leave I was employed by a business. For one year I worked for a major oil company. Personally, I took a leave of absence so as to get my feet on the ground. The leave accomplished this. Let me explain.

When I left college I was in the midst of a personal crisis and I arrived home to discover that my family was in a serious financial strait. Their money problem was so bad that I went to work to help pay the bills. Consequently, I was left without any time to worry idly over my future, personal failures and successes, etc. After six months of odd jobs, I landed the job at a major oil company. I was given a great deal of responsibility. Not only did my waning confidence become resolute, but I performed so well I was awarded three raises in one year and authority over five people several days a week. After one year I quit and returned to school part time. Later I returned to my original college as a full-time student.

The benefits? I'm exceedingly confident. I can control my frustration and anxieties. Most importantly, I've learned to live a day at a time and not worry about the future. Also, I've learned to manage my time. I attribute these changes in outlook to my ability to bounce back. The leave allowed me to gain these qualities early. Consequently, I will get a great deal more out of my remaining three years in college.

I do not feel that every college student needs a break from college. However, those who take leaves should be required to keep in touch with his or her college dean. As for the college and its part in granting leaves, it is imperative that the college realize the leave is the best therapeutic device it has to counsel students. It allows the students to solve personal problems at their own pace without needless pressure from threats of failure.

3: I've yet to discover any inherent disadvantages in taking a leave of absence. Moreover, I've not experienced any handicaps in pursuing social relationships or my education since my return. My leave was initiated because of personal problems. It was after I was away from college that finances became a problem. During the last year of my leave I took several courses at an accredited college. These courses -- the ones I want transferred -- are not accepted here. My suggestion is that the college administration make a particular effort to point out to people taking leaves-of-absence the proper procedure of getting courses at another university or college approved for transfer of credit.

SECRETARIAL - CLERICAL

45. Female - Employed: Medical Claims Processor - One Year

1: I want both to find a source of motivation to enable me to learn rather than just perform at school, and to find an area or at least a direction of interest to pursue after I finish college. More specifically, I would like to try to determine whether or not I am interested in business school and whether or not I would survive there.

I will be working full time, hopefully at some job which will expose me to the patterns and personalities of the business world. Also very helpful has been my six-week search for a job, still unsuccessful.

2: Because I was the first student from my university placed by the Venture Program, and because I desired placement at such a distance from this area (that is, I was already in Atlanta, Georgia), it is difficult for me to evaluate how the university might have been of greater help. Although my eventual placement was a sort of last resort, last choice job, in retrospect, I could never have chosen a job more related to my interests and abilities, nor one more satisfying intellectually and financially. I do not see how my leave could possibly have been more productive. I feel the value of the program to have been in placing me in a job in which I was respected and given responsibility, and in which I was financially secure and so could expand my independence and self-esteem. The placement was especially valuable to me because I spent six weeks looking for a job on my own.

3: During the academic year 1973-1974, I was granted a personal leave of absence from my university. The factors precipitating the leave were far from unusual: I felt that I had lost a sense of perspective concerning both my professional and personal goals. I felt that, rather than working from an inner conviction of purpose, I was motivated by external sources, by expectations of parents and peers, by guilt, by superficial pride.

I saw my capacity to give to other people being oppressed by my preoccupation with academic success. As a pre-med student, attending school only fifty miles from home, I felt my behavior to be guided by a nebulous code of values not actively chosen by myself, but passively assimilated from my environment. These were feelings which had troubled me since my third semester, but I had assumed they would resolve themselves if I applied myself to my studies. By the end of my fifth semester, however, it became apparent that ignoring my conflicts was not accomplishing their solution.

The following semester, therefore, I tried to lessen my external pressures and to examine my directions and goals. I took two academic courses, worked 20 hours per week, and was exceedingly active as a choral singer. While this move afforded me some degree of perspective, I was still operating in that environment in which I felt manipulated; I felt the weight of a large indecision. Accordingly, I decided to make an abrupt break, with family, friends, and the university community. I chose a city far from home where I could be my own person. In August 1973 I left for Atlanta, Georgia.

My year in Atlanta was a positive experience in every respect possible. Most notable has been my discovery of faith in my own abilities, of coherence in my life style and values, of my capacity to know and help people, my ability to work effectively and with concentration, and perhaps most importantly, my discovery of a field in which I could combine my background, interests, and abilities, namely, hospital and health services administration.

The year was comprised of three distinct phases. During the first phase, I looked for a job and a place to live, and acquainted myself with the city. After six weeks of wearing but illuminating job-hunting, I was hired by the Aetna Life and Casualty Insurance Company as a medical claims processor in the Group Department. My duties involved the payment of medical claims for employees of a large number of companies, and required daily contact with doctors, hospitals, insurance companies, collection agencies, policyholders, and employees. During the course of the year, a great deal of information crossed my desk with regard to relative frequency of illnesses, hospital costs and billing systems, physicians' fees, Medicare coverage, public attitudes toward the medical profession, and the medical profession's attitude toward the public.

I developed an intense concern that claims be paid as accurately and promptly as possible, and that each employee understand the nature of his coverage and the explanation of his benefit payment. Another aspect of the job experience was the work atmosphere created by a large insurance company. I met, worked with, and made friends with a great many fellow employees, most with backgrounds, values, and goals very different from my own. I was daily confronted, in and out of work, with situations new to my experience.

During the second phase of my year, I experienced a great deal of job satisfaction, achieved a stable living arrangement with three other women, and sang with the Atlanta Symphony Orchestra Chorus directed by Robert Shaw (one of the finest choral directors in the country). Choral singing has for eleven years been a major source of satisfaction for me. It was during the past year that I accepted the fact that I would derive maximum pleasure from music as an avocation.

The third and final phase of the year began at a time when I truly had established a home for myself in Atlanta. My close friendship with a male homosexual college student from the Symphony Chorus was probably the single most important relationship of my adult life to date. The friendship served to draw me out of myself, to make me aware of the daily problems and conflicts encountered by others, to make me sensitive to others' needs as whole people, to help me avoid sterotypes and quick judgments.

My experiences in business, in music, and in personal relations in Atlanta gave me the strength to return to college with the confidence for a successful senior year. In the academic realm I have been able to function far more effectively than two years previous due to my sense of purpose and my recognition of the value and privilege of obtaining an education of the sort which this college has to offer. In the personal realm I have found that I have something to give to others out of my experience, and that I have as much to learn from them.

I went to Atlanta uncommitted and self-centered. I returned firmly committed to helping people, personally by being as sensitive and open as possible, and professionally by helping America to develop a more efficient system of health care distribution.

I have been in no sense handicapped by taking a leave. I would, however, recommend that one's senior year is not the ideal time for a leave. It is difficult in one remaining year to remake an academic career, and it can also be difficult to find one's original college class virtually vanished from the campus. This can, however, also be a refreshing situation and an opportunity for a new start without old images of self to contend with.

I consider myself a fairly independent person. The chief value to me was the job placement assistance provided by the Venture Program. Beyond this, I think most of my successes at my job and in returning to school have come from personal motivation rather than university personnel. Of course, I can never emphasize too greatly how very supportive I have always found the university community to be. The attitude toward leave-taking and the College Venture Program are but two aspects of a university atmosphere which I value very highly.

46. Male - Employed: Trust-Remittance Clerk, Banking - One Semester

2: I worked as a trust-remittance clerk in a large Boston bank. It involved clerical work and use of simple math skills. I was able to gain some experience in a job situation to the real world as opposed to the fantasy world of college. I also learned some of the business dealings of handling people and the managerial problems that arise. I was financially independent and managing my own budget in my own manner. There were specific things learned in the area of banking that were very helpful. The job helped give me some direction in the things I do and don't want from a career. The job was often stifling; often became repititous and unchallenging. The only thing that might have been more helpful was for this opportunity to be better publicized so that it might have been taken advantage of earlier than when I embarked on it (as a sophomore or junior rather than as a senior).

47. Female - Employed: Accounts Payable Department - One Year

1: Gain a fluency in German and obtain understanding of German culture. Develop an appreciation for college, which has been somewhat diminished through two years of living there. I will be working in order to have money to study at a German University. I will pursue the above objectives by just living and studying in Germany and just being away from college (thereby seeing its value and good points more clearly).

2: For the first two months of my leave I had a vacation -- just relaxing and swimming, playing tennis, etc. In August I got a job in the Accounts Payable Department of a company in Connecticut, where I worked until the following June. From the end of June to the end of August 1975 I was in West Germany where I studied the German language in a Georgetown University (USA) Summer Program. I also spent two and a half weeks travelling in Germany and Switzerland.

The most immediate benefits from these were: 1) the money I made working, 2) the insight into and experience in the "business world" (which I thoroughly enjoyed and which will help when I try to get a job after graduation), 3) an idea of what I wanted to major in, 4) an opportunity to go to Europe, 5) a 1000% improvement in my German-language speaking ability and 6) meeting new people and making new friends.

I cannot think of anything which could have been done to make it a more productive experience. Except for occasional moments of boredom or "homesickness" for college and my friends here, I fully enjoyed the entire experience. I honestly would have preferred to have more time off but I want to finish school now.

Overall impressions of my year off: exciting, interesting, challenging, educational.

BUSINESS - SALES

48. Male - Employed: Field Service Representative - One Year

2: My leave originally was for the purpose of earning money to be able to return the following year. When I left school the job that "I was sure to get" had been filled, so I spent some time unemployed, which at first seemed rather disappointing but it did show me first hand the situation an increasing number of people, worse off than I, were facing. I also had a good deal of time for hobbies and limited travel, so both of these aspects of unemployment were valuable to me.

Most of my leave was spent in employment. I had a job with a large corporation as a field service representative which provided me with expenses paid travel to twelve states as well as a possible future with the company. This job ultimately provided me with the most beneficial aspects of my leave. The close association I had with the elements of the business world altered my academic plans and gave me an ultimate goal and incentive. Before my leave I was a history major with no definite career or graduate plans. Through my occupation, I developed an interest in business, management and the operations of industrial organizations. A resultant switch of my concentration area to economics/industrial organization is that I plan to enroll in a graduate MBA program.

Before my leave I had grossly underachieved in my academic work, I believe, because of a lack of motivation due to uncertain plans for the future. At this point in my first semester following my leave, I have had the proper motivation in my academic work to complete reading and assignments when they should be rather than leaving everything to the final weeks of the semester. Instead of approaching exams with apprehension, I am confident of doing well because I know that I have done the required work and am interested enough to do the extra work which I hope will show in a comparison of my achievements before and after my leave.

As far as the university is concerned, permission to leave was easily obtained, the deans I spoke with were most helpful and informative. The difficulties encountered with my leave were upon being readmitted. There was a tremendous amount of administrative red tape as far as registrar, controller, and financial aid departments were concerned. Rather than informing me of problems concerning my accounts beforehand, I was not informed until the day before classes and it was not for some weeks after that all was straightened out.

In summation, I would consider that my leave of absence was of tremendous benefit in finding myself and determining the path I want to follow. I believe that to fully appreciate your position in society, and where and what you ultimately would like to do, requires a taste of that society away from the academic scheme of life. Some people are able to find their role and determine their plans without leaving the traditional "four year plan," but for those who cannot, I would strongly suggest that they experience the operations of the real world and establish the course of action that is in keeping with their ultimate goals.

3: Basically, my leave was intended to provide some sort of new outlook on what I wanted educationally and vocationally. I was dissatisfied with my situation and needed time for self-evaluation and planning. My leave was successful in that I was able to discover what I wanted to do academically, and gave me the motivation I have lacked thus far in my education. For the first time, I looked forward to my studies instead of arriving with an apathetic outlook. I feel that I have matured and prospered as a person due to my leave of absence.

I have been disadvantaged somewhat by my leave in that I am behind my friends in terms of studies and graduation, but I feel that what I have developed and learned far outweighs this situation. What is distressing to me is that the course of study I have selected is poorly represented at my college, and essentially I am biding my time until I can get to a graduate school where I can become involved in these studies. The university made my return a bit difficult because of the tremendous amount of "red-tape" involved in registering for the semester.

49. Male - Employed: Salesman - One Semester

2: I worked to make some money for school and some comforts. Much reading in things that I myself chose to read, not what was found on a course syllabus. I received very few benefits from my work. Just a weekly paycheck. It allowed me to travel. I was a salesman for a vegetable garden seed company. A good job for temporary employment. It was a seasonal job. Most of the people I met on this job were older, middle-class, whites, some college educated. They were caught up in making as many bucks as possible and were not very stimulating mentally. It made me realize what I don't want to do upon graduating. I could never expect to do something like that for the rest of my life -- just too boring.

While travelling around I became very aware of my surrounding environment and also of my body, too. We can't continue to do what we are doing to our environment. I started by cleaning up my own situation. Yoga -- made me very aware of my body. I watched what I ate, drank and mostly took better care of my body then ever before.

I really can't pinpoint any major disappointments. All I know is that my time off gave me a chance to be me. I was a part of the real world (not the protected and sort of unreal existence of university life) and had to deal with certain situations that would not confront a college student. College has been very rewarding for me. There is no doubt in my mind that a college education combined with time off on a leave of absence has been good for me -- and might be good for others too.

3: My leave let me sit back and evaluate why I was really at college. At any rate -- for what reasons. Previously I was here because it seemed like the thing for me to do. Afterwards I began to realize what an education truly meant to me. It was not just a stepping stone to a high paying job in society but a means to fulfill a desire that I am only now becoming aware of. A desire to learn as much as possible about many different things -- intense curiousity.

The only handicap that I encountered upon returning to school was that I became unsure if I was spending a majority of my time in the right field. Was I involved with a major that was truly what I wanted to be studying?

50. Male - Employed: Retail Sales - One Semester

2: During the period of my leave, I stayed in the area of my college and continued to work full time at a camera store where I had been working on a part-time basis for the last semester. Besides working at the store, where I began to acquaint myself with some managerial practices and got a glimpse at the functioning of the business world in general, I also began to do a modest amount of freelance photography for institutions and private individuals. I also took up swimming on a serious exercise basis, and during the summer, after most of my college friends had recessed for the vacations, I took a summer school course at night at a college in the area of my major.

Working on a full-time basis, with a small amount of responsibility, made me develop an appreciable amount of discipline, and at the same time a feeling of accomplishment. I was able to gauge some of my fallibilities, as well as discovering some interests and hidden skills. Finally, it gave me the chance to try to run my own life independently of anyone or anything (institution or social setting). Frankly, there were few difficulties or disappointments. Sometimes I had difficulty tiding by financially, but as far as achieving goals or deriving satisfaction from what I was doing, there certainly was none.

3: My "leave" was for me a necessary break. During it, and almost without my notice, I matured tremendously. I worked at a store coming in contact with people who did not exist at my college and whose situations and life styles clashed with mine. This served to appraise and define my own interests and directions. I returned to college with a clearer understanding of what the world contained as far as possibilities and opportunities but also pitfalls.

I began to appreciate the value of an education, an idea often stressed while growing up but seldom verified. Therefore, I returned to school with a clearer foresight of what to do and what to expect once I received my degree. My leave did not put me at a disadvantage but, on the contrary, it gave me a clearer focus on what life was like outside of the college community compared to my college friends.

The university maintained a detached stance when I returned to continue my studies. I would have appreciated a more personal involvement on the part of the administration, perhaps a small reorientation talk with one of the officials or an advisor. Unfortunately, my return was more like a fight, having to make all the arrangements and efforts by myself.

FOOD, HOTEL, DOMESTIC SERVICE

51. Female - Employed: Waitress, Chambermaid - One Year

2: Lived in Jackson, Wyoming last winter, worked at ski area as a waitress and part-time chambermaid with two other people from college also taking a "leave." The benefits I derived were: living far away from New England and home -- travelling in the west -- skiing every day both alpine and nordic -- meeting people on non-academic level -- studying winter wildlife -- living in small mountain community -- making own living, cooking, rent -- intense involvement with characters for winter season -- social study of human behavior in such an environment. Experienced few disappointments -- nothing major.

In summary -- my leave of absence was the best thing I have ever experienced. I would recommend it, and almost suggest it as a requirement for all college students. If any student has doubts about their school or academic involvement they should take time off either exchange junior year abroad or complete "absence." I learned more about the inter-relations of people in seven months than I ever learned at school. A taste of the anti-intellectual life was a necessary process in my recent development and choice to return to the academic life.

52. Male - Employment, Travel, Self-directed Study - One Year

1: I have a list of about twenty things I want to do while out of school. These rang from learning to juggle to experimenting with drugs. I think that I am already more mature and better able to deal with works of literature (my main academic interest) and that a year away would help even more. I want to really want to go to school if I go, and to have alternatives.

Over the summer I read many hours per day. Since then, on the road or working a 12-hour day, I have not. I've been lonely and drunk and sometimes happy. I tripped and hiked in the Grand Canyon.

I've met people I couldn't have imagined. I vaguely try to ferment the Revolution. I have learned that there is a whole angry continent west of New England's ivied campuses and that the university is no more in the vanguard socially than intellectually; that before I can afford the luxury of studying French literature, I must learn some primary lessons, get some basic tools and get my shit together.

I have no program as such, no organization, only vague aims. I got support, which I needed, and help in various ways from a few professors and classmates. Talking with two friends, one who dropped out of Vassar and one who did not go directly to college, was very important. The hassles of application for leaves and leave-extensions seem undesirable, inefficient and unnecessary, no real guidance was provided by the university.

2: I worked my last job as a waiter. It would have meant $10,000 a year after R&B and taxes, as opposed to paying the college $15,000 for a job that would probably pay less or a chance for graduate school. I read, travelled, etc. More than ever, I wonder if the structure at this or any university provides any more desirable an environment for learning than those I enjoyed while away from college (including auditing courses for which I paid no tuition).

The university still seems pretty smug about its being "real learning, etc.," and thus it separates theory from practical activity. Because I was not in a formal program, my leave status was "inactive." The only problem with the leave was a sense of homelessness which I hope will not exist at school. Unfortunately most people I know are away from school this year and I have no sense of community.

53. Male - Employment, Travel, Self-directed Study - One Year

1: I feel that my experience at college has released me to grow personally, intellectually, socially, politically. I need to grow more completely on my own terms, without necessary academic structure, although allowing it when called for. My objectives while on leave are to continue this growth outside a structured academic environment. I hope to increase my sense as an active, initiating human being. I hope to recognize some things I may take for granted. I hope to increase my practical ability to survive. I want a sense of challenge and commitment.

I plan to live with friends and start playing music as a group, hopefully becoming financially self-supportive by this involvement. I want to pursue especially my technical and expressive abilities on reed instruments. I would also like to travel. I would like to see and get involved in different ways of living.

2: I decided to go on leave originally because I wanted to "bug out" those personal dimensions of myself which were pressing to get out, but were too often held in check, it seemed, as long as I was trying to play the student role. In other words, I felt myself growing in directions that I did not want to evaluate, be accountable for, take credit for, or even always make explicit. I just wanted to play sax and get a feel for that -- I did. I wanted to work as a skilled worker -- I did. I wanted to travel cross-country -- I did. A lot of my relationships worked out in ways I didn't anticipate, but everything stuck with me. I feel I got a hold of myself, got a solid sense of "certainty" or confidence that I can handle myself, that I can take care of myself.

3: Going on leave gave me a sense of personal competence that I have carried over into my continuing personal/educational development. During that time a lot of questions worked themselves out, either disappeared or became practicable, workable problems that I could openly work on. I don't think it is correct to say my leave experience caused any changes in my development. "Being on leave" allowed me a perspective on my direction as a human being, allowed me to realize a strong sense of self-determination in all ways, that I know I will never lose.

My attitudes toward educational institutions changed in that I realized that to become effective toward certain life-goals, I could submit to rigorous intellectual discipline without fear or confusion. In fact I could ride with my own weaknesses and idiocies and let them sort themselves out. I realized I could submit to "training" without losing control of the frail, sacred me, without getting lost. I knew in particular in advance the teacher with whom I was ready to engage in a disciplined educational encounter.

Being on leave has freed a lot of energy in me, because I realized I am responsible to myself and I enjoy that responsibility. No handicaps. The college had very little to do with influencing or directing or evaluating my leave. The college couldn't have done either.

54. Female - Variety of Activities - Three Semesters

2: I took a leave in the hope of finding a reason for being in college. I hoped to find more about myself through experiences other than being in school. My leave of absence was a very beneficial experience. When I first came to college I did not really want to come -- I came because of parental pressures and also because I did not feel that there was anything else that I could do. I stayed one semester -- beneficial in that it gave me the courage to leave. I did not spend my whole leave doing things that I liked. However, I did many things that I had never done, had always wanted to do and would not have been able to do in college. I began by working in a nursery school -- volunteered simply because I felt I should do something. It had its good and bad points. I did not thoroughly enjoy it, but I didn't hate it either (and I had hated college). The first semester I spent a great deal of time by myself (though living with my parents) and thinking about myself -- looking at what I was doing -- basic ways that I lived. I also worked the first semester on leave -- (for the first time ever). I had begun to feel very bad about having my parents totally supporting me. That summer I drove across the U.S. It was making a dream come true, which is a good feeling. The next year was spent working -- living with some friends, partly taking classes.

Through one of my jobs -- working in a greenhouse -- I discovered a new interest. Through other jobs I found certain things which I know that I never want to do again. A partial reason for coming back to college then is to avoid that type of job experience in the future. (That type of job experience being office work -- secretarial.) I found it a useful experience to be able to support myself and decide on my own living arrangements. It was interesting for me to see and actually experience what it means to have a family business and how much of a commitment that actually is. I feel few real disappointments with the leave. It was perhaps a bit too long. The last semester of my leave I often found myself wishing that I were back in school. For me, there is a definite feeling that there is so much to learn. It is often very difficult to really devote one's time to study while supporting yourself at the same time.

3: Basically I feel that the whole concept of leaves is an extremely good one. The academic community is a very sheltered environment. It is always helpful to keep a grasp on reality with some time away from academia before being "pushed out of the nest" for good. It gives one a much more realistic viewpoint on one's studies. I have not been disadvantaged except that I will be older when I graduate.

I strongly feel that the college should offer more guidance than was offered (none at all) -- there are many fellowships, crafts programs, apprenticeships, and so forth, across the country which I am sure would be interesting to many students. However, it is almost impossible to find out about most of them as they are not widely publicized.

55. Female - Various Jobs, Self-directed Activities - One Year

1: In taking this leave I want to take advantage of being out of school and having the opportunity for various and different sorts of job experience (both paid and volunteer). I plan to pursue various interests on my own (such as reading and art work). Hopefully, by the time I return to college I will have a better idea of which area(s) of study I'd like to pursue there.

I presently have a part-time waitressing job as well as a part-time volunteer job at the Eliot-Pearson School at Tufts University where I work with $2\frac{1}{2}$-6 year olds. In addition, I am taking a course in life drawing.

3: My leave was a very important part of my personal growth -- I could not have continued happily or productively in school without it. The time I had away from academics was just what I needed to rekindle my interest. My leave also helped me to decide what I wanted to do while in college. Under no circumstances can I see that I've been "handicapped" or "disadvantaged" by having taken a leave (except that I am behind most of my friends in terms of academic program and will graduate at a different time).

56. Female - Variety of Employments and Travel - One Year

2: I spent the first summer after leaving school working as a waitress on Block Island, a small resort community. I stayed on into the fall, and had a taste of the off-season life. I had problems dealing with the employers of the two restaurants where I worked; my values clashed with theirs and I was fired from both jobs. In October I went to Paris by myself. I lived in a pension and enrolled in two French courses. I went to classes and toured the city for two months. I met various Americans, and a few foreigners, but I met very few French people.

Failing to establish any real roots, I was restless and I decided to travel for two months. I covered most of the big cities in Europe and also spent some time in Greece, a week here, a few days there. I was alone sometimes, but more often I travelled with people I met. Tired of constantly moving around, I returned home in February. I moved into an apartment about a mile from my college. I worked a few odd jobs, babysitting and waitressing at a bar downtown until the end of May. At this time I moved on campus and became employed at the college pool.

I perhaps would have benefited more from this time off if I had gotten into one thing and stuck with it. I think I would have had an easier time readjusting to academic life, if I had become involved in some kind of employment that I found corresponded to my interests and personally satisfying.

3: Taking a leave of absence gave me a chance to get out into the "real world" and to broaden my perspective. It helped me to realize that college is only one part of the rest of the world. Since I choose to be here and am not forced into it, I don't get burdened with the problems I have here. I feel I can benefit from my experience here by having the contact with different people in this intellectually stimulating environment.

My leave consisted of doing a number of different things, which unfortunately only confused me more as to what I wanted to do with my life. That experience has persuaded me to finish my college education. In this way I will fulfill a necessary personal satisfaction of setting a goal in front of me and accomplishing it.

I feel taking a leave did handicap me in that it interrupted the flow of relationships I had had here previously. Good personal relationships are essential for me in order to effectively pursue other areas of interest. It is taking some time for me to re-establish that feeling of continuity which was lost from my year away, but this is also due to other circumstances which I am working to overcome.

My college could have helped to make my leave and return more valuable by more guidance. By not allowing such absolute freedom to leave but rather really questioning my reasons for leaving, such as what definite things I wanted to do, my interest, how the leave would help develop them, etc. would have benefited me. Also, giving me more definite advice about the remainder of my time here would have been very helpful to my particular situation. The freedom allowed here is great if a student knows exactly what he wants to do, but unfortunately, I feel very few people do. Since taking the initiative to seek advice is also hard, I think faculty and administrators could and should take a more active part in seeking out and questioning students periodically about their plans, and general attitudes.

57. Female - Various Employments - One Year with Subsequent Leave

1: Finding myself constantly overburdened -- of my own volition -- by commitments, unsure as to my own needs, goals and even true academic and vocational interests, struggling within the realm of a number of personal problems, as well as attempting to assert my independence (and escape from certain types of school-related decisions), I found the idea of taking some time off -- time for myself -- enticing and valid (once I escaped from the mental tyranny of the "graduate-in-four-years-do-it-like-everyone-else" syndrome). I felt a great deal of frustration and divided interests; I devoted huge amounts of time and energy to "extra-curricular" commitments while academically I was not doing the caliber work I believed myself capable of doing (my most rewarding "intellectual" pursuits were independent study). I found myself to be quite alienated (I know that's an overused term) from myself and my emotions, as well as my friends and work. I had been sick, I was tired, and the time seemed right for a change.

I think I sought, also, a broader perspective; I felt I wanted to be more aware of resources and how best to utilize them -- in the college community and elsewhere -- after I had acquired a little distance. I also realized with some dismay that the only thing I really knew how to do was to be a student. I decided to remain in the college town because of my need to assert an independent life style for myself, and also greatly because of the security of friends and a familiar setting in which I felt comfortable and thought I could find work.

I felt immensely freed and opened by my decision to leave school for awhile; excited, thrilled by the tremendous unknown potential and possibilities of the year, anxious and yet somehow not afraid.

During my leave of absence I plan to live in an apartment with friends, find some sort of full-time paying job and hopefully work with the Rhode Island Feminist Theatre in some sort of technical production capacity.

I would suggest some sort of program, open forums, seminars, counseling on alternatives to college; also, I see a need for emphasis on personal freedom and responsibility, a way to deal honestly, openly and creatively with the necessity for individual initiative coupled with more visibly accessible mechanisms for finding one's own way to make it (the "college experience") "work" for the particular individual.

2: Nothing worked out exactly as "planned." I did live in a house with several other people and supported myself financially for the first time in my life! I worked as stage manager for RIFT and as an administrative assistant in a campus affiliated office. My year off was a difficult one in many respects. I was being challenged on a number of fronts, facing situations and responsibilities which I had not had to deal with so completely before -- and often I did not deal with things well. However, on the whole, I would have to say that it was a tremendous challenge and a very important process for me to go through.

First of all, I learned to survive. Although money was (and still continues to be) a paramount concern, I think I have become more pragmatic in my understandings of personal/larger economics. It was very important for me to learn that I could support myself, to make my own mistakes and deal responsibly with the consequences. I feel I have become a more responsible and centered person -- though the growth was often painful, it was nonetheless certainly necessary. I was also receiving counseling at a local mental health clinic for three months during this time (March-April-May), which was helpful.

Secondly, I began and have continued to feel more concern for the Providence-Rhode Island-New England community, outside of the insular and myopic view of reality which many people seem to remain trapped inside of -- often voluntarily -- through privileged association with the university. I still have a great deal of respect and affection for academic communities -- they are very special places and the people who populate them often are as well -- but it sure as hell is not the only thing going on. I see more and more that a college or university is a very special/specialized place -- which has a great responsibility to the community which it often refuses to acknowledge. My perceptions of my role as "student" have changed also; I see universities (and other places, organizations, and people, as well) as incredible resources to be actively used, rather than allowing oneself to be used, overwhelmed, maintained by the institution itself.

I think that were I to be in a similar position again, I might well try to get as far away from the University as possible, to see things more clearly by contrast -- although it is true that one of the most important things gained from my experience here was a greater understanding and appreciation of the city itself.

3: I did find it somewhat difficult adjusting to being a student again -- worsened somewhat by being at first required to live on campus. There was somehow in me a feeling of great confusion and resentment which I did not know how to handle -- probably stemming from a great deal of financial frustration. It seemed that when I was out of school I spent an inordinate amount of time and energy trying to find the money to be enrolled -- and when I was enrolled (and, at that, part-time) I knew that it was temporary and I was not able to focus my energies on that but rather on how to support myself when I was out of school.

I also wish that I had taken more tightly disciplined "academic" courses (to give me a more defined structure in which to work) than the ones which I chose. My situation improved greatly upon moving in with a family in mid-October. Although I have experienced a lack of needed private time and space, it has been most valuable to me to live with a family not my own, deal with ages at great variance to mine and a very different schedule as well. The responsibilities I have had within the "household" have been important ones, and have brought me some valuable insights.

Please note that I have been forced to leave school again for lack of funds -- I am currently working at various jobs. I have also, since I received this questionnaire in February, travelled on my own cross-country for several weeks. This, too, has been a very expanding valuable aspect of my leave taking and my perspective has so shifted that I am at the point at which being in school is a leave-taking process from the rest of my life/supporting myself -- and no longer an entire end in and of itself.

UNUSUAL ACTIVITIES

58. Male - Delivered Boats to Central America - One Year

1_2. I'm living in a cooperative on campus for the rest of this year working part time on bicycle repairs and reading and studying botany and "natural philosophy" starting with Thoreau as an example. I hope to learn some Spanish and navigation for a job I hope to get delivering a small boat to Panama.

14. They could try to make the education more important than a degree.

1₅. I'm concerned and confused. I'm both proud and disappointed that I was too stubborn to make better use of what this university had. I like your survey. It helped me think things over some more.

2: I decided to take my leave just as school started last year because despite having organized a flexible independent concentration (natural history), I'd found too few courses I really wanted. I had already moved into a student cooperative and I stayed. I read more than ever before. I bicycled, canoed, walked -- watching and studying the natural history. I attended scores of university movies, lectures, concerts, political activities. I visited friends and places all around the northeast. I calmed my fears of my inadequacies to the point where I've needed to revive them.

In January I signed aboard a small boat being delivered to the Canal Zone. My trust in the authority of the captain was a good new experience. In Panama I sought out a volunteer job with C.A.R.E. and helped them to organize villagers to raise food and build kitchens for a school feeding program. It was discouraging except that we did more with less than most charities. Learning Spanish from scratch by submersion was harder than I'd anticipated, but the only way for me, though learning more of the basics beforehand would have been a good plan. I took two trips to Puerto Rico after hitching back through Central America. Being paid to deliver boats to interesting places was ideal. I did some quiet working with the land at home (southeast Massachusetts), then moved north of Boston to earn some money as a carpenter.

I've come back to school knowing I can learn informally but wanting to earn my degree so I can have it behind me. I've been able to organize this year to take better advantage of things a university offers which I can't do as well alone.

It turned out that most of what I wanted to do could be done outside of college. Even though it cost me my last semester's-worth of scholarship money when I left school towards the end of my senior year, I am glad of it. I wanted to learn how to live by farming and handcrafting and still have time left over to help those around me to learn and grow happier. Getting a degree wasn't helping me as working as a carpenter while working on a farm did or as taking a course in education at a state college while volunteering in an exciting school and a live-in half-way house (is?) now. Leaves of absence are a good thing, but it would be still better if people stayed out of college till they really want to be there, rather than staying in until they really want to be out.

59. Male - Apprentice in a Maritime Museum Boatbuilding Program - Two Years

2: 2 months climbing expedition in Alaska
2½ months employed at salmon cold storage, Alaska
3 months lived at home in New Hampshire, wrote, etched, read
16 months apprenticed as a wooden boatbuilder in Maine
2 months travelled in Europe (Scotland, England, Norway)

My boatbuilding experience has totally changed my life, or really, has fostered what I desired and had acquired already into an incredibly satisfying experience and way of viewing my life.

The college had nothing to do with my leave. My advisor was not interested in the least. This bothered me a lot.

3: I view my "leave," as not a leaving of academic, but rather a first step into reality. I see no connection between it and my course of study, directly, but it intensified my desire to complete my course of study as soon as possible, so as to get back to the "leave" situation.

60. Male - Racing a Sled Dog Team

2: My intention while on leave was to continue my work in studio art (sculpture). However, most of my time was spent managing, supporting, and racing a sled dog team (17 dogs). This relatively new experience brought about a change in my major, now involving science. It is my feeling that a leave option, as it is set up at my school, is most beneficial for a student, especially during this stage of his or her education. It forces you to ask more important questions of yourself. Learning how to ask the question is the key to becoming a good student.

61. Female - Walked the Appalachian Trail - One Semester

1: Practical application of things I've been studying -- want to lead my own life instead of having it controlled by others -- want to be truly self-reliant. I will be hiking the appalachian Trail with a friend -- keeping a journal, studying various ecological aspects of things I find -- do some photography.

2: During my leave I hiked the Appalachian Trail, a mountain trail which starts in Georgia and ends in Maine, covering a distance of 2050 miles, with another student from college. It took us $5\frac{1}{2}$ months.

I don't really feel like I can write about the values, or the disappointments. They seem self-evident. The joy of being in the mountains, living there, rather than merely visiting (the difference here is crucial), feeling alive and strong with all senses participating -- the disappointments all momentary, being soaked in a downpour or having boots frozen or the end of a love affair -- meeting so many different kinds of people, learning about them and how easy it is to love; oh it was all about life and living, self-reliance and dependence, continually and miles and miles more. An incredible perspective on life -- so much bigger and awe-inspiring, a reality so different from that of a college. My only disappointment, all in all, was that I am not super-human. And having to leave that way of life.

I do feel that this journey was a valid educational experience. I learned more during those $5\frac{1}{2}$ months than I did the previous year at school -- and yet the college will not recognize it as a valid educational experience unless I "write something." That's bullshit, and that's why I don't particularly value colleges and the educations one receives there. I think learning how to live, period, should be the focus of a college -- all other things are purely incidental and accidental. Anyway -- I wouldn't change my leave for <u>anything</u>.

3: My leave was the best thing I have ever done in my life. It was the healthiest, most stimulating, and most growing six months of my life. I learned much more in these six months than in any other six-month period of my life. Because of this, it is very difficult to write about it, in retrospect. I have been over my experience many times, know it intimately. In addition, I have used it for a portion of my academic work. It has become painful to me to write about it because I would like more than anything to be out doing it again.

I physically became stronger than I have ever been. I realized that my physical capabilities were much greater than I had previously realized. Correspondingly, my emotional strength grew. Every day was different, every day had a crisis with which I had to deal. I became more strong in myself, came to respect myself more highly. I became much more sure of myself -- my goodness as a person, my abilities and my goals.

There has been one way in which I was handicapped for taking a leave. My parents were very much against it and thus told me that they would count it as a semester of college (i.e., they would only pay for four more semesters, when technically I had five left). But I will graduate within that time and, therefore, have no qualms about their actions.

When I was on my leave I realized that I didn't want to continue my college education. But this action (of dropping out) would have several repercussions -- my family would have been very resentful and hostile, especially my parents. Since I only had two more years, I decided to finish up as quickly and start doing what I really want to do. I'm tired of being a college student and, moreover, do not value the mode of learning which occurs in colleges. I find it artificial and stultifying. I find it a deadening experience -- it is joyless and forced. It suppresses emotional growth. People in college tend to have overdeveloped minds and underdeveloped hearts.

62. Male - Employment and Training in Competitive Sailing

1_1. To learn about the sail making business.
To prepare for the 1976 Olympics in sailboat racing.
Hopefully win an Olympic gold metal.

1_2. a. Work as an employee of Van Zandt Sails.
b. Build three sailboats for racing.
c. Physical and mental preparation for sailboat racing. This includes working out and extensive reading.
d. Extensive racing throughout the year in North America.

TRAVEL

63. Male - Travel in the United States - One Semester

1: I expect to go back and find myself. I'm black, and while at school, I felt my ethnicity, my "blackness" slowly but surely being educated out of me. I'm on leave trying to get back to the person I was before I got to college. I recognize that I'll never be able to retain all of my culture, but it is very important that I sort out the aspects of my blackness that I must retain in order to survive. I plan to travel from one city to the next, just being myself.

2: On leave, I travelled around the country, met people, wrote a lot, and generally got back to the realization that there is an honest life without the pretensions and bullshit that I encountered in college.

3: The major problem which resulted from my leave was that I found that I had outgrown my college experience. Having lived for a while as a totally independent and self-supporting person I accepted the responsibilities of adulthood, and as a result "grew up." The shallow, childlike environment of college is extremely painful when you attempt to squeeze an adult consciousness into a post-high school group philosophy. I, as a person, have developed considerable as a result of my leave. I think that only in this last semester have I really begun to achieve any understanding of myself and what I want to do intellectually, and occupationally.

These advantages of a more "mature" awareness must be played off against the hassle of attempting to reconcile oneself to the playground mentality which seems to mindlessly dictate the entire functioning of a college; college, and the activities which go on in a college campus, seem more of a masquerade than anything else. But this is , of course, a personal conception and something which is not in the realm of rectifying.

64. Female - Study and Travel in South America - One Semester

1: Hope to see some of what I've been learning applied or confirmed (or disproved). Going to Peru. Possibly will visit other Latin American countries. Hope to intern in an international agency such as the Andean Pact Commission although the FAO is more likely. Possibly observe Agrarian reform at first hand. My advisor and individual faculty members here and at other nearby colleges are most helpful. I find the college and many other places have few contacts with Latin America.

2: I spent approximately four months in Peru and a little more than four months travelling through South America. The travel was mainly for leisure and also to see other South American countries for my "major" in Latin American Studies. Time in Peru was partially spent on an internship. Independent field study, arranged by me, of squatter settlements in Lima took up a major portion of my time. I lived with a Peruvian family.

The whole experience was very rewarding. I acquired a vast amount of information which will be applied to a thesis in progress. I learned a great deal of different life styles and cultures. I had few disappointments or difficulties other than while traveling. My college had nothing to do with my leave other than the official "leave" papers.

3: My leave was directly related to my studies and invaluable to me for that aspect as well as the complete dependency upon myself, alone. I was far removed from sources of assistance and managed most things myself.

65. Male - Extensive Travel in Africa, South East Asia and Europe - One Year

2: Last summer I worked in construction at a gold mine site in Tok, Alaska for three months. I broke my wrist, returned East and travelled to Italy with the hope of securing a job through the Venture Program.

Sadly, they dissipated before I could commit my time and monies, so I continued to southern France where I partook in the autumn harvest of grapes. Back to Italy where I joined two friends for an escapade through southern Italy, Sicily and Tunisia in the bitterest of winter weather.

After a Christmas at home I embarked on an eight-month wandering through West Africa, East Africa, Rhodesia and South Africa, Australia, Indonesia, Southeast Asia and meanderings westwards to Europe. Fortunately, I travelled in Africa through my father's company contacts, tracing roads through rural villages and markets with salesmen.

These adventures are a terrific human experience which subject the traveller to incredible intensities -- cultural learning, sharing, writing, reading, incredible deluges of thought, communication, novelties, curiosities and perspectives. A holistic education about humanity and the natural world. One inevitably learns about oneself and others. I think American universities should be far more receptive to global realities regarding their curriculums and foreign students.

3: For me this has been an unusually social year which I have enjoyed enormously. Academically, the semester slipped easily by; however, the compacted week of examinations in January was most tense, I noticed that I had lost much fluency in writing but that only reflects on practice. Without any doubt, my "absence" triggered much introspection and self-discovery which has carried over into the academic year. It tends to distract from concentration.

66. Male - Study and Travel in Java - One Semester

2: The first six weeks of my leave were spent at a Thai University, where I was instructed (in English) in Southeast Asian History, contemporary politics and Indonesian language. The program was separate from the university, but allowed informal contact between Thai and American students, which was more valuable than the classwork.

The remainder of the semester was spent in independent travel and study. I spent six weeks in Java studying the economics of the batik industry. Field work was infinitely more satisfying to me than reading books -- I was in control of my work, not interpreting the work of others.

There is no substitute for first-hand experience -- travelling in Asia has left a greater impression on me than any amount of college instruction could. Some prior academic preparation might have been helpful, however, particularly with regard to language. If I had been fluent in Indonesian when I arrived in Java, my stay would have been much more productive.

3: My semester abroad was more important to me in terms of "personal development" than the remainder of my four years of college combined. In particular, I gained an appreciation of the immense gap between developed and underdeveloped countries (I spent the semester in southeast Asia), and resolved to prepare myself for a future in the field of international economic development.

My career objectives are much clearer now for having been abroad, and my final semesters in college have been made much more personally meaningful. I plan to go to grad school -- an almost inconceivable notion two years ago.

Initially, after returning from my leave, I found the daily study regimen rather tedious. But other than passing feelings of boredom with book learning, I can see no disadvantages in having taken the leave. I have a better attitude toward my work now, because I have a better idea of what interests me and is important in personal terms. My return to the campus life was easier than I anticipated.

67. Male - Extensive Travel in the Pacific - Two Years

1: My aims are to gain competence in non-academic areas, to gain practical knowledge, especially in foreign places and peoples, to test myself in real-life situations, to decide if I should finish college or whether I am capable of educating myself through other avenues. I am travelling, working and living in the Pacific area. I've been in Hawaii for 2½ months, working in a day care center and reviewing nightlife establishments for a tourist guide. I utilize the University of Hawaii's library, film, etc. resources. Learning photography now to record travel experiences. Plan to learn sailing to get around by sea. Leaving for Samoa tomorrow, then Fiji, New Zealand, Australia, New Guinea, Asia, etc.

I'm glad the college did not impede on my LOA. When I requested a leave, they were cordial and quick. Some close friends had minor influence, but I decided to leave and made plans of my own accord. The Academic Development Office gave me helpful information on the NEH Youth Grant. I think it would be constructive to arrange a mini-colloquium or something of the sort on leave-taking, where enrolled students could meet with students who were or had been on leave. It might allow a more realistic conception of what to expect from a LOA.

2: Worked for a few months at an anthropology museum, teaching children, giving tours, doing a mural for the museum. Worked nights as an IBM computer operator. Then I spent one year working my way around the South Pacific, taking several jobs in Hawaii and New Zealand. Worked on a farm in Queensland, Australia. Stayed with native families in villages in Samoa, Fiji, Tonga, Niue and New Caledonia.

It was a chance to test myself in a variety of situations. There was much new information, exposure to new people and cultures, languages. More of a conception of being American. New skills learned in response to the new environment. And some important friends.

It was as bad, at times, as it was good. Failures to match up to demands of situations as well as successes. The loss of a friend off-setting gaining a new one. At times the loneliness and isolation from anyone remotely similar to me was a problem.

Essentially, I left feeling like an unviable (in this environment) kid, and came back considering myself a viable adult. A major claim. I would attribute this change to the time involved, to the risks I took and my degree of immersion in totally new world, also to efforts made in overcoming obstacles. I should mention that "culture shock" eventually became a problem as did "culture differences."

The college had nothing to do with what I did except to be cooperative in letting me leave and return on short notice. An involvement on its part would have changed the nature of my experience. I suspect it would have been more of a program than an adventure. Maybe there should be more of an information program for departing students or more of an effort to provide contacts through university-related auspices.

STUDY ABROAD

68. Female - GLCA Program, Antioch College, Bogota, Colombia - One Semester

3: My leave, a semester in Bogota, Colombia, gave me a rare experience from which I developed a new perspective, socially, politically and intellectually. I came back feeling more of an individual, less identified by my college and my experience here. I am more self-sufficient and have a greater understanding of people and the world. I have become more impatient and less understanding with my peers and traditional education. I find new opportunities for intellectual interchange between students -- most interaction is student/teacher, which ignores the rich resources which students have to offer.

My high school experience, in a public experimental school, is coming back to haunt me and I feel like I'm missing a lot in the university atmosphere. I find a lot more stimulation and fulfillment at my part-time job with a private social-research firm. I feel like it's time to graduate. I will go on to graduate school, but am not sure in what or when.

It was hard fitting in socially, when I came back, and has taken amost a year to find some sort of "milieu." Life goes on when you're away! Only other disadvantage -- my college doesn't accept grades from other universities study-abroad programs. Of course, they don't offer a program in a Spanish-speaking country, although they publicize it in the catalogue and admissions information. I tried to have them reactivate the Mexico program, and although a number of students were interested, the administration did not respond. I think that's really sad. My college is behind the times in a response to increased student interest in Spanish and related areas. The lack of courses is appalling.

69. Male - Institute for Mediterranean Studies, Rome - One Semester

1: I hope to obtain new insights, knowledge and my own character development not possible at college at this time in the following important ways: (1) additional elements to my major that aren't offered at college, (2) opportunities for field research with concomitant personal and academic growth, (3) travel and new experiences.

2: I was on an academic leave of absence and enrolled for the semester program with the American Universities Field Staff Program at the Institute for Mediterranean Studies in Rome. There were twenty students in the program from all over the States and several European countries, we took three concentrated courses on modernization in the Mediterranean area -- one a general course with numerous speakers from government, business, etc. and two regional courses. I studied the Balkans and the Middle East.

After two and a half months of classes we were given six weeks for field research for a thesis that had to be completed before the end of the term at the end of May. So we had approximately two and a half months to research and write a thesis, with the emphasis not on pursuing all academic sources but delving into a people's culture, politics, society and value structure and seeing/understanding what was going on in that environment. I chose a topic on Egypt -- problems facing manpower planners -- and spent most of my time in Cairo talking with the educated Egyptians in government, research, business and education that could give me insights into the topic.

On the way back to Rome I traveled up through the Balkans - Greece, Yugoslavia, Hungary -- with a fellow student who had spent most of his life there, and received a very brief view of those countries. I should also mention that I did a lot of traveling on weekends and during vacations while in Rome, seeing most of Italy, Austria and southern Germany.

The benefits were many. Academically none of the regional courses I took were offered at my college so I feel I enhanced my major enormously by studying in Rome, I learned a great deal about the people and their institutions that could never be properly explained in a classroom in the U.S., was taught some of the finer aspects of interviewing and getting information, especially from difficult sources, most of all was exposed to a whole new environment that not only stimulated me intellectually but personally and emotionally, i.e., I learned a lot and matured a lot, and which has given me new stimulus and interest in the fields I'm studying.

Difficulties mainly surround what can be called "biting too much off to chew," there was just too much to learn and experience and not enough time, but knowing there is so much more is probably an added factor in wanting to continue academically and personally to learn about the areas I saw. Language was also a hassle, especially in Egypt. I could get along in Italian and German so southern Europe wasn't bad, however. The amount of work required, or I should say the type of work required was vastly different than my college experience and that took some adjustment.

College classrooms and seminars didn't prepare me very well for sitting around a table with the planning minister from Iran and talking about the implications of the oil increase. And I don't mean in the sense of being able to ask him intelligent questions, and knowing something about the situation, the economic factors, etc., which college did educate me in, but in being able to understand his answers and criticize/analyze on the spot -- critical debate I guess it could be called, when your cards are damn few and he has a royal flush. It was in those types of circumstances, and there were too many of them for comfort, that I learned the most and had the greatest joys and disappointments.

3: I still consider the leave as an important and extremely valuable continuation to my personal development, intellectual interest and career direction. It has been the major stimulus in my independent studies, course work and honor thesis that I'm presently engaged with. It has also been an integral component of my desire to continue in higher education and return abroad to study and do research.

I have had problems readjusting to the college curricula and life style -- back to the grind is the best description -- as well as just getting used to the States and a more structured and restrained life. I can't leave for a weekend skiing in the Alps, for instance, and get away with only spending $15 for the whole thing.

College has been great with helping with the red tape and getting settled back in, the lack of courses in my area of interest are still a headache but the lack was a major reason for leaving in the first place. Now I can set up some valuable independent study projects and write a thesis. I now know enough men here and at Harvard to get some advice.

The only way that I have been handicapped with leaving is in extra-curricular activities in which I could have had leadership positions and really enjoyed if I had stayed, and several year-long courses that were, be broken up and now can't be taken because the professors are on leave. Both were losses I knew of before leaving, however, and were considered in the debate of whether to go or not.

70. Female - Smith College in Florence, Italy - One Year

2: My program (Smith College in Florence, Italy) provided an excellent opportunity to those students especially interested in art history. The courses were all taught in Italian and we were required to take at least one course at the University of Florence. Perhaps the greatest difficulty was in meeting Italian students. Actual contact was brief and superficial.

I personally was quite fortunate. I managed to meet some lovely people who made my stay most enjoyable. But above all else, I managed to apprentice myself with wood restorers. They opened my eyes not only to the profession of restoration but also to the whole new socio-economic set-up that was in all senses foreign to me -- the real working class. Being with them facilitated my understanding of the culture, improved my language ability and helped to teach me a trade.

For some there will always be difficulty in meeting other people. What my program offered was, compared to other American programs in the city, a more realistic approach to a foreign culture. We spoke the language, we were fairly free to travel if and when we wanted and we lived with Italian families. I would suggest, however, more contact with Italian students, private living quarters (an apartment) and more concise information regarding expenses prior to departure.

3: My experiences abroad (i.e., on leave) not only helped to formulate opinions about America (i.e., greater perspective) but also to be objective about myself and where I stand, what I do, where I am going. Out of necessity I grew up in terms of being more dependent upon myself -- I had no choice, really and that was most instructive. Also, I became more serious about academics -- my interests were stronger and also I became, frankly, scared about the encroachment of just one more year!

The most difficult matter involved in returning after a year away is friendship. Many new faces, some old ones no longer around. . . . But that's an individual matter which has to be dealt with on an individual level. The college can't help.

More meetings before and after the "leave" so one not only has the opportunity to be with people but also so one can share experiences.

I criticize the college for only dealing with people who went to France en masse and those involved in its own "Rome Campus." Equal attention should have been paid to all people who were gone regardless of where they were. If people can't share, then how else can other people learn by mistakes.

71. Female - Kent State University Semester on the United Nations, Geneva, Switzerland - One Semester

2: During my leave of absence I attended the Kent State University Semester on the UN in Geneva. I had approximately sixteen hours of classes a week, studying with professors from the University of Geneva and the Graduate Institute. Educationally, the program was a perfect complement to my major program in international relations. We had free access to the UN in Geneva -- were allowed to use its libraries and to attend all conferences.

While I was there, I sat in on the Law of the Sea Conference, the Nuclear Non-Proliferation Treaty Review, and the Human Rights Commission discussions on political torture in Chile. We had briefings at the headquarters of all international organizations in Geneva as well as at NATO, the Common Market, OPEC, UNESCO, UNIDO, the IAEA, and others, in their home cities.

Since we had classes only four days a week, and were provided with Eurail passes, I travelled quite a bit. I saw all of Switzerland and managed to get to Spain, Morocco, Germany, Italy, Austria, France, and Belgium.

I think the most beneficial part of my leave entailed my living in Geneva for four months. I did not live in a student dormitory, an "American ghetto" so to speak, but out in one of the neighborhoods. By the time I left I no longer felt like I was a traveler, on the outside looking in.

Four months is not long enough to transform oneself, but it is long enough to acquire a real understanding of a foreign culture. My only regret, I believe, is that I did not take a whole year off instead of just one semester.

Perhaps it should become required for students to take a leave of absence during their college careers. This campus is often like an island unto itself -- leaving the routine for a while, whether for work or other study, gives one an added perspective on the world which is essential for a well-rounded education. You can get just a little too stunted sitting around the old college town for four years.

72. Female - Sweet Briar Junior Year Abroad, France - One Year

1: It is my desire to deepen my education during this year abroad. My long-growing interest in the French language and culture determined my decision to live in France. Sensing the great importance and value of observing, examining, questioning, in short, thinking -- in a manner other than the one to which I am accustomed, I look forward to returning with a broader perspective into the issues with which I am concerned (urban aesthetics, humanistic psychology).

My advisor was perhaps most helpful in advising me with regard to course offerings and programs. However, the decision is essentially mine. Since I had made up my mind to live in France several years ago, the university could not have been more helpful in the decision making process.

3: As far as personal development is concerned, last year's leave was immeasurably valuable. The varied situations I found myself in demanded novel responses and decisions. Perhaps the most poignant realization I came to was the fact that the success or failure of my year abroad depended solely on me. This understanding, that my happiness could only be determined by my decisions, has now become an integral part of my modus operandi.

The intense cultural exposure provided much personal enrichment, which correspondingly led to certain decisions regarding my academic and future career. It led to extreme confusions at first; it was not until several months after my return that I was able to resolve these conflicts.

A third insight stemming from my year away from the highly sheltered academic world is concerned with perspective. At no time was it as clear that the universe does not revolve around the corner of the globe I had been limited to, as last year. This reminder has given me a broader vision as regards everyday life. Unfortunately, the pressures of the academic experience threaten at every instant (and often succeed) in eradicating this perspective.

The unprecedented freedom which I was granted has had an effect on my motivations concerning my continuing education. My desires at the present are to experience more of the same types of situations, places. The world of books is a fine supplement to a fulfilled life, but can never be a substitute. Before going on to graduate school (if I do, in fact, choose to go), I feel it is necessary for me to get out into the non-academic (I refrain from calling it "real") world once again, preferably to travel/work. Compared to the 24-hour-a-day environment college students in the U.S. find themselves in, the European intellectual experience is much less intense. Also, perhaps healthier, because academic life is not cut off from the other realities of daily living. A certain feeling of suffocation, of stiflement, permeated the first few weeks of my return to the university. Time has tempered this dissatisfaction, of necessity.

73. Female - Hebrew University and Work in Israel - One and a Half Years

2: My leave was divided into two parts. I spent a year studying at Hebrew University on the One-Year Program. I lived in the dorms and my friends were of similar background except ethnically some were Arabs and Sephardic Jews. Most of my time was devoted to studying and social and cultural life. My studies were in fields not offered at my home school - mostly Middle Eastern and Jewish studies, and hence very valuable.

After the year I volunteered to work in Kiryat Shmona on the Sherut L'Am Program for six months. In contrast to the modern, metropolitan, cultural Jerusalem, Kiryat Shmona is small, rural and underdeveloped. The ethnic makeup of Kiryat Shmona is Moroccan, Persian, Iraqi, etc. and, of course, there are always Americans. I was provided housing but later I moved to personally arranged accommodations. The socio-economic level of Kiryat Shmona is fairly low.

I worked as a camp counselor, social worker and school teacher. I taught English, arts and crafts and painted murals. The experience was a most valuable one and I intend to return upon receiving my college degree.

There is little my college could have done to make this a more productive experience as it was basically non-involved. There are always things I could have done to have made any experience more productive. The difficulties were primarily those of adjustment - learning the language and coming to understand how things are done. As far as the latter is concerned -- the Israeles themselves have this same difficulty or least the same frustrations at trying to get things done.

74. Female - Stanford University Center in Taipei, Taiwan - One Year

1: The main reason is to fulfill a strong desire in me to be able to really speak Chinese. To devote myself fully to it is the only way. Secondly, having lived in Taiwan before, I felt there was a lot to the country that I had missed by not knowing the language and I wanted to try and find that. Also, going to school in the East while living in California has separated me from my family. My sister will be in Taiwan this year and I will live with her so we can try to re-know each other.

2: I spent four quarters at the Inter-University Program for Chinese Language Studies in Taipei (Stanford Center) studying Chinese intensively. I learned a lot, both Chinese and personally. Living overseas and realizing that American culture isn't the only culture is an incredibly important and growth-inducing experience.

I would recommend going overseas to anyone though maybe not to Asia. I experienced culture shock both going over and coming back. It was not so much the environment (it is amazing how quickly three-inch cockroaches seem commonplace) that caused the culture shock but rather the fact that people thought in ways totally alien to what I was used to. To accept and live with that requires a lot of growth. My only regret was that I spent so much time studying the language that it limited the time I spent dealing personally with Chinese people.

3: I never left formal study -- I worked much harder in Taiwan than here. The only handicap has been that I have only had three years in college to study courses other than Chinese. But I still think that living overseas was the most valuable experience in college because being forced to deal regularly with things that before had been totally outside my experience contributed greatly to my personal growth.

75. Female - University of Nairobi - Currently on Leave

1: I wanted desperately to get away from my home college. I was interested in my studies, economics, but they were becoming increasingly abstract. I was also upset with its oppressiveness. Yes, there is a good deal of personal and academic freedom but the students can sleep with whomever they choose, recycle whatever they choose, study whatever they choose. But the range of choice seems to be dictated by our extreme homogeneity -- we are all rich, white, predominently eastern.

In taking this leave, I am studying African Economic History and Development. The abstract social and economic theory is becoming concrete. I am experiencing people with none of the assumptions that I and my college friends have grown up with. I am, perhaps most importantly, learning to live and travel by myself, something I never could have learned living on campus.

I take courses with the University of Nairobi one year long. I am also writing an independent research project. During vacations I travel by myself (train and/or bus). I have applied for an internship with the United Nations in Ethiopia for fall semester 1976. I hope to follow this with a teaching job back in Kenya. (My total leave will be 2-2½ years). I hope to return with a much better idea of my own abilities and the direction in which to apply them.

I applied to several African universities on my own, following a course in African history. Nothing could have prompted me to think more seriously of taking a leave than two years straight, on-campus. I didn't need any help. When I began to consider taking a leave, I did so because I was upset with my home school. I was feeling more and more as though my experience there wasn't relevant to important issues. I applied to Nairobi, because it seemed a way to have my cake and eat it too. I could be experiencing a new political, educational, cultural environment, while still making progress towards my degree.

I must admit that had I not gone to my home school I might never have gotten this far (spiritually as well as physically). At a more traditional school I might not have been exposed to the political ideas that made me dissatisfied with my academic experience. At any rate, though I criticize my home college relentlessly, it has given me the opportunity to experience a unique year here at Kenya.

76. Female - University of Madrid, Spain - One Year

1: Personal reasons plus the hope of escaping the closed world of academics. I will be studying in Madrid, travelling, exploring Spain.

2: I feel that the college was in no large way responsible for my decision to take a leave. I spent the year in Madrid studying at the University and informally exploring Spanish art at the Prado, galleries and museums. Living more or less on my own in a huge city gave me increased self-sufficiency and initiative. Although my reasons for studying at the University of Madrid were not tied in with my major in college, I found that my knowledge of Spain and Spanish was terrifically increased. This has kindled my interest (heretofore very unenthusiastic) in my major (Spanish).

Appreciated my leave for teaching me that my college years form a false unit and that the campus is a miniscule world. Now that I'm back, I recognize far more clearly the dynamism and freedom of the university. My difficulties were those values that I have described.

3: My leave was the best thing that happened to me during my ill-starred college career. For a year I was spared the preoccupations of a university struggling to perpetuate itself, the anxieties of students struggling to make themselves. . . .

Outside of the college world, study was a pleasure, and learning came easily, as much through osmosis as through rigor. My interests solidified, my thirst for knowledge developed.

Disadvantages are the fragmenting of continuity which renders the term "college career" meaningless -- changes were made in my major requirements, and I was not accurately described those changes. This made my return somewhat unpleasant. The university should begin to establish precedents for credit transfer, rather than discussing each case after the student is back, especially for a junior year leave.

STUDY AT ANOTHER AMERICAN COLLEGE OR UNIVERSITY

77. Male - University of Alaska, Fairbanks - One Year

1: I want to learn more about Alaska, study the environment and ways to preserve it, spend a winter in Alaska, get a new and different perspective on myself, Alaska, eastern U.S. society and my college.

2: The objectives of my leave were: to learn all I could about Alaska so that some day I can do something to protect its natural character and environment; to take a break from the rigorous academic pressures of college; to learn more about myself and people of the North; to try to get a genuine feel for Alaska, by spending a winter there (I had spent three summers there before my leave), and by getting out as often as possible into the wilds of Alaska. I did achieve these goals to a great extent, although, as usual, I felt I could have done more -- I am generally very satisfied, though.

I spent the 1974-75 academic year at the University of Alaska, in Fairbanks, pursuing a heavy load of studies there, taking courses that dealt with various aspects of Alaska (its history, literature, native people, politics, geography, geology, natural resources, etc.). To support myself I had received a grant from a special fellowship program sponsored by my high school, a loan from the University of Alaska, and I spent 15-20 hours per week working at the University of Alaska Campus Center.

The greatest benefits I reaped from this experience were the ones gained outside the university. Although I learned a great deal through my classes, which I had much enthusiasm for and interest in, the most meaningful activities were the memorable adventures I enjoyed -- a 100 mile sheep hunt in the Alaska Range, snowshoeing, cross-country ski trips, and the like, all over interior Alaska throughout its infamous cold seasons -- and the community events I participated in -- public hearings on political issues, environmental group meetings, community forums and symposiums on problems of Alaska's growth, native festivals, speakers, demonstrations, etc.

I experienced few difficulties that the college could have helped me with, except for the hassle of transferring credits, which might cause me to lose up to a year. It was worth it, though -- I gained maturity, confidence, valuable experience in the North, made some valuable friendships and gained many important insights of myself and Alaska and people and life in general.

The biggest problem I now face is re-adjusting to the relatively severe academic pressures of my college. I have come to believe that either it has gone over-board with its expectations from students to "produce," or that I do not belong here. Most students here sacrifice all other aspects of life to maintain an acceptable academic standing -- at the University of Alaska it was practically the opposite. Yet, there must be a reasonable middle ground -- I believe college should encourage students to spend much of their youthful vigor (and physical energy) on aspects of life not purely academic. Because I can't see spending all of my waking hours with books or in class, I was eager to escape, and enjoyed the "year off" immensely -- even my job at the student center was largely enjoyable -- largely due to the change of pace it offered.

I think that all students, before they leave this college after graduation to become part of the system and immerse themselves in work for the rest of their lives, should take a year, or a semester, or a summer off, to obtain a first-hand view of the "other side of life" -- the view beyond the Ivory Tower, beyond the college town, beyond the East Coast. If this is indeed one of the centers producing the leaders of the future, the college should encourage its students to get out and get a feel for the people and the country they plan to influence and guide.

Equally important is the opportunity to do things, experience raw life, while students are still young and able to get the most out of this -- travel, living in strange places, testing one's stamina and capabilities whatever they naturally are -- these should be done when there are fewest bonds restraining such desires, before immutable obligations and responsibilities make such experiences impossible. I have found that after taking a year off I can return to the task of obtaining a degree from this school which, though frighteningly formidable, has taken on new and greater meanings, which I can approach with clearer and more confident direction, increased certainty and perceptive appreciation.

If taking a year off can improve one's education like this, then isn't it a good idea to encourage others to consider? The time it takes is never lost -- it is wisely invested with continual and compounding returns.

3: My leave gave me new perspectives on life, greater insight into people by exposing me to a variety not represented at college, yet perhaps more typical of the people I will live with after graduation. By opening me up for new experiences, I greatly matured during my leave. My leave did not answer all my questions or satisfy all my appetite for non-academic challenge, and this was a very difficult problem for me to face and surmount during my first semester back. Yet, my time off gave me a confidence and increased motivation that has aided me in my greater enjoyment, appreciation, and educational achievement at college since my return.

I value college and its opportunities and offerings now more than ever, partly in contrast to the university I attended during my leave, and partly due to its intrinsic qualities that new perspectives, time, and personal growth served to clarify and bring to my attention. My attitude toward my college now is one of respect and pleasureable understanding. Before my leave, I was fighting it, to make it something it wasn't (or shouldn't really be at this time), and this (though possibly admirable) was terribly frustrating. Not that I have lost my idealism -- now I just know how and where to most effectively apply myself.

Along with this, I have much improved my personal attitudes towards and relations with other students. I feel more comfortable here now, more a part of the place. I rarely question whether this college is really the place for me now, a way that I frequently tended to torture myself before my leave. I have come to see that it is where I belong, and desire to be, at this stage of my life.

78. Female - Barnard College/Columbia University, New York City - One Year

2: Attended Barnard College. Worked with several dance companies. Taught at summer dance camp.

I was extremely disappointed with my college in respect to the opportunities in dance. I was happy with other aspects of the college. Barnard offered so much in terms of dance -- technique classes, dance history, seminars on choreographers and other exciting classes concerning the dance field. New York is a haven for anyone in the arts -- many performances, lectures, a constant opportunity to surround oneself in the arts. I had the opportunity to immerse myself in all aspects of the performing arts, an opportunity totally lacking here.

There were almost no disappointments or difficulties - adjustments to N.Y. and Barnard were quite easy. I had a great year and I enjoyed all my activities and courses, not just the dance related courses. I'd recommend Barnard to anyone in my situation.

3: My "leave" at Columbia University was the best move I have ever made. Even though I have very warm feelings for this college, its friendly and warm atmosphere, and the close friends I have made here, it just doesn't offer enough in the two fields that I study now and plan to do further study in: dance and sociology of education. There is only one dance teacher here, who, in my opinion, is unqualified and totally unstimulating. I spent three incredibly frustrated years trying to combine my interest in the arts and academics.

At Barnard/Columbia I had wonderful dance teachers, an excellent dance curriculum (history and seminars on choreographers) as well as NYC, which is the best dance resource center in the world. Dance was treated as a vital field, an art comprised of actual studio technique, choreography, dance history. . . . It was really a comprehensive program.

I also took a French literature course with an excellent professor, a German philosophy course, educational psych., Japanese art, and acting. I got to know all my professors personally and have great admiration for all. I lived in a dorm one semester (not very happily) and in an apartment the second semester. I made some wonderful friends in New York. I loved my leave and definitely did not want to return.

My last semester here would have been horrible except for two things. I took an educational sociology course and worked on a research survey project which was thrilling. It stimulated me so much that I plan to go on for a M.A. in educational sociology. I stage managed "As You Like It" which took up so much time that it kept me from being lonely and frustrated. When I came back I couldn't stand to dance here so I really put myself into these two activities all semester.

My leave helped me to make priorities in my life -- knowing what I wanted to do after graduation. Again, I say that it was the best thing for me. To realize for once that this college had nothing to offer me and to stop living in the past of my glorious, carefree freshman year and to commit myself to dance and sociology and education, even though they aren't status-filled occupations.

79. Male - University of California, Irvine - One Year

1: I want to know my new home. California is impossible to compare to the East -- climate, people, mores -- all so very different. I'd like to get to know them better. I also will be attending a state university and commuting from home, and probably working at the same time. This way I'll add another facet to my leave. Moreover, I cannot under-estimate the fact that I hope to go to a California law school and would like an inkling of what that might be like.

I plan to pursue a similar program of studies as I did at this college and take some courses which UCI will have a stronger department in (e.g., Latin-American politics). I plan also to carry on an active roster of social and extracurricular activities here, and as I said, to work as well. It should be an exciting year.

It was a pretty good survey. Some of the questions taught me a few things about my leave of absence.

2: I attended the University of California at Irvine for one year (three quarters, fall, winter, spring 1974-75). All of summer 1974 and 1975 and much of the school year I worked as a sales representative for Time-Life Books in Irvine. Through late spring and all summer 1975 I spent much of my time writing, rehearsing and recording music with a professionally-produced rock band.

The year was great. I would rather be in California now than back here. Last year accomplished that much. Having just moved to California at the beginning of last year, I was unfamiliar with the place and the people. But after a year and a half of working, going to school and playing music there, California is really my home.

Education at UC Irvine is surprisingly similar to that of the Ivy League. Many of the professors I had there were Ivy-educated. The ratio of great-to-terrible courses there was about the same as here. A major difference I noted was that UC offered many courses more immediately applicable to the outside world. One such course was Introduction to Criminal Justice, a fascinating course of contemporary legal systems and systems of justice. I know that an Ivy League school would never offer a course so immediately usable.

I can think of no disappointments I had in going to school in California. My social life during school was meager, though outstanding in the summers. But social life at my college has hardly been productive for me. All in all, it was a very productive year; I learned about California, I learned what being a commuter student and going to a state school is like (it's not half bad); I enjoyed myself immensely, and I wish I could do it again.

80. Male - University of Wisconsin - One Year

1: To experience a larger university and its department in my field of study. Also to reconfirm some personal relationships which I feel are important. Many of my close friends and feelings are in Wisconsin.

I will enroll as a special student at the University of Wisconsin for one semester. I will then travel overland to India after having spent two months in western Europe. I want to see another culture in as full a sense as possible.

2: University of Wisconsin - Madison. Primarily I studied in their philosophy department, i.e., taking an undergraduate course and a graduate seminar. (I filled in with three other -- history, French, music -- undergraduate courses.) My primary reason for going was to evaluate and consider the department with the possibility of going to graduate school there. However, two things occurred: first, I did not like the department that much (they were philosophically very competent, but their personalities weren't), and second, I decided against philosophy graduate school altogether (I no longer desire to be a professional philosopher for the rest of my life).

However, I did learn that Madison, on the whole, was an excellent university in many aspects. In a certain sense it helped me avoid a type of academic provincialism that I had been developing. The academic and social atmosphere was more diverse than that of my college. Although I left Madison dissatisfied with a future in university-level professional philosophy, I did develop helpful insights to two different types of academic atmosphere. From this experience (academic), I would highly recommend others to spend at least one semester of their undergraduate years at another academic institution. The college was quite helpful in allowing me to attend Madison for that semester.

3: My semester of traveling throughout Europe enabled me to see my situation in both academics and life to an extent that would not have been possible if I had remained in school. I am now able to approach people and institutions with much more ease and clairvoyance. Furthermore, I can laugh at that which I once seriously venerated (i.e., the supposed omnipotence and omniscience that the academic community has; and the "necessity" of "making it" in the rat race outside of academia).

My semester at Madison helped me realize that education need not cost $6,000/year (i.e., formal academic training). Although I am very satisfied with the high quality of education that I am receiving here, I discovered that a state school can provide similar opportunities (if a person has the true motivation to learn). Why, then, did I return? Established academic and personal ties; parental investment; prudence, in light of a tinted vision towards Ivy League schools held among many.

No handicaps (although a short 3-4 week period was needed to get back into the swing of intense academic life).

81. Female - University of Massachusetts, Amherst, Massachusetts - One Semester

2: During my leave I attended the University of Massachusetts in Amherst. My major there is the same as it is now; mechanical engineering. I was required to take five courses; zoology, physics, public health, computer programming and calculus.

I lived in a dormitory suite with three other girls who I became very close with. I didn't have much of a social life there. I have a boyfriend who goes to school in Boston and either I went home on weekends, or he came for the weekend. My sister and her husband also attended U. Mass. and while I was there I became very close to them: probably closer than I ever have been or ever will be. This means a lot to me. I think it is the part of my experience that was most important and valuable to me. I left my college partly because of the effect some of the people had on me. I felt that many of them were cold and unfriendly and I was often lonely and unhappy there. At U. Mass., I found much of the same behavior which was disappointing in a way.

I learned that many of the things I was trying to get away from were at U. Mass. also. I am very happy that I took a leave of absence. It was a very valuable experience for me to be able to attend another university. It made me appreciate what I had at my first school. Now that I am back at college I am able to tolerate more of the things that bothered me so much before. I am much happier because of it.

3: I think that after my leave of absence I became more independent. I lived on campus but my home is close by. While on leave I was away from home and it did me a lot of good. Also, after going to another school I was able to see the problems with this school in a better perspective. Many of the complaints I have with this school I found exists in other schools also. I am still bothered by many aspects of this school but I know that it would be the same anywhere else.

I have been handicapped by my leave in the following way: there is an attitude that no other school can teach a course. I had trouble getting credit for a couple of courses I took while on leave. As a consequence, I did fall behind a bit.

82. Female - A West Coast University - One Year

1: Easterners, generally speaking, whom I came in contact with at my home school, could not recognize my need for cultural identification with my own people during my college career. The college I will visit has sixty enrolled Alaskans. It is known everywhere that the Eskimo is a cohesive group. The presence of fellow Alaskans, the association with them will provide the personal satisfaction I am looking forward to.

My college, as is characteristic of many private Eastern schools, takes on a very snobbish attitude toward other schools when it comes to accepting credits from other schools. They were unable to see my reasons for visiting a West Coast school.

Despite these somewhat negative comments, my college has helped me immensely in recognizing my capabilities and has instilled in me the determination and self-confidence necessary to pursue a successful career.

83. Male - State University in Western State - One Semester

1: Study coursework in academic area not available at home institution. Do research on topic for which material and people are not available at home institution. Give attention to personal matters and career plans.

2: During my leave I enrolled in a large state university in a western state in which I went to high school. An American history major, I went there to study western history at a well-known, somewhat distinguished department. I also went to pursue a topic for my senior thesis.

My classroom experience was better than I had expected. I had both the smallest class I've ever been in and the best professor I've ever had. The research paper was a bit of a problem, however, because professors seemed reluctant to help me with something not a part of their classes or not assigned to them.

Two difficulties I experienced were: problems in my living situation while on leave, and a lack of communication from the home institution. I think they should have kept me on certain mailing lists -- housing, registrar, etc.

3: The most significant observation I could make about my leave would concern the process of transferring credit. My home institution has been unwilling to give me credit for all the courses I took. My Dean and the faculty of both schools have been cooperative, but the registrar at the home institution has not. Despite several faculty recommendations and a complete official transcript from the other school, the registrar has arbitrarily decided to allow credit for only three of four courses I took.

(From subsequent communication) I was later able to get full credit for my coursework. However, this required pressure from my Dean, parents and faculty members at both schools. The rules were bent by the registrar, but not changed to afford other students.

84. Female - Boston University Marine Program (BUMP), Woods Hole, Massachusetts - One Semester

1: Objectives in taking leave were so that I could learn something about marine biology (none offered at college I go to) -- also, when I originally started checking schools to attend for a semester, I was somewhat tired of college and wanted a change -- also, good to get a sample of different courses, people, etc., since my college is so small. I went to Woods Hole specifically so that I could do concentrated marine biology and really find out what is done at a research level. I'm considering graduate school in this field and wanted to see what it's really like before applying.

I am participating in the Boston University Marine Program (BUMP) at Woods Hole.

I really did all the footwork myself -- I talked to several professors and went to the Dean in charge of leaves of absence, who was fairly helpful in listening and suggesting who specifically to write to -- I learned about BUMP through the Chairman of Biology, who was familiar with the program. From there I applied directly to the program.

I think for the most part, the college was as helpful as possible. Everyone very willing to help. Hardest decision was deciding whether I wanted to go away, but once I was accepted I didn't feel I could afford to pass up such a great opportunity.

3: I cannot over-stress the value of my leave in giving me a great amount of insight into a field which I had seriously contemplated as a life career. I was fortunate to be a part of a very unique program and to have the facilities of the most reputable marine lab in the East available to me for the semester. One course was taken at a time, each for a six-week period. Each course consisted of 3-5 lectures a week, depending on the professor with the majority of the time being allotted to laboratory work. In some cases we did specific labs, whereas in others, we studied samples which we had gathered on field trips. We also carried out independent research projects. The whole orientation was towards independent work. Even though we were a mixed group with extremely varied backgrounds (PhD and master's candidates and undergrad students), we were able to function quite well as a single class of 7-10 people.

Things were very informal. Of course we got to know our professors quite well. Woods Hole has lectures every day, sponsored by either MBL or the Oceanographic Institute. It is a fantastic place to learn. My only regret was that I didn't have more background before I took the courses. Probably the most valuable part was being in a place where first-hand and significant research was being done and to get the feel for what the field of marine biology is really like. In many ways I have been deceived about marine biology. I had tended to overdramatize it but found that much of it consisted of very tedious lab work. I learned the frustrations of trying to get a simple experiment to work, of equipment failure, etc. A semester taught me more about what is actually done in marine biology than I would have learned by attending graduate school. Besides academics, it was a great and needed change from college. We lived in a house, and there was always time for bike-riding, etc. We worked, but we were never incredibly pressured. The whole environment was extremely healthy.

I can't say that I missed anything by being away from my home college in comparison to what I gained from my leave. I was close enough to school to go back a few times to see people and keep in touch with things at the college. In many ways I had the best of both worlds since I was spending my time completely entrenched in one subject which I wanted to study, and yet I was part of a very closely-knit group and able to be outside and by the ocean for a semester while receiving full credit.

My attitudes toward college and towards my college professors has changed. I lost some respect for many of my teachers and no longer think of them as "sacrosanct" as previously was the case. At Woods Hole, we had no tests or quizzes, and there never were any deadlines to meet for papers except towards the very end when grades had to be in. I have found it very difficult to study for tests all this year. I haven't felt pressured at all, and as a result, I haven't done well academically in comparison to other years. My motivation to do well has dropped severely. I don't attribute all of this to my leave. I am a senior and indecisive as to my career and life goals. I cannot see a clear reason to give up as much as I have in the past in order to do school work. I say this as a person who was extremely self-motivated in high school and the first years of college. Of all my college experiences, I consider rowing on the women's crew and my Woods Hole leave of absence to be the most worthwhile. I have not yet found any experiences that surpass these two.

85. Male - College in California - One Semester

3: That sagacious prophet, John Cage, tells me that "nothing is isolated." So? What happened to me when I went to California? The corniest and truest word I can use is "maturation." There is something about the junior year of one's educational existence, coupled with turning twenty-one years of age, that makes the head reel and the brain spin at speeds henceforth unimaginable. I got a chance to experience another type of collegiate institution, approach and living arrangement. I didn't get "stale" like my friends who stayed here did during that year. I was forced into a reawakening; I knew nobody and nothing when I went to California. . . . I even had, I now realize, dillusions of grandeur. Perhaps I was shown my shortcomings in a gentler way than most, for I survived with only a brief major depression during the autumn when I returned to my original college.

You know what people always say about reflections, "If I could do it over again I would . . ." Well my leave did exactly that. I got away from my college self and was almost feeling like college was over and that this California thing was a new phase. When I saw that I was still very much in the thick of my educational development (formally) it was like finding out that there are twelve days of Christmas. I could return with a fresh outlook and "do it over again" while going forward. Exhilarating as it was, it fucked up anyway. I fell in love.

I do not have to quote Shakespeare, Dante, Lawrence, Faulkner or Brautigan for you to understand what love can do to a human being. For the last six months that I was in California I had the most beautiful relationship that I have ever had with a woman in my meagre lifespan, I had my own musical ensemble playing my music and becoming locally famous, I had a house on the Pacific Ocean, where I could go to sleep listening to the coastal waters, I had friends that I cared for. It sounds idyllic in the telling, doesn't it?

As everything, it was a combination of beings aligning themselves right at a certain point in time and my development. I don't know whether it would have happened anywhere. . . . But California always represented the dream state of life to me, before and even now . . . maybe from all of that counter-culture, social revolution, love-in stuff during the sixties, but I was very open to new experiences and new ideas. Why the hell did I return? It's like leaving Tahiti for a frozen tundra in Nome.

Having these goddamn lofty ideas of what an artist is, I decided that it was time for me to move on. In the midst of all of the California incredibility, all plans were focused on my departing in September and I felt that if I changed those, everything else would change, perhaps diminish . . . like knowing that you are going to die . . . maybe you live more intensely.

When I came back to college everything looked weird. My friends looked older -- eyes a little more carved into the face -- a few more hairs gone. It was insane but I, as a flood, got a feeling for age and growing older and that this perpetual youth business that America is so big on is such a farce when one is trying to understand anything about living. So here I was back at college. Things with my best friend here (who came out to California to spend the summer with me) were going very sour. I missed my lover like I never believed and I was totally out of touch with the college community.

Perhaps if I hadn't played so much the part of the tragic play role I would have found it easier to assimilate once again, but it was one of the hardest things that I ever have had to do. Getting used to cold weather, coming back to a life that I left, and especially applying to graduate school all took their toll on my sanity and left me totally blitzed. For a while I was paralyzed with indecision and the void that surrounded me. I was distant from my friends. I was writing a musical with my friend and every attempt to get it produced by the university failed and we were thrown into despair over that. I don't really see how the university could have eased this craziness. I have very close relationships with some of my professors. I was so unmotivated, though, I had to take "incomplete" grades in some of my courses in order to even get by in the semester.

Since everything is so interrelated to everything else, I am affected every minute by things that happened in California, visions, people, work. I am struggling to come to terms with things that I had been so incredibly naive about before. I mean you wouldn't believe how I viewed things before I left -- and I guess this is a necessary growing process for every inhabitant of this planet in some way or another. I wonder . . . I don't think that I would have my California experience changed in any way. It's adjustment. Like coming back from a war. Only more like paradise. But that's all bullshit. Dealing with change. Coming and going. Has it ever been different?

MEDICAL - PSYCHIATRIC

86. Female - Maternity - Currently on Leave

   1: Unfortunately, my objectives are not educational per se. During my leave I will be giving birth to my first child and breast feeding that child. Since I live a considerable distance from college, my leave is of indefinite duration. This college, as others, is oriented toward unmarried (unharried) students. There is little or no flexibility afforded undergraduate women who are married with children.

87. Male - Illness of Fiance - One Semester

   2: I took my leave due primarily to the serious illness of my fiance. Her death climaxed a grueling semester of emotional turmoil. My leave was a rest, a recouping of my goals and purpose for life.

   My questions are very real and, at the moment, unanswerable. I know only that I must go on. My leave was unavoidable, invaluable, and regretably too long. I found myself ready to go back to school before school was ready to start up again. I'm not really as excited about school as I was, but my degree is something that I have wanted for a long time.

   Nothing could have been done to make my experience any better. It was a sudden development as opposed to a thought out program with goals. Its purpose was very basic, and to that extent I'm afraid it is not of much value to the study. My particular circumstances are rare, fortunately.

I believe in what this study is trying to accomplish. I know I thought often about taking time off during my early undergraduate years, but I shied away because of the hassles involved and lack of prospects of anything better than school. My orientation has been: go to school <u>now</u>, while you've got the study habits, momentum, etc. I think it imperative that one have a specific, <u>positive</u> reason for taking time off. One needs that to <u>justify</u> the loss of time to oneself in terms of career development, personal development, etc.

88. Male - Surgery, Employed in Drug Store During Remainder of Leave - One Semester

2: I had very little choice in this matter of my leave. The diagnosis was "bleeding peptic ulcer," and surgery was an immediate (if not sooner) possibility. After a week of in-hospital observation, I left for home. Another few weeks of recovery and I was essentially all set to go. Unfortunately, college was by then a month into the semester. Due to the nature of my new-found ailment, I decided to "bag" the first semester.

However, during this period which we shall loosely refer to as a "leave," I became very interested in stero speaker design and did a "moderate" amount of research into the subject. This line of activity would probably not have been duplicated here at college, as I would have undoubtedly been engaged in my studies to a significant degree. In this regard, my time was well spent. I derived a moderate amount of satisfaction during my leave.

My college could have done very little for me during my leave. The whole debacle decended so rapidly that no time was available for the college to attempt to make my leave a more productive experience. Perhaps, though, a get-well card would have been in order!

89. Female - Psychiatric Therapy

2: The majority of my leave was spent dealing with my health problems. Much of the time I spent in psychiatric hospital or so heavily invested in therapy I had little energy to do much else. When I could, I engaged in adult education courses, dance classes, and volunteer work. I sorely missed the availability of young people or people actively involved in intellectual pursuits so available at college.

Many of my days were unstructured. I, of course, found most people working and that most of the public education classes offered in daylight hours were of a homemaking nature. The general experience of isolation -- particularly academic isolation -- while painful, taught me much about seeking out the people and resources I needed.

Generally, the time spent working in a day-care center or mixing with young working adults did much to change my perspectives of life. I found people in general no longer fit into categories I had once placed them in. Non-academic daily life is not well described in college lectures or books.

Throughout my leave I visited with one of my professors who often spread word of my activities to colleagues I knew as well, and who gave me their thoughts and caring. The caring I felt, the consideration I received in talking over a decision to return to school, and the high level of interest maintained by faculty about me during my leave persuaded me to return to this college. Without that I would have had much to cynically think of, of impersonal schools and colleges where individuals do not matter -- unlike big business or adult education classes, like factories.

90. Female - Psychiatric Consultation and Full-Time Employment - One Year

1: I was afraid of feeling (a) left behind by my classmates who would be going forward without me, (b) that I'd rather I just got college over with. Both of which I decided were NOT the right reasons for continuing my education at this time. I wanted to "find myself" -- all of my reasons for leaving school were my own personal difficulties that I was having dealing with myself and which interfered so completely with my academic life that I could not enjoy anything anymore.

During my leave I have held my first full-time job and am living on my own 2,000 miles away from home. I have learned a great deal from my waitressing experience, supporting myself, etc. Also I am seeing a psychiatrist during this year, and her counselling has been an incredible source of energy for me. I feel that I have accomplished "finding myself" and am eager to go on from here on my own.

I have two very good friends who were the entire influencing force behind my decision. Through them, I began to see that school was not the only form of life and that taking time off was no tragedy, and might be a very good experience. They also believe in therapy, and by talking with them, I began to realize that if I went to a psychiatrist for help, it wasn't the end of the world either. They showed me all of the positive aspects of both.

I have done very well on my own and I even prefer it this way, because I had to make the decisions and decide where to go and for what and it has all turned out very well. I did it all on my own instead of having the college hand it to me, as if I were a child.

I want to stress the fact that my leave has made an incredible difference for me, and I feel it was the best thing I have ever done for myself. I have a very different perspective on myself in the world, and now when I come back to school I know why I am coming, I know the world that I am leaving and will be going back to. My head is together instead of apart, etc.

2: I took my leave so that I could devote my energy to my psychiatric care and because I felt that I could not deal with the pressures of school effectively. Psychiatric treatment has been very successful for me, as well as the experience of supporting myself for a full year and gaining some insight into what it is like to hold down a full-time job for a period of time extended. Living in a small winter community, I developed a very close-knit community feeling with my friends, which was very valuable to my learning about social relationships. (Problems with social relationships was a major factor which drove me away from the pressures of school.) I worked as a full-time waitress at a country inn which is a summer resort area -- quiet winter community -- lived on my own, with female friends, male friends and in a house with both. Overall, I feel that the year has been very well spent.

RELIGIOUS ACTIVITIES

91. Female – Studying and Teaching Transcendental Meditation – $1\frac{1}{2}$ Years

1: I intend to complete the first half of the six-month course in Switzerland for becoming a teacher of Transcendental Meditation. The second half I hope to complete either next summer or next fall.

I was helped by Students International Meditation Society and the teachers of Transcendental Meditation at college.

3: After my freshman year I took a year and a half off. I spent six months on a teacher-training course in Europe to become a teacher of Transcendental Meditation. I then spent a year teaching TM full time in New Haven, Connecticut. I had reservations about returning to school, i.e., the readjustment to academic work and dorm life. But I have been amazingly happy with both situations since returning this February. It almost seems like there has been no adjustment at all. Considering the fact that my freshman year was not particularly rewarding, I feel that I must attribute my increased satisfaction with my life to the practice of TM.

92. Male – Way Biblical Ministry – One Year

1_1: To grow in a knowledge of God and his World, to gain practical experience in living the Word in a less pressured environment than college, to share the Word with different kinds of people, to see how far my believing can take me in this world. When I get back from my leave, I will have clearer objectives for the time spent at college. I will be more effective in ministering the Word to college people because I will have walked the Word for another year and have real practical experiences to back up (to confirm) the preached Word.

1_2: I will be leading a twig (Bible study) group in my home. I will study the Word much and grow in fellowship with God by renewing my mind. I'm going to talk to lots of people and learn better how to relate to people, beyond just understanding what's going on with them. To learn how to reach people by growing closer to God and to talk effectively with all kinds of people.

1_3: Nobody really helped me. I'm linked with the Way Biblical Research Association located in New Knoxville, Ohio.

1_5: In many ways this form and the quest for statistical, book-knowledge and the like (academic research) represents in a large way my objections to the orientation of academic centers. The "pretty" precise language, the "neat" structure, the coldness of the format, the standard answers accumulated from past experience, all combine to reduce this evaluation into another intellectual exercise. When I stated that my interest in college is purely vocational at this point, I sum up my position. Unfortunately, many others, who continue to "grind it out," also are motivated by job opportunities as they deaden the feelings and emotions of their minds. Furthermore, the world outside of college is caught in the same web of mediocrity. Yet God loves us and man is unlimited in his potential for peace, joy and love when he walks with God.

93. Female - Various Employments, Spiritual Enlightenment - Two Years

2: I left school because I had no reason to stay. I could not see any sense in having a degree just for the sake of having it, I had no inclination to pursue my major (English) and I didn't want to use up time and money that would otherwise be available if I did want to pursue a college education later. There was no fulfillment for me in schoolwork and even though I had only one semester left, I just couldn't stay at college. I needed something else and wanted to find it. It was difficult too. Many friends and relatives were disappointed, but I knew that I was doing what was necessary and healthy.

After three horrendous weeks in a factory, I worked as a barmaid/waitress after which I took a month off and went to Europe. Shortly after I returned I rented a house with several people. I realize this doesn't sound like very much, but it was quite an incredible time for me. I knew many people and I was learning things about the world and myself that just cannot be expressed and I was so glad to be away from school, to be relieved of the awful pressure I had felt while I was there. I was beginning to study spiritual books and I was involved with a feminist group and I was very sensitive to people making jokes about my being an "intellectual." It was an intense period of searching.

I had my fill of waitressing by mid-winter and I quit my job. It was depressing after a while, all the heavy drinking that so many people did day after day. I had a lot of security invested in that job, however, and I was a bit scared about giving it up, but I knew I really didn't have any choice. Something was "pulling" on me and I had to move on.

I took part-time work which included working in a friend's bookstore. I loved that. I was still dissatisfied, however, so I bought a car and decided to leave in mid-summer for parts unknown, searching for something that I could call a "home" or "school" in the "esoteric tradition" and that would involve finding "my people." Again I was frightened in going away on my own, in giving up my security, but I knew it was necessary.

As it turned out, the "odyssey" was not necessary, only the resolution to do such a thing was necessary, for in July I had the experience of "receiving knowledge." This is the initiation into pure meditation which is given by Guru Maharaj Ji. There is considerable bad press about Maharaj Ji, but somehow I got beyond it, received knowledge, and stayed home because I had found what I had wanted to find.

I had no idea what I really wanted to do and I hadn't yet learned to really trust the meditation, but again it was a time of growth. I began reading some "esoteric" literature and I would go to the town library with my books and read in the mornings. One morning while I was there, the idea of returning to school just popped into my head. I hadn't been thinking about school -- I had only been trying to keep my mind open to whatever came next, I considered all the "reasons" for it, but I knew that I didn't really know why I should go back, I just knew that I was meant to try to go back and finish.

I reapplied, was accepted and returned. I also ended up going to summer school and that was a very good thing. I had been out of the academic community for two years and needed the "warm-up" and as it turns out I also needed the two credits. I earned them. But even when I was in summer school I didn't know for certain that I would be in school in the fall. I knew that whatever happened would be the best thing.

So, it hasn't really been as if I've come back to school, I've simply come to school. I was extremely happy to be in college at first. I loved my courses and teachers and the classroom setting. It was only gradually that I came to see how restrictive the environment was for me. The things that I had learned were not generally well received. A university is just not the place these days for a "spiritualist." I found that the schoolwork was generally tedious, standing in the way of my real education. I saw that I needed to finish up this fragment from the past and I saw more clearly than before just what it was that I truly wanted to study and how and with whom I wanted to live.

There is just no way to evaluate these last few years. I feel I've learned more than most people learn in a lifetime and I feel that I am in training for something that involves the whole world. And I am speaking not only of myself but of others who have grown from the experience of this meditation. I feel that a revivified way of being human is now possible for many people in ordinary life circumstances and I wish to work for that. I see most institutions as old forms which probably will break before they bend, and I am very happy now to follow my life toward the ideas which more and more people are sharing.

3: First of all, I must admit that I did not experience "taking a leave," for although I was granted a leave of absence, I had no intention of returning to school. I left the confines of an academic environment in great joy and relief -- as if I could breath again, as if I were finally free to pursue the business of me. Who was I and what did I really wish to experience in life? Academics had worn me down. I finally saw, despite the reputation of being an egg-head type "good student," that I was not the academic type at all. I couldn't fake the role and I had no desire to pursue it any longer. There had to be something else.

Through a lengthy and baffling series of coincidences I became interested in "The Knowledge" which was being revealed in the West by Guru Maharaj Ji, and in mid-summer "received" this Knowledge. It answered all my needs for the missing "something," it gave me a sense of true community with the brothers and sisters who had also received this primordial experience, it gave me the tools with which to work all the rest of this life (and beyond) on my own spiritual evolution. It gave me everything I had ever wanted and more.

Since then the path of my life has opened before me like a beautiful flower. In simply practicing the experience of Knowledge, I have been led to and through all that I have needed for further realization. It "happened" that I was inspired to return to school to complete the unfinished project of my degree and I tried not to have expectations about what school would be like and why I was returning. I knew that I would learn what I needed to learn when I was there. I was very happy to be back at first. The campus is lovely and my courses were stimulating, but after awhile I found the work to be rather limited.

In the course of my meditation I had broken through the bonds of "intellectualism" and had experienced flights of the mind that were impossible in an "intellectual community" (these words are controversial and ambiguous, and I use them with care) and very soon I could see that people (both students and faculty) either did not understand me or were embarrassed by my lighthearted enthusiasm or both. I really didn't feel too much at home, but it didn't bother me because I knew I would be there only a short time. It was a terrific challenge and I accomplished a lot of inner work.

So everything has worked out perfectly. I have tried to answer your questions sincerely but I admit that some of them are rather difficult. Who among us is an "average leave-taker"? Who among any of us is an "average" anything? Mankind has so much potential, the seed of divinity is within us all, but the inertia of the myths of our institutions (education, religious, medical, political) acts as a lid on the germination of that precious seed. The seed must be released to grow freely in the manner best suited to its need, and I can only hope that this study has brought those of you involved with it closer to the realization that true education, the actual bringing up and out into light of the individual consciousness, is a process far more precious than the perpetuation of inert heritage.

A FINAL WORD

94. Male - Employed: Child Therapy Aide, Attended Two Universities - Two Years

2: At first my job consisted of filing and doing 20 hours of behavior modification with autistic children, teaching them sign language for communication. In several months it expanded to include psychodrama with learning disabled kids, play therapy with childhood schizophrenics and individual treatment with "disciplinary problems." I simultaneously attended night school, taking a total of three psych courses in two semesters. During the second year, I attended a university in the morning and worked in the afternoon.

College work went much better than it ever had before, was more rewarding, more fun and had better grade results. I studied psych and humanities. Socially I never felt better and found the students to be more accessible. Attending these two schools and having success academically, improved my view of myself as a learner, as did success in my work. One of the schools that I attended is as academically high-powered as my home college but is not nearly as impersonal, difficult or exhausting, due in part to its trimester system which is light years better than the despicable semester system in force at my college. My experiences at these two schools helped me put my earlier college years in better perspective.

Working and studying also had the effect of taking pressure off me. If a class was discouraging, I had the immediate release and successes of work, and if work got too heavy, I had the uplifting aspects of school. Living in the city was also socially and intellectually enlightening for me, especially because of the diversity of neighborhoods and because it allowed some distance from school: exchange of ideas and life styles with non-students, feelings of self-sufficiency, and deflated the old feelings that "I am a student and only a student, and what I do in school is what I am, and because I got C's in school, I am a C̲ person."

Off-campus living adds a second and third dimension to life and allows you to be an 'A' cook and a 'B+' tenant union member and an 'A+' organizer of a food co-op, even if you are still a C student."

This may seem way off track and like an ax-grinding diatribe, but its purpose is to share some of the conclusions that I was able to arrive at regarding educational forms after attending three schools.

Additionally, a small school makes all the difference. I knew more teachers and fellow students after one year there than I ever will at my home school. A new life in the academic world, as well as the fabulous opportunity to work in the field of my choice and begin to see what aspects of mental health most interest me and where my abilities lie, were my two greatest gains (next to putting the pieces of my personality back together). Work also made me more responsible because I could not afford to miss it and got only 21 days off per year. This structure was very good for me after more instructual and less productive college years. I have no major regrets about my hiatus except that I didn't do it after my freshman year. The only way that my college could have been more helpful -- they were very cordial and informative when I wrote to them for academic consultations -- would have been to occasionally (perhaps bi-annually) drop me a line to find out where I was and if alumnae in the area could be of any help to me.

3: Basically it allowed me to view myself outside of the school context and to elaborate my self-constructs that were non-academic (i.e., to develop other pegs to hang my self-worth on besides my grade point average). My motivation to work hard and do well were always high and I always knew that I would get at least one degree. I did not know that I would need at least two to do what I want to do. Well, now I know.

I was disadvantaged in transferring credits. There were no handicaps except that I only knew a handful of people when I returned here. Also, it meant that I did not get the opportunity to know my department's faculty very well.